# Courage: The Heart of Leadership

Courage lies at the heart of leadership. Leaders need courage to make wise decisions, not self-interested ones. They need to be able to set aside their egos, to feel vulnerable, to face challenges, yet remain principled and hold the course. This book presents many suggestions on how to make a real difference in organizations, and explains how one can develop the courage to be an effective leader, step by step.

The book is designed to give leaders the self-awareness and the tools to overcome the obstacles that prevent us from leading effectively. Leadership requires working through the systemic barriers that serve as forcefields pulling and pushing us in various directions. Drawing on interviews with over 20 organizational leaders in a variety of industries, the book helps leaders to address key areas that are rarely discussed: the personal baggage attached to authority, self-esteem and self-differentiation, ego management, and the terror of the group. It highlights – with examples – how fear impairs our ability to make good decisions, and how our tendency to reactivity and the quick fix vitiates our attempts at being courageous. The hallmark of courage is the ability to have courageous conversations that invite transformation.

The book is ideal reading for organizational leaders who are seeking ways to break through some of the personal and systemic barriers to leading with purpose in a way that makes a real difference.

**Annabel Beerel** has worked with multinationals as well as educational and non-profit organizations. She was the founder and CEO of an international AI company, has been a corporate financier and investment banker in the City of London, and was the president and CEO of the New England Women's Leadership Institute. She is currently an executive leadership consultant and is the author of ten books.

"In all my many years of reading books on leadership and taking leadership training, I've never read a book as tightly focused on the courage that is lacking in leaders today and so effectively presenting why and how courage should be self-developed by leaders in all sectors of life as Annabel Beerel's book on courageous leadership. Dr. Beerel does a commendably thorough job of using story telling from her own life and literary works to provoke thought and make her points more vivid and memorable. She is extremely well read in a topic on which she is clearly passionate, and she explores each facet with thoroughness and diligence. Her lists of references and self-examination questions at the end of each chapter invite the reader to dive more deeply into the inextricable links between courage and leadership and live more courageously. This would particularly be an excellent book for all women and men in leadership positions in businesses, nonprofits or the government to read and cultivate more courage in their leadership, but it would also be valuable to all those who are willing to take up its challenges of becoming more courageous in their decision-making and life choices."

**Tom Raffio**, *President and CEO, Northeast Delta Dental*

"In *Courage: The Heart of Leadership*, Dr. Beerel motivates and inspires the reader to reflect on their own character and capacity for courageous leadership practices. She encourages each of us to scan our environment for areas of opportunity for practicing courage in the face of ever-changing realities and provides a solid framework for developing and implementing a foundation of courage. Through her extensive research, Dr. Beerel illustrates the importance of ethical behavior as it relates to personal and professional freedom and happiness. This is an insightful resource for those in or aspiring to be in a leadership position, educators at all levels, and students of business and leadership studies."

**Kelly A. Duggan**, *M.S.; Broker and Co-Founder, Maximum Results Realty, LLC*

"It's not often you find a leadership book that's a page turner but this storyline of firsthand observance, acute social and financial commentary, plus scholarly teachings makes for riveting reading. The status of where we are, where we could be and how to get there is relevant at all organizational levels. May you have the courage to pursue it."

**Diane Smith**, *Retired Senior Executive of International Supply Chain*

"It was hard for me to read the first three chapters of this book because I became so dismayed at the lack of ethical leadership in the workplace. However, Chapter 4 gave me hope that some people have the courage to tell the truth despite the consequences. After reading the later chapters, I gained new insights into why people lack the courage to be truthful. I learned a great deal about myself and others in reading this book."

**Janet Laatsch**, *Former CEO, Greater Seacoast Community Health*

"Dr. Beerel's book on courage taught me that true leadership involves reflection, vulnerability, and embracing uncertainty to grow from every experience. Courage is about facing one's fears, making tough decisions, learning continuously and being mindful. This book was an extremely stimulating read."

**Dr. Nicole Parsons**, *Co-Director, Associate Professor,*
*Program for Advancement of Learning, Curry College*

# Courage: The Heart of Leadership

Annabel Beerel

LONDON AND NEW YORK

Designed cover image: CreativeFire – iStock / Getty Images Plus

First published 2025
by Routledge
4 Park Square, Milton Park, Abingdon, Oxon OX14 4RN

and by Routledge
605 Third Avenue, New York, NY 10158

*Routledge is an imprint of the Taylor & Francis Group, an informa business*



*British Library Cataloguing-in-Publication Data*
A catalogue record for this book is available from the British Library

ISBN: 978-1-032-60561-6 (hbk)
ISBN: 978-1-032-60560-9 (pbk)
ISBN: 978-1-003-45964-4 (ebk)

DOI: 10.4324/9781003459644

Typeset in Adobe Garamond Pro
by Apex CoVantage, LLC

This book is dedicated to my many friends, colleagues, students and clients who model courage, character and compassion. You are the unsung heroes of this book, yet your presence is the backdrop to every word on every page. Your fortitude and perseverance bring light to any darkness and provide inspiration and hope for our embattled world. Thank you!

# Contents

# Preface

## The Hunt For Courage

### *Hidden in Plain Sight*

On January 5, 1970, at 8 am sharp, I arrived at the Johannesburg offices of Cooper Brothers to begin the 6-year apprenticeship required of aspiring public accountants. My grand title was "articled clerk," for which I was to receive the grand salary of Rand 30 per week.

After two torturous weeks of staring despondently at a formidable training manual of impenetrable density and enormous proportions titled *Fundamental Audit Procedures*, I was instructed that on the following Monday morning I was to accompany someone on an audit. What that entailed, I had no idea, but at least it held a promised relief from the dark training room in which I had been entombed.

On day one, I learned that every audit began with what was termed "reconnaissance day." On this day, every person on the audit team was assigned the task of investigating what was really going on inside the company. This detective work entailed talking to those people one did not normally talk to in the normal course of the audit. There was the janitor, the people who worked in the canteen, the CEO's chauffeur, the person responsible for the building and the grounds, maybe a truck driver, the in-house nurse, the security guard, a warehouse worker, the switchboard operator and so on. (We had switchboards in those days!)

Each encounter with the chosen party was styled as an invitation "to chat." Casually we would inquire as to how things were going, what was new, what changes had occurred recently, were there departmental restructurings, why the canteen had been moved to a new building, what happened to the CEO's old Mercedes, when did he get a new one, what was in all the stacked crates of inventory, why there were now two security guards, and so on. Our intent was to sniff out anything that seemed vaguely different or out of the ordinary. We would chat and question, seemingly nonchalantly, with no apparent agenda, just getting the feel of the place and what was going on at the grassroots level.

Come 4 o'clock in the afternoon, the audit team would then gather in an office and share the spoils of the day. My, what a lot we had learned without opening a book or looking at one canceled check! We had learned about hirings and firings, misappropriated money, scandals, new homes purchased by the senior management team, court cases in progress, inventory being stolen, overseas bank accounts, office affairs and the true picture as to whether the company was doing well or not. The "low-level" employees knew it all. Delighted with the attention they received and the opportunity to talk about what they observed and longed to gossip about, they eagerly engaged in seemingly idle chatter, unwittingly spilling the beans. The audit after that was a piece of cake.

The brilliant theory that underpinned reconnaissance day is that (1) people low on the hierarchical totem pole immersed in the daily minutiae of the organization, observe, and know what is really going on. They revel in unexpected attention and are disarmed by the casual questioning that does not put them on the spot. (2) If a fraud or any form of corruption is in process, everyone knows about it even if, or when, they feign ignorance. There are no secrets in organizations. (3) Almost all schemes of fraud and corruption require collusion, hence the big deal about division of duties as the backbone of internal controls. Very rarely is just one person involved.

Fraud and corruption require a network of multiple players, and it is not always just senior managers who are the bad guys. More often than not, many layers of employees are involved.

After our debriefing, having digested the information we had garnered, if we suspected any malfeasance, all we needed was the evidence. And, it is always there, one just needs to know where to look. The real story of how the firm is performing and its ethical behaviors are invariably hidden in plain sight.

In my naiveté, I used to often wonder why no one tattled; why, when everyone somehow knew something was going on, no one had the courage to stand up and to challenge the offenders. What was this collusion of silence? That was before I knew about groups and group dynamics, the fear of challenging power, and the fear of standing up and standing alone.

Those many long days and years of auditing all kinds of businesses taught me a great deal, not just about financial accounting but about human nature, temptation and courage – or the lack of it.

And so my hunt for courage began.

## Leadership and Reality

In 1995 (I had now emigrated to America), I had the good fortune to be given a scholarship to study leadership at the John F. Kennedy School of Government at Harvard University. Week after week, I, along with over 100 other students from around the world, participated in Ronald Heifetz's challenging discussions on leadership – what it is and what it isn't. I was riveted. It was a deeply transformative experience.

While being stimulated by Heifetz's insights, I also participated in seminars and training offered by the A.K. Rice Institute for the study of social systems. A.K. Rice is the American affiliate of the London-based Tavistock Institute of Human Relations. These two institutes promote the field of object relations, and what we colloquially refer to as group dynamics.

Object relations refer to how we relate to others. Group dynamics is a term for the behaviors that take place within groups, and the factors that impact these behaviors.

From these two experiences, I gained many critical lessons that have stuck with me over the years. The first is that the key task of leadership is to identify, frame and mobilize others to adapt to changing realities. This task requires huge courage – courage as most of us dislike change and resist it, courage because we threaten those leaders whose message threatens our existing reality, and courage because it shakes up the status quo. Courage, I decided, lies at the heart of leadership.

Regarding object relations and group dynamics, I learned about the complexity of relationships and the conscious and unconscious dynamics that influence them. I gained insights into how the power of the group can make a person lose their sense of self and how they begin to over-identify with the collective. I also learned, and observed, how groups in distress sink to the lowest common denominator. Fear and anxiety turn them into irrational, unethical mobs. Leading a group, especially during challenging times, I learned, takes great courage. Who is role-modeling this courage, I wondered?

## *Ethics Chair*

In 2006, I was awarded the Distinguished Chair in Ethics at Southern New Hampshire University. At the time, the United States was still reeling from the enormous frauds of, among others, Adelphia, WorldCom, Enron, and to crown them all, Bernie Madoff's gargantuan Ponzi scheme. Thousands of people lost their investments and thousands of people lost their jobs. New regulations were passed – the Sarbanes-Oxley Act of 2002 – which had no teeth and failed miserably to curb the next tide of greed that led to the 2008–2009 financial debacle.

In my role of Ethics Chair, I was tasked by the president to implement a program that provided "Ethics Across the Curriculum." This type of initiative was in vogue at the time, especially once it was revealed that many of the corporate crooks had MBAs from Ivy League schools.

Within no time, universities took to boasting that in their university ethics education was included in every discipline, be it marketing, operations, accounting, science or biology. Many professors, however, resisted inserting specific ethics classes into their curricula as they claimed that they were insufficiently versed in formal ethics theory and that they covered "the ethics thing" by way of case studies. Many university administrations pushed back by instructing ethics professors to run ethics seminars for fellow faculty to educate them in the theory and language of ethics. As you might imagine, this went down like the proverbial lead balloon. Faculty members dislike being "instructed" by other faculty, and often during the seminars and discussions their poor grasp of ethics became apparent, which further fueled the fires of rebellion. In my university, several members of the faculty had the courage to invite me to come and address their classes directly. In these instances, I was disappointed to witness students' absolute lack of ethical education and the minimal attention given to justice and courage in any of their discussions.

## *Courage: The Lost Virtue*

In June 2014, I was the keynote speaker at a women's leadership conference. In preparation for my presentation on Courage and Leadership, I scoured my personal library of leadership books as well as the internet for literature that linked courage and leadership.

My search confirmed my suspicions; discussions on courage and leadership were nowhere to be found. Having taught in many MBA programs and having been privy to the curricula of other business schools including the exalted Harvard, MIT Sloan, Tuck (Dartmouth) and Yale, I knew that courage was not directly addressed in any program and was only given attention if it came up in case study discussions.

In general, business literature gives scant attention to the issue of courage, and surprisingly few business ethics books even mention courage at all. The fact that "Corporations Rule the World" and that business leaders radically impact the quality of life of millions of people seem to obviate the need to give attention to courageous or honorable behavior.

So where are leaders going to learn about courage? What is going to inspire them to be courageous?

My hunt for courage gained new urgency.

## *Courage in the Corporations*

As a corporate consultant and executive coach, I rarely hear about acts of courage. My clients are usually enmeshed in trying to resolve issues they mishandled from the get-go or trying to repair situations they previously ignored. Most leadership work, it seems, is clean-up and covering one's tracks.

Sadly, I find the effectiveness of many senior leaders appalling. Toxic cultures abound, stop-go strategies are the order of the day, and profitability and senior management pay seem to be leaderships' major pre-occupation. Caring for customers and employees is most often pure lip service whatever the fussy PR brochure or social media post may posit.

Regrettably, from the top down, companies want talent not character. They want technical smarts, not ethical courage. They want people who will "fit in," not stand up or stand out. They want savviness, not wisdom. They want action, not reflection. They want results – to hell with the process! Everything is a means to one end – more money. And, as I discuss in the chapters that follow, many of us are complicit!

## *Looking for Courage*

In the chapters that follow, I begin with a discussion of our desire for happiness, and how our being truly happy depends on our being in a state of inner freedom. Without inner freedom, we will never be truly happy. Our search for happiness in external, material things will continue to fail and disappoint us. However, finding inner freedom takes courage. It requires us to face our inner demons and to work with and through them so that they lose their hold. With courage we can conquer the forces that hold us back from being our best selves and this courage will lead us to the happiness we all long for.

Having set the parameters for our discussion, I begin with a review of the need for courageous leadership and how the free-market system has created an environment of excess, greed and temptation. Chapters 1 and 2 expand on the challenges we face, both individually and in our role as leaders, and how it takes nerve to be a self-defining person in the world of the quick and easy fix. I also highlight the dangers of relying on data, statistics and artificial intelligence (AI) as panaceas for our problems. Decision-making requires wisdom, intuition and common sense, not a reliance on statistical probabilities.

Chapters 3 and 4 detail stories of corruption and greed and how these plague our society. I shine a light on what we do to whistleblowers, who are rarely recognized and honored for their heroic courage in the face of dismissal and persecution, and I point out how many of us are complicit in not standing up and speaking out for honesty, justice and fellow feeling.

In Chapter 5, we dive into the original meanings of virtue, courage and character, and we see how these form a cohesive framework for living a good life and being happy. Throughout the chapter, I provide many examples of what courage is and isn't and I set out a synopsis of the key elements of courage that can be used to guide one's daily life.

Chapters 6 and 7 discuss the many factors that inhibit us from being inwardly free and how these factors lead us into temptation, and into being thoughtless, cowardly and losing our sense of self.

Chapters 8 and 9 are filled with suggestions of how we can, both in our personal capacity and in our professional role, overcome the inner shackles that rob us of our freedom and the strategies we can adopt to cultivate our courage.

Chapter 10 includes the research results, described in the following section, while Chapter 11 discusses the importance of including the cultivation of virtue, character and courage in our education systems and how this might help us to be more informed and more active citizens creating and sustaining a vibrant democracy.

The book ends with a reminder that in our deepest selves, courage is part of our existence and how we all long to live a good life, a noble life and a courageous one.

## Primary Research and Surveys

While I was researching material for this book, I partnered with the Center for Ethics in Society at St. Anselm College in New Hampshire. Professors who were teaching business ethics agreed to survey their students on the topic of courage. The survey was designed by me. I also approached several professional adults and their colleagues to complete a separate survey distinctly designed for working adults. Both surveys and their results can be found in Chapter 10.

Along with the surveys, I also interviewed 18 CEOs or senior executives as to their understanding of courage and their experience of courage at work. The discussion was guided by several orienting questions – see Chapter 10, Primary Research Results.

Given the small, nonrandom sample of survey and interview participants, the results are in no way representative of any group. They do, however, give us some insight into the lack of understanding of courage as an essential character trait and its intentional practice in everyday life.

## The Invitation

This book is about courage: courage in everyday life. It is about courage at home and at work. It is about courage and the way we lead our lives. It is about courage and the way we lead others. It is about courage being a fundamental trait of who we are as human beings. It is about courage for you and me. This book is an invitation to live a courageous life.

I hope it speaks to the courage that resides within you.

Annabel
Boston/Belgooly
August 2024

# Acknowledgments

This book is the culmination of many years of personal reflection on my own personal path in life as well as on my over 40 years of professional experience in almost a dozen countries, in all kinds of businesses, for-profit, nonprofit, quoted, private and government departments.

I would like to extend my gratitude to a multitude of people for the wisdom, guidance, advice and courage they have so generously shared with me over the years. If I were to thank you all, it would double the number of pages in this book. I hope you know how indebted I feel to you.

Besides the many colleagues and friends who have informed my writing, there are several people I would like to thank especially for their ideas, feedback, insights and conversations that have informed the pages of this book.

In alphabetical order these are:

- Kelly A. Duggan, M.S., Broker and Co-founder, Maximum Results Realty, LLC
- Janet A. Laatsch, former CEO, Greater Seacoast Community Health
- Max Latona, Executive Director, Center for Ethics in Society, St. Anselm University
- Rhaea Maurel, Founder and CEO, Rhaeart Creativity and Pottery Studio
- Tom Raffio, President and CEO of Northeast Delta Dental
- Diane Smith, former VP of Operations, Medtronic, New Hampshire

As always, I want to thank Rebecca Marsh and her team at Routledge. I am fortunate to have such a thoughtful, helpful and understanding person in Rebecca who makes the publishing process a pleasure.

## Note to Readers

All the case study narratives provided are true. However, all names of persons and companies have been changed as have the dates.

Annabel Beerel, PhD
August 2024

# Introduction

## Courage – The Secret to Happiness

### A Program for Life

Many years ago, as my hunt for courage gathered momentum, I came across an ancient quotation that subsequently changed my life. The quotation is an excerpt from the funeral oratory by the great Athenian leader, Pericles,[1] in honor of the soldiers who died in the first year of the Peloponnesian War:

> The secret to happiness is freedom and the secret to freedom is a brave heart.
>
> Pericles (494–429 BC)

In this one commanding sentence, Pericles links three significant ideas, happiness, freedom and courage, as the path to a meaningful life. A meaningful life is a happy one in a deep, abiding sense of happiness.

Let us begin with this idea of deep, abiding happiness. I doubt anyone would dispute that we all desire happiness and that we spend a great deal of our lives pursuing it. But what is this happiness? According to the ancients, happiness is a state of being that derives from one living one's full potential. Our sense of purpose in life, that enduring happiness we all long for, arises out of our living fully who we are. It is not a possession; it does not require having anything, no job, no status, no partner, no anything, just being fully oneself. Happiness IS our purpose, our mission, whatever you want to call it. The happiness we seek is BEING happy, not having it.

Now let us consider freedom. Beside our pursuit of happiness, we also expend an enormous amount of energy demanding freedom as we believe that without freedom, we cannot make the choices that will make us happy. What we misunderstand

DOI: 10.4324/9781003459644-1

is that it is not external freedom that makes us free (tomorrow there will be a new dictator or a new law), but internal freedom. Internal freedom is freedom from our conditioning, freedom from our fears, and freedom from our projections and inappropriate expectations. Internal freedom enables us to make choices freely uninhibited by any pressure or need other than to be our true selves. It is internal freedom that leads to happiness.

And what about courage? Courage arouses awe. It gives hope, it inspires. It reveals the incredible strengths and possibilities of the human spirit. Alas, often we assume that only certain, special people are capable of courage. We do not realize that courage is innate to who we are as human beings, something explained beautifully by Paul Tillich.

What Pericles's powerful oratory reminds us of is the transformative power of courage. Innately, we know this to be true in that we have been documenting stories of courage since the beginning of time. We call it history. The earliest mythology, ballads, sacred tales and epics are all stories of courage, and we love stories of courage as they touch us deeply because courage is our story too.

While there are certain identifiable conditions that define courageous acts (explained in Chapter 5), these acts are not the preserve of the elites, nor do they always refer to big, momentous, media-attention-grabbing actions. Courage, as we explore together in these pages, begins with small things that invariably have huge impacts.

Courage is a commitment – a commitment to being true and resolute when the chips are down and when escape of any kind seems preferable.

We all have this capacity, but being courageous does not just happen. It must be cultivated – cultivated not only as a way of acting, but as a way of being. If we desire abiding happiness, if we want true freedom, we must practice courage. With practice, courage becomes our fundamental disposition. It informs and shapes the way we live our lives. We explore what this means in the chapters to come.

## The Courage to Be

In 1952, the well-known twentieth-century philosopher and theologian Paul Tillich (1886–1965) wrote a remarkable book titled *The Courage to Be*. Courage, Tillich writes, "is an ethical reality rooted in the whole of human existence and ultimately in the structure of being itself" (Tillich 2000, 1). What Tillich means is that courage is part of existence, especially our existence, and that acting courageously affirms who we are as human beings. Courage is an act of self-affirmation of our essential nature. It is our ability to affirm ourselves despite fate or the reality of death. This self-affirmation is not selfishness in that it is the affirmation of our full humanity, not just its selfish aspects. It is self-affirmation that makes love of others possible. Self-affirmation and love, writes Tillich, are interdependent.

In his book, Tillich puts right before us our human responsibility to be courageous. If we wish to live a full and happy life, a life of well-being and flourishing where we avail ourselves of all the possibilities presented for our fulfillment, we are called to consciously develop our capacity for courage.

Tillich acknowledges that being courageous is by no means easy in a world of uncertainty and clashing opinions. It takes great courage to pursue our principles and not concern ourselves with public disfavor. It takes courage to refuse the attraction of dogmatisms, to be open to exposing our ideas to challenges and critique, and to live willing to be different. And it takes great courage to always live out of the best of our humanity.

Tillich points out that acting courageously demands sacrifices that if we fail to make, prevent us from being fully who we are. These sacrifices may include our own happiness and even our existence. Courage, therefore, always includes risk. Most often our submissive self wants to escape the pain of hurting and being hurt, or longs to overcome the existential anxiety of our death and the awareness of our mortality. Courage helps us transcend these anxieties and fears so that we can live a full life and experience a meaningful death without regrets.

Courage is morally praiseworthy in that it is through courage that goodness and truth are realized. Courage is a strength of mind capable of conquering whatever threatens the attainment of the highest good, and therefore it is also inherently noble. Courage is the very best of us, and it is only by being courageous that we have any hope of being happy, deeply happy, a happiness of which no one or no thing can deprive us. And we need good, courageous role models and leaders to help us step into our own courageous shoes.

## The Need for Courageous Leadership

Not since the 1920s have we faced such a torrent of uncertainty. In the intervening years we have told ourselves that we have brought the world under our control. Technology has catapulted us into space, into multinational corporations, and into global capitalism. As a result, we have exploited the planet and one another, and we have created the motto of growth as our saving way out of everything – poverty, mismanagement and other structural imbalances.

But where has all this technological progress got us? It has certainly not brought peace and prosperity to many people on the planet. Rather, we have landed ourselves a boatload of problems in every possible domain, and it is going to take astute leadership to help us navigate through this mess. A huge question is how to stop, take a deep breath, and look thoughtfully at our pile of seeming insurmountable challenges. Where should we begin?

Our first step must be to face reality, something we often loathe doing as then we would have to behave in ways that might be uncomfortable or inconvenient. It is far easier perpetuating the fallacies around which we have constructed our present lives. If we must face reality now, we will have to step out of our comfort zone and show some humility. We will need to develop an interest in learning new ways of being and behaving. This requires energy and commitment, and above all, courage.

We would far rather keep doing what we have always been doing and that is reacting with our favorite tricks and solutions even when these don't work.

To achieve the first step, we need the help of new and different leaders. We need leaders who understand their role as leaders, and who grasp that leadership is a role of service. What this service entails is identifying changing realities and unpacking what these changing realities imply for humankind. The critical piece is that reality cannot be countered or rationalized away – it can only be acknowledged and adapted to. It must be faced head on.

Well, what are these realities? Reality number one is that everything is impermanent and uncertain. The universe has been revealing this truth to us for ages, but we refuse to accept it at face value. We insist that we are in charge with guns, vaccines, fancy financial instruments and the promise of trips to Mars. But the universe will not be tamed, controlled or exploited. It will not be treated as a means to everyone's partisan, material ends.

Reality number two is that the universe is a live, intelligent, comprehensive system in which everything has its purpose and place. It thrives on balance and harmony. It is in continuous movement marked by creativity and life cycles of birth, maturity and decay. It demands respect and reverence. Nothing on earth escapes the universe's rules for any length of time. The universe will prevail. That is reality – the reality which we must stop resisting. This is what the new breed of leaders must help us to face.

This brings me to the main thesis of this book: the prime leadership skill that is required, and required urgently, is courage – courage to face reality and courage to deal with people's opposition and resistance.

Stories of leadership courage usually cover examples such as a food recall or a major case of quality control failures. This is not the courage I am exploring here. I am calling us to a far more profound notion of courage. I am concerned with courage that underpins character. Courage that is infused with wisdom, fortitude and resolve. I am referring to courage that is concerned with facing the truth and not winning a confrontation. A courage that initiates transformation. A courage that is not dependent on accolades but thrives on advancing goodness and well-being. A courage that is persistent and not erratic. A courage that is motivated by the desire to promote goodness and is not a matter of expediency.

We need leaders now who have the courage to dismantle our many broken systems, not fix, or repair them. We must start again based on new principles, the principles of the universe, the principles of reality. We need leaders who can usher in a new vocabulary of moderation, limits, and enough, who can demonstrate what these terms mean in practice – in your life and in mine.

We know that the only way out of a problem is by going through it. Well, the only way out of our current mess is by going through it. This means not fighting it but in good Taoist fashion, reading the energies of change and riding the waves. This requires courage of another order. A courage that can hold steady during uncertainty. A courage that knows when to respond and that does not become reactive. A courage to trust one's deepest instincts and a courage that can stay clear of defensive behaviors. It requires true courage of the heart – from which the word courage (French *Coeur*) is derived. This is the leadership courage we need right now.

Courage is the hallmark of an effective leader. Courage refers to the quality of a person's intention and action. While we tend to treat courage and leadership as separate concepts, effective leadership is intrinsically courageous, and courageous people are natural leaders. We are all leaders in that we all lead our lives. Some people are called to take on a role of leadership in and for a group, an organization or a nation. While the demands are the same, the complexities are compounded.

Where are we going to find courageous people who will help us deal with reality? Are we perhaps one of those courageous people? If so, let's get cracking. If we want to become one of those new breeds of leaders and are not sure where to start, let's start here, now, in this moment and the next.

## The Web We Have Woven

In 2015, David Korten penned his prescient book entitled *When Corporations Rule the World.* Using the backdrop of laissez-faire capitalism, a type of capitalism that has radically strayed from capitalism's original blueprint àla Adam Smith, Korten underscores how capitalism has become grounded in an elitist ideology of individualism devoted to the concentration of the wealth of a select few, mostly senior corporate leaders.

He, like many others, argues that the financial sector produces nothing of value, yet it accounts for an increasing share of the Gross Domestic Product (GDP) and of corporate profits. Government bailouts, for example, the TARP (Troubled Asset Relief Program (2009)) being a frightening example of corruption and mismanagement,[2] followed by the most recent Silicon Valley Bank debacle, feeds the excesses of the financiers, and fosters moral hazard. As a result, banks have become "too big to fail" and the cycle of supporting them without any consequences for their reckless behavior continues.

Korten states that greed has become sanctified and that American culture is focused on actions that yield the greatest financial return believing that this is in the best interests for society. Everyone, he claims, is oriented toward financial gain based on endless growth.

Korten is right. Due to our focus on growth and amassing more we are stuck. We want salary increases because costs keep going up. Costs keep going up because monopolies keep raising prices (see Chapter 9), and everyone wants salary increases to try to maintain their standard of living. Firms need to grow revenues to cover these escalating costs. We want the return on our investments to increase because costs keep going up. To increase returns we need to sell more because costs keep going up. Increasing returns means investing more and investing increases costs. So, we need to keep selling more to cover the costs of investments. We try to grow faster than costs do, which is like trying to run faster than our shadow. But resources are limited and exploiting them not only depletes them but puts up costs.

Growth is pursued in a frenzy to outrun costs. Corporations consolidate and create monopolies so that they can dominate markets and maximize revenue streams. Corporations lobby against regulation so that they can pursue revenue, control competition and grow to attract investment so that they can grow some more. We are caught in a capitalist web we have created for ourselves.

Corporations cheat, exploit, commit embezzlement and fraud and massage their results to prove that they are on top of the growth game. Corruption, as we discuss in Chapter 3, is pervasive. Whether it is WorldCom, Enron, Tyco, the Volkswagen Dieselgate saga, the Wells Fargo falsification of accounts episode, the manipulation of results by Bed, Bath & Beyond,[3] and the huge interwoven network of corruption in the financial services sector, thousands of people are complicit. Then there is big Pharma, the extractive industries, the universities and colleges, not to mention many government departments. People would rather get their bonuses and hold onto their jobs than blow the whistle. Blowing the whistle takes huge courage and the price is exceedingly high – something we discuss in detail in Chapter 4.

Corporations do rule the world, especially financial corporations, as their intricate international network of money, contracts and backhanders influences every aspect of life. These notably have an impact on the climate, the supply of food and water, demographics, economics, politics, and the quality of life in societies. There is no corner of our existence that escapes the extractive, manipulative powers of the corporations' tentacles.

Raghuram Rajan, formerly the Chief Economist and Director of Research at the International Monetary Fund, and currently the Distinguished Service Professor of Finance at the University of Chicago's Booth School of Business, raised multiple warnings in 2005 regarding the imminent collapse of the financial system. In a recent book, *The Third Pillar* (2019), he discusses how the three pillars of society, the state, the markets and the community, are out of balance and how this has led to an imbalance most especially of market power.

Rajan claims that the neglected pillar is the community. He argues that the bonds of communities are frayed due to the invasion of states and markets. Industries have become dominated by large firms who all but control everything and everyone. Markets no longer work for the community but for themselves. Real human networks have been eroded due to our transaction society. Government and state bureaucracies have reduced local control, crowded out community engagement and weakened the community as a key pillar of democratic vigilance. People have become less engaged citizens. They need to reclaim their sense of self-determination, he argues, and to feel that their actions can make a difference. Without engaged citizens who are "en-couraged" to stand up for what they want, the health of a democratic society is at great risk.

## Greed Rules

In 2012, the Harvard School political philosopher Michael J. Sandel wrote an eye-opening book titled *What Money Can't Buy*. Sandel's text is filled with examples of the expansion of greed and markets into areas in which they do not belong. He demonstrates convincingly how everything in American society is up for sale. He shows how we sell things that should never be up for sale such as unborn children. He explains the growth of the viatical industry where one can buy the policy of someone who is physically ailing at discount and then take over the premiums and collect the policy when the person dies. The moral implication lies in the hope that the ailing person dies sooner rather than later. The question this raises is whether there is a temptation to speed up the person's demise.

Sandel argues strongly that the virtues in American society languish and that market thinking and behavior invade every human activity. He poses the question "Do we want to live in a society where everything is up for sale?"

Here are some examples from Sandel's book:

1. In Santa Ana, California, nonviolent offenders can pay for a prison upgrade. They can get a clean, quiet jail cell, no doubt with a TV.
2. The services of an Indian surrogate mother to carry a pregnancy is $6,250. (This is in 2012.)
3. If you have $500,000 and promise to create 10 jobs in an area of high unemployment you can buy US citizenship.
4. You can pay someone – the price varies but in the thousands of dollars – to ensure your child gets into a prestigious university. You call it a donation!
5. For several hundred dollars, you can rent out space on your forehead to advertise – a tattoo displaying an ad – as Air New Zealand did to encourage people to fly with them.
6. You can buy the insurance policy of an ailing person, pay the premiums, and collect their death benefits when they die.
7. You can rent out your time to lobbyists who want to get into Capitol Hill and plead their case but don't have the time or do not want to be bothered to stand in line to get in. You can line up for them at $XX per hour (negotiable) and they can take your place when you get to the doors.

(Sandel 2014)

By this time – 2024 – no doubt the options for buying something or someone have grown exponentially since Sandel penned his book. True to the title of his book, is there anything we cannot buy?!

The philosopher, artist and award-winning filmmaker, Raoul Martinez, in his book *Creating Freedom: Power, Control and the Fight for Our Future* (2017), exposes the systemic mechanisms of control that pervade our lives, and that inhibit our external freedoms, along with the myths on which they depend. He points out how the language of freedom dominates the political and economic landscape – free markets, free trade, free elections, free media and free speech – and how ironically none of these are actually "free."

Of course, one must question what this term "free" refers to: free from what? For what? In practical terms it appears that free refers to being free from democratic control and being free for the subjugation of corporate interests. Surely this is not the freedom that enables people to make free choices to live the life they choose.

As discussed in the opening paragraph to this chapter, freedom is an ideal we clamor for. It is central to our concept of human dignity and hailed as the key to a meaningful life. Yet despite all the hoopla about free this and free that, few people enjoy this freedom. The system we have created is designed otherwise. Inequality has soared, economic corruption is ubiquitous, people work longer for less, refugee populations have grown in alarming proportions, forests disappear, sea levels rise and mental health is now a monumental problem, worldwide.

The regulation of business has been reduced to a bare minimum. US Senate members represent the views of their richest constituents. Over half the senators are millionaires. Winning a seat in the senate costs more than $16 million (2018) and a seat in the House of Representatives requires at least $2 million.

In 2011 the Occupy Wall Street movement sought to highlight the power of the 1%, the corruption of the financial industry, corporate greed and the extreme equality produced by the economic system. The movement was branded as a "left-wing populist movement" by the press and politicians. Due to lack of clear objectives and a cohesive storyline, the movement failed, yet, among a growing number of people resentment lingers. And this resentment is on the rise fueling the desire for someone – anyone – who will make promises, whether they are true or not – who will fix the problems. That is what the search for external freedom does: it lurches us from one form of leader to another.

But can we find the courage to seek and secure true freedom where not only can we make choices in our best interests but where we take full accountability for those choices? Where there is no one to blame? Where the buck stops right here with you and me?

Aye, there's the rub!

## How Much Is Enough?

In their book *How Much Is Enough* (2012), the brothers, Robert and Edward Skidelsky, challenge our current materialistic culture by asking how much is enough? They argue that capitalism, as currently practiced, has exalted greed, envy and excess. The commitment to growth at any cost has been fueled by motives of greed and acquisitiveness and the limitless desire for wealth. But when is enough, enough?

The two Skidelsky's claim that we have now taken the utilitarian ethic to the extreme where any means is acceptable in the service of material and financial ends. The idea of virtue has been discarded and supplanted by value neutral language such as utility and preferences. Being rich is deemed virtuous and being poor a vice.[4] Avarice is now called self-interest with wants and needs being both voracious and insatiable. We have lost all sense of moderation, of limits, of anything being enough. More is our motto, and we will do anything personally, organizationally and as a society to chase an endlessly insatiable desire for more. Where will it end? When will we have the courage to say "Enough"!?

## Money, Money, Money

What does money mean to us? What kind of relationship do we have with money? How deeply is it tied up with our identity, with how much or how little we have, and our ability to get more? Do we make worldly success the justification of our lives?

These are some of the questions Jacob Needleman, Professor of Philosophy and Religion at San Francisco State University, poses in his book *Money and the Meaning of Life* (1991). He points out that the issue of money dogs every step of our lives. Like Sandel, he asks whether there are things that money can't buy.

In prior times, Needleman reminds us, there were laws against usury as interest on loans was considered the exploitation of another's misfortune because only people in dire need borrowed. Interest was considered avarice and was forbidden. Nowadays we borrow money (profligately) to satisfy our insatiable wants, and the interest we pay for our desires is funding hundreds of thousands of people who thrive on our human condition.[5] We no longer need to be pitied but exploited.

Needleman explains how capitalism fuels our desires and makes having money or access to it a vital necessity. Money has now become the solution to everything. The meaning of life is tied up with our material wealth and our souls have been abandoned. The money changers have taken over the temple and we feed their coffers rather than our souls.

Money can never buy meaning, claims Needleman, even though we believe it to be a determiner of our worth. Money tests us, he writes, tests whether we can live a soulful life, a life of true meaning that can withstand anything and transcend everything.

Sadly, when we look at the thousands of people willing to sell their souls for jobs they hate or for money, through corruption, fraud and complicit behavior, it seems clear that we no longer know how to render to Caeser what is Caeser's, and to God what is God's.

## Who Do We Choose to Be?

In her thought-provoking book *Who Do We Choose to Be?* (2017), Margaret Wheatley challenges the reader to consider the choices we make as we are the sum of our choices. She highlights the need for islands of sanity amid a world that has lost its way – a world filled with failing systems, violent reactions to waves of uncertainty, a clamoring of conflicting manufactured identities and humans preoccupied with approval ratings rather than decency and courage.

Wheatley claims that we desperately need leaders, not more entrepreneurs, or more technological breakthroughs. We need leaders, real leaders, she claims. These are people who put service over self, who can be steadfast during times of crises, and who are not power-hungry or who manage by fear.

We need leaders who can face the fearful complexity of life, face reality head on and accept uncertainty. We have enough corrupt leaders with false promises.

Wheatley is known for taking a systems approach to leadership based on a systems view of life. In her book she points out how many of our systems are in disarray and that they foreshadow our decline and even possible collapse. She rails against our handing over our skills to technology, and our arrogance, and stupidity in the face of uncertainty which makes us keep on repeating what did not work in the past. She points out that chaos is an opportunity for new things to emerge and how organizations should use self-organizing systems to address problems during times of uncertainty and change. She pleads for leaders to step up to the nobility of leadership and not to flee reality or fight it. She asks us how we can evoke our best human qualities.

Wheatley cites the works of Joseph Tainter in *The Collapse of Complex Societies* (1988) and Sir John Glubb in *The Fate of Empires and Search for Survival* (1976). Independently, Tainter and Glubb studied many different societies. Both noted that a recurrent feature of every society is collapse and that the patterns that precede this collapse are almost identical no matter the geography, ethnicity or spiritual tradition.

According to Glubb, the *Stage of Decadence* always precedes collapse and can always be identified by the following traits:

- Politics are increasingly corrupt, and life increasingly unjust
- A cabal of insiders accrues wealth and power at the expense of the citizenry, fostering an opposition between haves and have nots
- There is increased narcissism, materialism and consumerism
- The masses are distracted by entertainment, sporting events and a celebrity culture
- There is a general abandonment of moral restraint, and leaders are in charge who believe they will govern forever

Are we perhaps entering this stage of decadence? What do you think?

## Where to Now?

The sanctification of greed, materialism and excess appears to dominate American culture. Individualism and self-interest are now the prevailing values. Virtue and courage are no longer part of our public lexicon. As I describe in detail in Chapter 5, and what emerged from the Courage surveys (Chapter 10), few people can articulate what virtue, character and courage mean as concepts and means to them personally. Alas, courage is an almost forgotten trait that has been supplanted with the idea of success in the form of fame, recognition and wealth. The idea of "the good life" no longer forms part of public discussion; instead, we talk about choice, efficiency and the protection of rights. Utility is the prime value expressed as what I want not what I ought to want. If I prefer crack to wine, then crack has more utility for me, and this justifies my desire as it gives me greater happiness than wine. There is no longer any objective sense of the good; it is now the good as each individual person conceives it. And sadly, the greatest waste of all is not material wealth but the best of our human possibilities.

Where we now stand:

- Principles are out and relativity is in
- Virtue is out and opportunistic success is in
- Self-mastery and self-discipline are out, and self-justification is in
- Self-determination is out and seeking of approval is in
- Character is out and high performance is in
- Courage is out and expediency and herd conformance are in
- Courage is out and self-justifying the ego's needs are in

So, where to now? Tillich, Korten, Rajan, Sandel, the Skidelsky brothers, Needleman and Wheatley, all challenge us to rethink our fundamental values. Who are we? Who do we choose to be? Can we return to a society based on virtue where courage is the cornerstone, and where we have the courage to face reality no matter how inconvenient it may seem? Will we awaken to the truth that the secret to the happiness we hunger for is freedom – freedom from avarice, pride, conditioned dogmas and opinions, and the need to be liked and affirmed. To attain this freedom, we must be courageous. We must respond courageously when we are called to act beyond our ego selves despite the call for great sacrifices but where we live a life of self-affirmation of our full humanity by having the courage to be.

This book explores both the concepts of freedom and courage and how these are essential traits for an effective leader. I also argue that the virtue of courage has been sorely neglected, and as a result our world is suffering. We no longer understand the depth and breadth of what courage means, which is much more than saving people from burning buildings.

Courage is an activity of the heart. Let's begin with that.

## Your Turn

- How responsive are you to changing realities, especially inconvenient or unpalatable ones?
- What is your relationship to money? Is it a determiner of your self-worth? Think carefully as you review your choices, your lifestyle, your job, your house, your neighborhood and the kids' school or college.
- Do you consciously practice moderation? Is it one of your lived values? How, when?
- Which leader/s are your role models? On what grounds?
- Do you practice courage regularly, intentionally?

## Notes

1 Pericles was a Greek general during the Golden Age of Athens. He was prominent and influential particularly between the Greco-Persian Wars and the Peloponnesian War.
2 Described in alarming detail in *Bailout* by Neil Barofsky, the Treasury appointed special inspector general, in charge of overseeing the allocation of TARP funds and ensuring that banks would not abuse the system. Here we see a firsthand account of how the United States Department of the Treasury bungled many initiatives and decidedly took the side of banks at a huge cost to taxpayers, where some lost everything they owned. See Chapter 3.
3 Bed and Bath Bankruptcy – After the stock hit an all-time high of $70 per share in January 2014, the stock fell below $40 a share in the latter half of 2016 amid softening sales. In 2019, year-over-year quarterly revenue growth began consistently coming in negative. On October 9, 2019, the company tapped Mark Tritton, Target's former chief of merchandising, as CEO. The stock soared 21 percent that day on hopes of a big turnaround, denying the reality of declining demand. Gustavo Arnal CFO, who jumped to his death on September 4, 2022, and others of the executive team made misleading statements and omissions when communicating to investors regarding the company's strategic plans and financial condition, and delayed disclosures about holding and selling their own shares. *New York Times*, September 6, 2022.
4 See Chapter 11 and the discussion of *The Tyranny of Merit* 2021, a book by Michael J. Sandel.
5 See the compulsion of consumerism in Chapter 3 and the need to keep up.

## References


Barofsky, Neil. 2012. *Bailout: How Washington Abandoned Main Street While Rescuing Wall Street*. New York: Free Press.

Glubb, Sir John. 1976. *The Fate of Empires and the Search for Survival*. London, UK: William Blackwood and Sons, Ltd.

Korten, David C. 2015. *When Corporations Rule the World*. Oakland, CA: Berrett-Koehler.

Martinez, Raoul. 2017. *Creating Freedom: Power, Control and the Fight for Our Future*. Edinburgh: Canongate Books.

Needleman, Jacob. 1991. *Money and the Meaning of Life*. New York: Doubleday.

Rajan, Raghuram. 2019. *The Third Pillar*. London, UK: William Collins.

Sandel, Michael J. 2014. *What Money Can't Buy: The Moral Limit of the Markets*. New York: Farrar, Strauss and Giroux.

Skidelsky, Robert, and Edward Skidelsky. 2012. *How Much Is Enough? Money and the Good Life*. New York: Other Press.

Tainter, Joseph. 1988. *The Collapse of Complex Societies*. Cambridge, UK: Cambridge University Press.

Tillich, Paul. 2000. *The Courage to Be*. New Haven, CT: Yale University Press.

Wheatley, Margaret J. 2017. *Who Do We Choose to Be?* San Francisco, CA: Berrett-Koehler Publishers, Inc.


## Recommended Reading


Twist, Lynne. 2017. *The Soul of Money*. New York: W.W. Norton & Company.

# Chapter 1

# Understanding Leadership

## New Realities

The following passage from the *Lord of the Flies* provides us with some powerful insights:

> "I should have thought that a pack of British boys – you're all British, aren't you? – would have been able to put up a better show than that –"
> "It was like that at first," said Ralph, "before things –"
> He stopped,
> "We were together then – "
> The officer nodded helpfully.
> "I know. Jolly good show. Like Coral Island."
> Ralph looked at him dumbly.
> Simon was dead – and Jack had . . . the tears began to flow, and sobs shook him. He gave himself up to them now for the first time on the island; great shuddering spasms of grief that seemed to wrench his whole body.
> Ralph wept for the end of innocence, the darkness of man's heart, and the fall through the air of the true, wise friend called Piggy.
> (William Golding, *Lord of the Flies* 1969, 223)

Some of us may recall William Golding's grim novel *Lord of the Flies*, which begins with a group of young boys evacuating from Britain because of a nuclear war. Their plane crashes, all the adults are killed, and the boys find themselves stranded on an uninhabited island.

The plot unfolds with the fight for leadership between Ralph and Jack and the disastrous attempt by the boys to create some kind of social order. Instead, they

DOI: 10.4324/9781003459644-2

devolve into brutality and savagery where three of the boys die – one disappears and is presumed dead, and two become the victims of manslaughter – or murder – depending on your perspective.

While this masterpiece of fiction reflects the dark side of human nature, let us not dismiss it simply as an entertaining tale. Sadly, we do not have to look far to see how rapidly we, supposedly civilized people, become a murderous mob or how often we demolish or "kill" others who stand in our way.

The horrific repercussions that whistleblowers encounter as chronicled in Tom Mueller's powerful tome *Crisis of Conscience* (2019) (discussed in Chapters 3 and 4), and the dishonest and disreputable national and global networks that eliminate everything that obstructs their rapacious paths so vividly described in Sarah Chayes's book *On Corruption in America: And What Is at Stake* (2021), remind us that our evil shadows are very close. This is no fiction! It is the most ethically challenging and deepest truth we can, and must, face.

Fear and uncertainty were factors that played no small measure in the boys' tale. Similarly, when we are devoid of constraining structures or we're fearful, we become murderous in the middle of Manhattan, not just on an uninhabited island.

The two main characters of the *Lord of the Flies* are Ralph and Jack. Jack, who is jealous of Ralph's leadership capabilities, attacks him as being a coward. Jack believes hunting is what the boys should engage in, while Ralph wants to build huts. Here we see some different approaches to dealing with new realities and radical uncertainty. Either the leader endeavors to tame it by "building huts" or fight it by "going hunting" – that is, finding someone or something to kill. In the tale, the majority prefer to follow Jack and go hunting. We too often choose to fight new realities rather than adapt to them. The choices here, which are not the only ones we engage in, also reflect the tension between our more civilized and primitive instincts.

Jack seeks to convince the other boys that Ralph has no stomach for hunting and that he would flee if attacked by a wild pig. How could such a coward be a leader, he asks?

Ralph tries his best to resist Jack's taunts but vacillates, thus losing his authority. How often don't leaders pick the wrong courage – the courage to defend their ego called their honor, that façade courage masquerading as the tough fighter ready to fight the hard fight and win? The real courage of course is staying true to what is true – true to one's own principles of goodness and principled resolve regardless of the temptation to succumb to bravado or popularity. How often don't leaders vacillate just to hold onto their power only to find themselves on the slippery slope of fighting the wrong fight for the wrong reason. And how often don't we follow suit?

The only steady person in the entire story is the short, fat boy, with asthma, Piggy. Piggy, the one who wore the glasses that could light the fire to attract help, the glasses that represented vision and insight, the glasses that had to be snatched away and broken; Piggy, the fat boy, discredited by others as he bravely stood for civility, kindness and wisdom; Piggy, who demonstrated courage by speaking the truth and by advising Jack repeatedly to take the high road; Piggy, the short fat boy, who would not normally be seen as courageous as usually we ascribe courage to tall, strong, good-looking men. Piggy had to die. That is what evil does. Corruption, destruction and unscrupulousness kill all kindness, all fairmindedness and all wisdom. And those who are not the perpetrators most often just stand by, their silence being their lack of courage to counter the corruption, and the evil. Cowardice is everywhere.

While the story is both sad and damning of human nature, in it we see some hope. Ralph's self-awareness and grief remind us that at our roots we know and long for goodness and truth. We recognize our ethical fragility and our struggles between the pulls of light and darkness. In Ralph's tears lies his redemption and ours too – the humility to face our shadow and begin anew.

In Ralph's story we see the struggles of the human spirit and how it is amplified when one takes on the role of leadership. In these next pages, we will travel back and forth between the person as leader and the person in the role of leadership and the enormity of the need for courage both personally and professionally.

We begin with looking at the significance of the role of leadership.

## No Courage = No Leadership

Despite hundreds of books on leaders, and millions of courses and seminars on leadership, not to mention the billions of dollars poured annually into leadership training, we still do not understand how leadership works.

Admittedly there is a mystique to the power of leaders, especially the great ones, and how they have influenced and changed millions of people's lives, sometimes for millennia. Having studied these leaders over the centuries, one would have thought that by now we would have grasped the essentials, defined the character traits required and figured out how to cultivate them. Alas not so. The record of our leadership efforts is abysmal. Evidence lies in our fractured world, our determination to ignore or fight realities that do not suit us, our fixation with fighting rather than peace, and the massive corruption that exists in every corner of society. We have discarded the importance of character, virtue and ethics in favor of relativism, opportunism, technical savvy and charisma. And we continue to exchange justice for power, and courage for expediency.

The tragic result is that we have very few good leaders – and by good, I mean both ethically good and effective. Whether it is in politics or business or any other arena, good leadership is scarce. What is in ample supply is people in power who know how to line their pockets and who unfortunately encourage others to do the same. There are a multitude of leaders who happily abuse their authority and never really lead people anywhere, other than into the same grimy unethical pit in which they dwell.[1]

What add to the complexity in describing the magical ingredients of leadership are the different arenas in which leaders operate. Let us take a few examples from documented history: the Buddha, Plato, Pythagoras, Alexander the Great, Jesus,

Mohammad, Leonardo da Vinci, Martin Luther, Florence Nightingale, Albert Einstein, Sigmund Freud, Mahatma Gandhi, Franklin D. Roosevelt, Angela Merkel, Bill Gates and Steve Jobs.

Based on this very short list, and despite the variety of landscapes and circumstances in which they exercised their leadership influence, we find, however, a clear commonality in their actions. For example:

- They all came to the fore during times of uncertainty marked by upheaval and change
- They played an instrumental role in responding to and shaping the changing environment
- They initiated movement; that is, they lead people from one physical, emotional, psychological, or spiritual place to another
- They oriented people to adapting to the new realities
- They held people's feet to the fire to change and adapt, often at a great personal price
- They all demonstrated great personal courage

What we note from these commonalities is that leadership is first and foremost about the processes of change during times of uncertainty. It is concerned with aligning a society, a group or an organization to changing realities that, in most cases, are muddy and have not been clearly formulated or explicitly articulated. In response, many people fight the new order and/or resist out of fear of the unknown.

As we saw in Ralph's story, and we know from our own experience, the work of leadership is dangerous, and it is no surprise that few people have the mettle for it. The stakes are high, and leaders are vulnerable to making all kinds of mistakes – physical or other. To prevail and survive, leaders need courage, determination and perseverance. They need to be able to deal with uncertainty, to make decisions when faced with new and complex problems, and to have the confidence and self-determination to hold steady despite not having all the answers and being challenged by others. Effective leadership therefore requires foresight and insight, and undoubtedly strength of character, which includes having courage.

No courage = no effective leadership. It is as simple as that.

## The Inner Call

The above discussion applies directly to you and me. We are all leaders in that we lead our lives, and our lives are in continuous movement and transition. Nothing remains the same. From one day to the next, there are new realities, new dramas, new problems and new opportunities. We too then, as leaders of our lives, are change agents continuously grappling with the process of change. We are also perpetually facing uncertainty, something which many of us dislike intensely and try to deny, or fight. We too, like organizational or societal leaders, must make decisions in new situations where we do not have all the facts, or, in many cases, previous solutions to turn to. Regrettably, in our desire to rid ourselves of the discomfort of uncertainty, we often cede our personal agency to some charismatic authority figure who promises to take away our discomfort by giving us simple answers in return for our allegiance.

### The Flight From Uncertainty

> People have a psychological need to feel certain. To have shifting sand continuously underneath their feet makes their life difficult. This gives an opportunity to those cunning people who can pretend that they deal exactly in the commodities you need. . . . The leader only has to be this clever, that he goes on watching the mood of the people, where they are moving. He always stays ahead of the crowd. The crowd will have moved with some idiot who does not bother to wonder about where they are going. You may be going to hell, but you follow the leader as he is ahead of you. . . . And the leader will go on promising whatever the crowd is asking for – nobody will expect you to fill your promises, they are only asking to be promised. The leader does not worry about fulfilling promises. Whenever they catch up with you, you can just give bigger promises. . . . And people believe in promises because they want to believe.
>
> *Intelligence: The Creative Response to Now*, OSHO 2004, 57–58.

Our personal lives are stories of the continuous adaptation to changing circumstances, be it marriage, divorce, death, a new job, the end of an old one, babies arriving or college kids leaving. Sometimes we just cope. At other times, we find opportunities that allow us to explore and live into new possibilities. We know that our attitude counts, our resilience matters and our courage is called on almost every day as we step into new situations and new uncertainties.

We also know in the depths of our hearts when our courage fails us. We know when we have sold ourselves out and made promises we could not keep, when we denied the truth and lied, when we sabotaged someone else rather than face some challenge we needed to face, or when we turned a blind eye to unethical behaviors at work or within our community. We know deep inside when our so-called leaders are lying or obscuring the truth, but often it seems easier to act dumb and to succumb than to stand up and call out what is not right. Hopefully someone else will do it, or the whole issue, whatever it may be, will go away.

We know – but we don't talk about it much – that to live honestly, reliably and responsibly, to be faithful and true to who we want to be require courage, and we know too that many times we fail. We also know that it takes courage to admit our failures, courage to pick ourselves up and try again, and again, and courage to be able to live up to an inner motto of living a life of character based on well-tested principles.

Having courage day in and day out is difficult. When we are courageous, we feel good. We know that we have shown the best of ourselves, and that we have, in Paul Tillich's language, had the courage to be who we truly are. There is no better feeling than when we stand up for what is true or good or just, when we do not succumb to temptation and when we act out of our higher selves.

How often don't we wish that we could always act from that place. That longing is the call of courage, the inner call that is part of our full humanness, the call to be all that we can be. The call of courage exists in all of us, and that is why we have such a need to justify ourselves or convince ourselves of our innocence as facing our own self-condemnation is more than we can bear (see Chapter 7 – Why Can't We Be Courageous).

## The Courage to Face the Truth

Leadership expert Margaret Heffernan, in her book *Wilful Blindness* (2012), explores the forces at work that make us deny the threats that stare us in the face. Through stories ranging from broken marriages, X-rays given to pregnant mothers knowing that radiation damages prenatal children, the lingering presence of asbestos, the 1987 financial collapse due to derivatives that several people predicted would play a major role in the next financial debacle, and did, the Catholic Church scandal, Enron and the BP environmental disaster, Heffernan highlights people's fierce determination not to see what is right before their eyes if it in any way hints at change and conflict, or creates cognitive dissonance. She points out that we don't want to know what challenges our values and deeply held beliefs. We filter out, edit, rationalize, ignore, defer and become quite blind to truths we do not want to, or cannot bear to, hear. Our fragile egos serve as virulent gate keepers.

Not only do we willfully ignore or deny what scares us or does not suit us, we frequently engage in self-deception. This is eloquently explained in Shankar Vedantam and Bill Mesler's book, *Useful Delusions: The Power & Paradox of the Self-Deceiving Brain* (2021). Here the authors claim that we all seek beliefs that tell us we have a purpose, and that our lives are okay. We eschew the hard truth, as, according to them, our eyes and brains are not in the truth business but in the functionality business (Vedantam and Mesler 2021, xxi). We are gullible, and once deceived, many of us defend ourselves by denying the reality that we were duped.

The situation of both blindness and self-deception is worsened when it comes to the collective. The cultic nature of groups encourages groupthink, the denial of contradictory realities and the need to feel invincible. Groups readily rationalize away a reality that does not meet their own. (This is expanded upon in Chapter 7.) For our universal collusion, see No Surprises – Everything Is Forewarned.

As discussed in my book *Ethical Leadership and Global Capitalism: A Guide to Good Practice* (2020), not only do groups share common understandings and outlooks; they also share secrets and defense mechanisms. They learn to see things the same way, and how not to see what they do not want to see. For example, if the group wants to deny the reality of unethical behavior, it will. The group also has the potential to "kill" anyone who breaks the unconscious agreement of deception – see Chapter 4 on whistleblowers. Collaboration at all levels is the name of the game and the passport to safety. These are some of the things I did not know or understand when I witnessed the conspiracy of silence in those early days as an audit clerk.

Can denying reality, as Vedantam and Mesler imply, serve us? Can we avoid the truth, and live with deception and be happy? Well, that depends on whether one wants to live a self-accountable and authentic life or not. The truth about the truth is that in the end, truth, that is, reality, always prevails. It does not wait for anyone's acknowledgement, acceptance or approval. We can ignore it, deny it, dilute it or fight it, yet the sea tide of change always arrives. And the longer we wait to embrace the truth, the fewer options are available to us and the higher the cost, not simply in inconvenience, but to our very existence.

**No Surprises – Everything Is Forewarned**

***2001 9/11 attacks***

Approximately 3,000 people killed.

Starting in the spring of 2001, the CIA repeatedly and urgently began to warn the White House that an attack was coming. The Bush government shrugged it off and did nothing.

***2004 Tsunami in Indonesia***

Approximately 230,000 people killed.

One week beforehand many animals fled to higher ground.

No one was watching.

***2005 Hurricane Katrina***

1,800 people killed.

Deaths due to flooding were caused by engineering flaws in the flood protection system created by the Army Corps of Engineers. In April 2007, the American Society of Civil Engineers termed the flooding of New Orleans as "the worst engineering catastrophe in US History."

***2008/2009 Financial Crash***

Predicted by many people beginning in the 1990s – see my Chapter 4 on corruption.

***April 2013 – Boston Marathon Patriots Day Bombing***
Three people killed, 254 injured.

Two years before the Boston Marathon bombings, Tamerlan Tsarnaev and Zubeidat Tsarnaeva came to the attention of the Federal Bureau of Investigation (FBI) as adherents of radical Islam. In September 2011, based on new information received Tamerlan Tsarnaev was added to the terrorist watchlist. Nothing further was done.

***2018, 2019 – Boeing 737 MAX***
Two crashes – 346 people killed.
Boeing admitted that it knew well over a year before the first crash of a 737 MAX in Indonesia that a warning light linked to a key sensor on the 737 MAX wasn't working on most of the airplanes. They failed to inform the Federal Aviation Administration (FAA) or the airlines operating the jet about the problem until after the crash.

***2020 COVID-19***
Estimated deaths worldwide – 3.5 million people: US 1.1 million (April 2023).

Disease experts have been issuing warnings about a massive pandemic for decades. COVID-19 showed how unprepared the world is. In 2005, the George W. Bush administration published a pandemic plan, which included the distribution of medical supplies from the Strategic National Stockpile in the event of an outbreak. In 2009, a federal task force recommended that the Obama administration replenish that stockpile of N95 protective face masks, which had been depleted during that year's swine flu outbreak. Nothing was done. The Trump administration abandoned the US health and security team and the stockpile altogether.

***February 2022 – Russia-Ukraine War***
Approximately 30,500 people killed to date (February 2024).

In October 2021, US intelligence warned of a near-certain mass-scale Russian invasion of Ukraine. Despite repeated warnings from the US, President Volodymyr Zelenskyy and his officials played down the possibility of an incursion, delaying the mobilization of their troops and reserve forces. Ukraine was totally unprepared for the initial attacks, leading to hundreds of deaths.

***August 2024 – Hamas-Israel War***
Estimated 40,000 Israelis and Palestinians killed so far.

Israel's military was aware of Hamas's plan to launch an attack on Israeli soil over a year before the devastating October 7th operation that killed hundreds of people, according to the *New York Times*, December 2023. They did nothing.

Because we tend to dislike new realities – unless they suit us – effective leaders are often the unwelcome messengers. In the face of our denial or resistance, it takes great courage to hold our feet to the fire so that we acknowledge the new realities and adapt. Unfortunately, many leaders lack the nerve to follow through if our clamor of discomfort is too loud.

## Leaders Need Nerve

A failure of nerve affects the entire American civilization and is especially prevalent among its leaders, wrote ordained rabbi, therapist and leadership consultant, Edwin H. Friedman (1932–1996), in his book, *A Failure of Nerve* (2007).

According to Friedman, American society is one plagued by chronic anxiety, reactivity, a tendency toward blaming, a desire for herding and a quick fix mentality. In this environment, he argued, leaders are not developed or encouraged to have clarity and decisiveness. They are poor at understanding problems and lack the important ability to frame issues. What would Friedman say now in 2024, I wonder?

Friedman claimed that there is a general failure of nerve by leaders to be self-differentiating and self-determining. Many lack self-regulation where they monitor and manage their own anxiety. They tend to appease others who claim to support them, and sabotage or work to destroy any resistance. They are reactive, blame others and are not personally accountable. They look for symptom relief rather than creating or inspiring fundamental change, and they lack the courage to stay the distance.

Friedman also discussed the misuse of real empathy. He cites examples of where a leader feels overwhelmed or powerless and instead of doing the hard work of leading, engages in empathy talk, thereby trying to unite followers into a sympathetic consensus.

Friedman claimed there needs to be a revolution in leadership training. He stressed the need for leadership self-differentiation. With self-differentiation, leaders have no need to fuse with others. They have a well-defined self and a principled presence. They have the capacity to go it alone and not try to change others. They can demonstrate endurance during a crisis and can withstand reactive sabotage. They are willing to be transformed by their experience and they understand the importance of self-regulation. They can tolerate the pain of isolation, the pain of loneliness, the pain of personal attacks and the pain of losing friends. They have a strong sense of self, they can be vulnerable and they can take a well-defined stand.

According to Friedman,

> Self-differentiation includes a capacity to be a non-anxious presence, a challenging presence, a well-defined presence, and a paradoxical presence. Differentiation is not about being coercive, manipulative, reactive,

> invasive but being rooted in the leader's own sense of self rather than focused on that of the followers.
>
> (2007, 230)

Friedman claimed that having nerve is,

> A willingness to be exposed and vulnerable. One of the major limitations of imagination's fruits is the fear of standing out. It is more than a fear of criticism. It is anxiety at being alone, of being in a position where one can rely little on others, a position that puts one's own resources to the test, a position where one will have to take total responsibility for one's own response to the environment. Leaders must not only not be afraid of that position; they must come to love it.
>
> (2007, 84)

While Friedman's critique appears to be right on the money, his approach is different from the many leadership theories currently in vogue. Contemporary theories devote copious attention to leaders' responsibilities for taking care of employees and are effusive in their praise for empathetic leadership styles. Everything is about the emotionally sensitive leader.

Friedman does not discount the importance of these attributes but argues they must have their appropriate place. They are necessary but by no means sufficient. Friedman focuses instead on the psychological strength and bandwidth that effective leadership demands. Alas, while psychology is at the root of understanding and influencing leadership behaviors, few corporate leaders appreciate the importance of psychology and its role in their own and others' sense of identity, self-esteem, motivation and performance.

Leaders need to have nerve – they need courage! They need to understand that sabotage comes with the territory of leading. They need to be able to withstand the risks of displeasing and refrain from being held hostage by victims. They must be separate while being connected, being their own well-differentiated selves who can admit mistakes without cowering and being able to weather a storm of protest.

Self-defining leaders with courage must cease trying to regulate toxic forces with reasonableness, love and empathy. They must be able to take a stand where they focus on their own integrity and strength of presence. Alas, writes Friedman, in efforts to be collaborative and understanding, leaders frequently allow dependent and weak people with regressive tendencies to set agendas.

And, sadly, we see everywhere weak, ineffective leaders who cannot handle facing the reality that an organization or a project is failing and choose instead to resort to cooking the books. (See Chapter 3 on corruption.) Global Crossing, WorldCom, Bernie Madoff, Wirecard, Theranos and many more provide examples of failing organizations where executives tried to mask the reality by fudging the numbers and pilfering what they could from the dwindling assets as fast as they could.

Then there is Volkswagen, Wells Fargo, and Credit Suisse, all large companies who did not face their new realities and chose to engage in fraud and noncompliance rather than face the hard work of significant change that new realities were demanding of them. What is also significant is that in all these companies many employees actively participated either in massaging financial results or in engaging in outright fraud. Some, under pressure to perform, were responsible for initiating the corruption.

The repeated mantra is that leaders need to be ethical, courageous and strong. They must be able to withstand bad news and they must be able to hold steadfast through crises and failures. They need to cultivate habits of reflective thinking and they must resort to grounding principles that guide their decisions. Courage needs to be part of their character; it needs to be who they are and not just what they do.

If we think back on Ralph, he did not have the courage to stay true to himself or to take Piggy's advice – Piggy the fat boy that was supposedly ineffectual and incompetent. Ralph was challenged to be self-determining, to accept that sometimes hard decisions do not win one popularity and that strength often lies in not fighting but holding steady.

We note too in Golding's story how most of the boys just wanted to be led, and the person who spoke the loudest and who gave them a distraction from facing the real issues, Jack, won out – note the OSHO quote above! Most of the boys just wanted to be part of the herd, relieved not to have to decide and just to follow whomever led. Is that not something that we frequently witness too? Are we perhaps one of the herds?

If we cast our minds back to my opening story in the Preface, when leaders display a lack of courage and are tempted to abuse their authority and act unethically, people in the organization not actively engaged in the abuse, fraud or corruption are aware that something is going on. Why do they tolerate it? Why do so few people challenge leaders or the leadership team if they sense foul play? And why do those who choose silence or feign ignorance attack and ostracize those who have the backbone and character to protest, like Piggy or the whistleblowers we meet in Chapter 4? These are some of the questions we tackle in the next chapters.

## In a Nutshell

Courage lies at the heart of leadership. Leaders need not only courage to face their own uncertainties, fears, limitations and shadows, but the courage to hold other people's feet to the fire to do the same.

It takes courage to take risks; it takes courage to take the high road in the face of opposition; it takes courage to stand apart from the group and break the pact of collusion; it takes courage to create new precedents, new norms and new conventions. It takes courage to have difficult conversations around ethical and moral matters.

Effective leaders have character and courage. As Paul Tillich insisted, they have the courage to be.

## Your Turn

- What are your strategies during times of uncertainty – personally, professionally?
- How well do you respond to new realities? Are you able to adapt to them immediately or are you someone who says "let's wait and see?"
- How dependent are you on the opinion of others? Are you self-defining and self-determining or are you always playing politics and trying to be admired by the group?
- Are you able to take the high road in the face of opposition and go it alone, or do you back down and just go along with the group or your peers?

## Note

1 In this text, I am focusing on people who exercise leadership and not on people who are simply authority figures and are mistakenly referred to as leaders. There is a great difference between the role of authority and that of leadership. See Annabel Beerel, *Rethinking Leadership: A Critique of Contemporary Theories* (Abingdon, Oxon: Routledge, 2021).

## References

Beerel, Annabel. 2020. *Ethical Leadership and Global Capitalism: A Guide to Good Practice.* Abingdon, Oxon: Routledge.

Beerel, Annabel. 2021. *Rethinking Leadership: A Critique of Contemporary Theories.* Abingdon, Oxon: Routledge.

Chayes, Sarah. 2021. *On Corruption in America: And What Is at Stake.* New York: Vintage Books.

Friedman, Edwin H. 2007. *A Failure of Nerve: Leadership in the Age of the Quick Fix.* New York: Seabury Books.

Golding, William. 1969. *Lord of the Flies.* Glasgow, UK: Glasgow University Press.

Heffernan, Margaret. 2012. *Wilful Blindness.* New York: Bloomsbury.

Mueller, Tom. 2019. *Crisis of Conscience: Whistleblowing in the Age of Fraud.* New York: Riverhead Books.

OSHO. 2004. *Intelligence: The Creative Response to Now.* New York: St. Martin's Griffin.

Vedantam, Shankar, and Bill Mesler. 2021. *Useful Delusions: The Power & Paradox of the Self-Deceiving Brain.* New York: W. W. Norton.

# Chapter 2

# Leading in an Uncertain World

## Cassandra's Gift

In Greek mythology, Cassandra, the daughter of Priam and Hecuba, was one of the princesses of Troy. Allegedly she was astonishingly beautiful and was blessed with the gift of foreseeing the future. The god Apollo, in retaliation for Cassandra's spurning his amorous advances, punished her by ensuring that no one would believe her prophesies.

In the "Aeneid," Aneas, a Greek hero, recounts how Cassandra foresaw the destruction of Troy.[1] When the Trojans found the big wooden horse outside the gates of their city, Cassandra warned them that the Greeks would destroy them if they brought the horse into the city walls. Ignoring her prophesy, the Trojans found to their chagrin that the Greeks concealed within the horse had emerged during the night, opened the gates to the waiting warriors, and proceeded to decimate Troy. Hence the famous phrase "Beware of Greeks bearing gifts."

Cassandra's curse persists to this day as we observe many modern-day Cassandras being frequently mocked or ignored. And as many of us have learned, individually, organizationally and nationally, failing to heed Cassandra's prophesy, which comes in many guises, can have dire consequences.

## We Were Warned

As mentioned in Chapter 1, leadership is about identifying new realities and mobilizing people to respond to them. Reality being what is real, what is true and not some fabricated ego job pontificated by someone in authority.

DOI: 10.4324/9781003459644-3

To respond to new realities, leaders must be committed to wrestling with the forces of surprise, uncertainty and change in the context of complex systems. They need to be aware that signals always exist alluding to the imminent arrival of a new reality even though these signals may be difficult to detect or decipher. The signals may come by way of a hunch, a rumor, a sudden change in patterns of behavior or a few people in a faraway city most people have never heard of getting a strange flu. As pointed out in Chapter 1, there are no surprises; everything is forewarned. We just need to be attentive, curious, persistent and open to change.

Leaders need to be Cassandras. They must always be on the lookout for change signals. They need to be like lighthouses continually sweeping the horizon for new patterns. And they need to be open to the arrival of both positive and negative change signals – the earlier the better. They must have the willingness to be overwhelmed and the capacity to handle uncertainty and to stand alone.

## Reality Means Radical Uncertainty

Since the beginning of history, there have been seers, shamans, prophets and fortune tellers. Their role has been to bring reassurance in times of uncertainty. They were the soothsayers, interpreters and magicians who helped humans deal with the fear of the unknown and who pandered to their refusal to accept that the future is unknowable. Prophesies have always been in demand.

Over the centuries, our dislike and fear of uncertainty has not dissipated. On the contrary, what makes things different now is that, due to our interconnected world, uncertainty appears to be more enveloping and more overwhelming, moving faster than before, revealing seemingly new and different dimensions and trajectories. We don't like this at all. We have all kinds of strategies to try to grab uncertainty by the neck and take charge of it. Here willful blindness and self-deception trip us up again. Rather than accept and live with the uncertainties, and see what we can learn from them, we ignore, deny and fight them. We feign that we are in control, that things are overblown and that the past is simply repeating itself at a faster pace.

With the rapid progress in science and technology, we have become even more determined to control the uncontrollable. Entrepreneurs and business leaders have now assumed the role of framers of reality and as self-appointed prophets and God-ordained appointees responsible for seeing and controlling the future. Meditation, trances and visions are out, science and technology labs, and AI are in. The current focus of education and employment is on the sciences. Philosophy and the art of living are deemed a waste of time. Who cares about comparative religion, history and literature when there is data analytics, biotech, AI and algorithms all set up to provide solutions. Forget questions. Questions are philosophical, abstract and a waste of time. Let's get to solutions as quickly as possible!

Our modern mind believes that we can control the future or at least influence it in some dramatic way. Our fantastic scientific progress has, or soon will have, everything under the control of some telescope, formula or computer code. We are within the finishing line of being invincible – COVID shook us up, but that is already forgotten – and now we are determined to move even faster to ensure we are masters of the universe and can combat or manipulate anything that might be in store. We HATE uncertainty. We are determined to squeeze certainty out of any unpredictability and make it manageable. For many, AI will be the magical elixir.

Pride followed by greed heads the list of the seven deadly sins, and our egos have become so large that we can barely walk through any normal portal. Despite our continuous self-assurance, science and technology cannot totally save us or insulate us from what is real, and because we refuse to make necessary corrections in response to new realities, we lie and cheat and pretend that things are going well. We tell ourselves, and others, we just need a little correction here and there. This is where our courage fails us and where the slippery slope of ethical misdemeanors begins. It starts small with that little cover-up, that minor adjustment, and the promised correction never happens. Before we know it, our company is in trouble, big trouble. Our product quality is down the tubes, dysfunction has set in and our cash flows are shaky.

## Early Warning Signals

In 1985, I was invited to be a visiting lecturer at Henley Management College in Oxfordshire, UK. I had recently completed my MBA and was working in corporate finance in the City of London. My great interest, which began in my days as a strategic planner in South Africa, lay in identifying companies in trouble long before they got into trouble. Maybe it was those early audit reconnaissance experiences that convinced me that the early warning signals of trouble are always there, hidden in plain sight.

Back in my strategic planning days, I devised a framework for analyzing the health of companies with a view to their likely survival and sustainability. Over the years, as I gained more insights, and with the help of Michael Porter's *Competitive Strategy* (1998), I kept tweaking my framework. It was this framework that I introduced to my classes at Henley.

The Henley students were all working adults from a variety of industries. Eager to evaluate their organizations, they gladly volunteered their company's information. Using my framework, we analyzed their organization's strengths, the imminent threats and their likely longer-term survival unless the company took some corrective action or drastically altered course. Some of the questions that underpinned the framework included industry and environmental trends, current competencies, stage in the life cycle, culture, product mix, markets, resource mix and financial strengths. The questions were aimed at detecting any early signs of impending problems. In a high percentage of instances, much to the students' amazement, there were blaring warning signals – as always, one just needed to know where and how to look.

Within the three years of my hosting my sessions and diagnosing student organizations, which I then continued to track, a significant percentage of my predictions of impending failure came true. At the time, I was not focusing on the ethical behavior of the companies' executives, but more on how, given certain parameters, the writing on the proverbial wall as to their imminent demise was painted in orange and purple graffiti. It could not be missed if one was paying attention.

It was at that time too that I became aware of the ethical shenanigans that CEOs and their leadership teams get into to conceal their emergent problems. My diagnostic framework provided the basis of my first AI expert system (discussed in *Expert Systems: The Strategic Implications and Applications*, 1987), which began my nine-year stint of founding and running an AI company that developed diagnostic tools for corporations.

Marianne M. Jennings's book, *The Seven Signs of Ethical Collapse: How To Spot Moral Meltdowns Before It Is Too Late* (2006), points out, as I did, that the signals of collapse are always evident well before the organization either takes remedial action or, as in too many cases, takes the cowardly action of lying, cheating or stealing.

Jennings identifies seven key signals that predict corporate moral failure that inevitably lead to the organization's demise. These are:

- Pressure to maintain those numbers
- Fear and silence
- Young 'Uns and Bigger than Life CEO
- Weak board
- Conflicts
- Innovation like no other
- Goodness in some areas atone for evil in others.

(Jennings 2006)

While I agree that these are important signals, I believe there are other causal indicators that arise prior to many of the items she identifies. For example, the type of industry plays a significant role as does how the organization is financially structured. Then there is the organization's stage in the life cycle. Once an organization experiences a high growth phase, usually early in its life cycle, the hubris begins and the desire to perpetuate double digit growth indefinitely takes hold. Also, industries whose products are abstract or complex, for example, financial services, or extractive industries, make it easier for management to be less transparent to consumers and regulators alike.

It is most unfortunate that, in the 1980s, the whole idea that the most important goal of the firm is to maximize the value of the firm by advancing the share price, known as shareholder capitalism, took such a rabid hold of the US (and UK) corporate mind. The rise of share options as a popular method of compensation in the 1990s added to this phobia. These trends created a shift to a shareholder ideology where the only stakeholders that mattered are those who hold stocks and the CEO and his or her senior executives.[2] This ideology has fueled an obsession with numbers where employees are dutybound to deliver or else. When difficulties arise or new realities have been ignored and things are not going well, they are typically told "to figure it out." Since in many cases their jobs depend on it, figure it out they do and the slippery slope either begins or gathers momentum – note Enron, Tyco, Bed Bath & Beyond and so on. Over the years, nothing has changed. Many still passionately embrace shareholder wealth as the normative goal.

In my experience many, many companies and their leadership teams are very poor at reading the environment systemically. They might identify a few blatant new trends in their industries, but the more subtle tidal movements across the globe and the reconfiguration of industries along with rapid innovation and intense competition from unexpected quarters invariably catch them unawares. While I put much of this down to hubris and complacency, I also argue that a lack of courage plays a huge role – courage to think out of the BOX, to ask the scary "what if" questions and to make certain radical decisions that may include taking new and different risks. There is also the courage to admit that they do not have all the answers and that they need to invite other's ideas and opinions with an open mindset that is looking for guidance rather than posturing that they know it all. It is often the so called "lower level" employee who is at the coalface and who has developed an intuition for the business who has the greatest insights. Alas, they are rarely consulted.

Once an organization feels it is losing its image as a fast growth, highly profitable company, the ethical shenanigans begin. Earning restatements, capitalization of expenses, payments in advance treated as current revenue, and all other kinds of accounting tricks are put into practice. Often employees are coerced into making fake revenue such as Wells Fargo and Theranos, to name just two.

Sadly, as we discuss repeatedly in the next chapters, most employees keep their mouths shut and comply. Pacts of silence and acts of collusion are all hidden as best as possible so that jobs can be kept, salaries earned, promotions attained and bonuses banked – anything rather than being laid off or facing the abuse that often goes with whistleblowing. And yet, if employees could understand that if a dozen of them marched into the CEOs' office or the boardroom and protested false claims, poor quality (Boeing!!!), fake accounting and so on, they would have enough clout to make a difference. Instead, human nature makes us hide among crowds.

The repeated refrain is that ethical collapses do not occur overnight. As Jennings writes, the patterns of ethical collapses are obvious and consistent. Many might ask what happened to the internal checks and balances, or the auditors or the board? Well, a lot has been written about their ineffectiveness, ineptitude and in the case of auditors and the board, collusion, so again where will we find the courage to face the truth?[3] Many companies have weak CEOs, sycophant management teams and a differential board of directors.

How many organizations can fly the flag of courage full mast?

## Decision-Making in a Radically Uncertain World

In a radically uncertain world, leaders are increasingly called upon to make decisions without fully understanding the situation or the effects of their actions. At a press briefing shortly after the attack on the World Trade Center on September 11, 2001, Donald Rumsfeld, United States Secretary of Defense is known to have said:

> There are known knowns; there are things we know we know. We also know there are known unknowns; things we know that we do not know. But there are also unknown unknowns – the ones we don't know we don't know.
>
> (Kay and King 2020)

John Kay and former Bank of England governor, Mervyn King, highlight in their book, *Decision-Making Beyond the Numbers* (2020), how often leaders delegate the management of uncertainty to the risk professionals who generate statistical probabilities that can at best be unhelpful and at worst misleading. In the world of risk, everything is assigned probabilities, and probabilities are not appropriate in the case of radical uncertainty.

Radical uncertainty is due to our incomplete knowledge of the world. It is the world of unlikely events, uncertain futures and unpredictable consequences. Black swans are examples of radical uncertainty. True black swans are states of the world to which we cannot attach probabilities because we cannot conceive of these states. In these states we cannot talk about tails on bell curves and frequency distributions.

Probabilistic reasoning depends on the sum of the probability of all events adding up to 1. In a radically uncertain world, we cannot describe all possible events, and even if we could guestimate some, their outcomes are not stationary. When we rely on statistical probabilities during these times, Kay and King argue, we are not using helpful information. There is a great appeal of probability theory in that it leads us falsely to believe we are assigning a measure of certainty to what in fact is uncertain.

In the case of uncertainty, Kay and King insist, the most important thing is to ask: "What is going on here?" This is a key question and requires a "thick" description which means making sense of something by asking many questions from multiple perspectives. It requires understanding the story that is unfolding.

Kay and King claim that behavioral economics has given human decision-making a bad rap as our so-called irrational biases that lead to nonrational decisions are demeaned as noneffectual. Yet, we humans are adept decision-makers. We bias our responses to the complex world of radical uncertainty. We are in the main survivors and learners. We use subjective probabilities and frame our thinking in terms of narratives. While we may not solve the puzzles, and in rational terms we appear to be irrational, humans can work better with the mysteries and with radical uncertainty than any statistical program or artificial computer system can.

The world of economics, business and finance is non-stationary. It is not governed by unchanging specific laws, like roulette wheels or games of chess or chance or even stock market data trends. Radical uncertainty presents unique challenges that require complex judgments for their interpretation. And, as we know from systems thinking, living systems are reflexive – this means they reflect on themselves and adapt and adjust to changing information. This reflexivity undermines stationarity. Data cannot reflect on itself. It is non-alive and non-adaptive. It can only provide a "thin" description.

People routinely make decisions with imperfect information. Our brains are adaptive mechanisms for making connections and recognizing patterns. Human minds approach problems in ways markedly different from computers. They excel at coping with open-ended mysteries. Storytelling is a central element of that ability. We organize our lives around reference narratives. Storytelling is how we interpret complex situations. We make decisions based on judgment, instinct and emotions woven in and out of the fabric of experience and narratives. In statistics we use samples and express confidences displayed in a normal distribution. But most models are minimally useful but usually wrong. We cannot rely on forecasts in planning for the future. We cannot split the world into the known and the unknowable. We can only become better at asking the question "What is going on here?"

The implications for leadership lie in having the courage to deal with uncertainty and to refrain from rushing into statistical reasoning, probabilities, over-rationalizations, data analysis and computer-generated solutions.

## Our Flight to Data

Edwin Friedman, who we met in Chapter 1, argued that rising mental health problems are due largely to the substance abuse of data – this was back in 2007 (2007, 114) – where amassing data has become an obsession: a form of addiction. The fixation on data, wrote Friedman, has resulted in the replacement of information over expertise, and knowledge over wisdom. Many leaders rush to data before even understanding the problem they are trying to address. Data is also used to justify decisions without leaders understanding the assumptions and the filters used to collect the data.

Yuval Noah Harari, in his book *21 Lessons for the 21st Century* (2018), writes about what he calls our global predicament. He highlights the power of Big Data algorithms that might create digital dictatorships in which power is concentrated in the hands of a tiny elite. As a result, many people, he predicts, will suffer not from exploitation, but from something far worse, irrelevance. He claims that due to the multitude of significant systemic challenges in evidence, we are experiencing an era of bewilderment (2018, 6). Harari claims there will be a general mood of disorientation and impending doom exacerbated by the pace of technological disruption.

Margaret Heffernan, in her insightful book *Uncharted: How to Navigate the Future* (2020), also writes about our fascination and addiction with data as the way out of dealing with uncertainty. She points out that since the beginning of time, there has been a fortune to be made in prophesy and that now we have swapped the fortune teller's globe for data analytics and technological solutions. We tell ourselves that data can give us assurance, forgetting that history is a poor forecaster. New problems need new solutions for which there may be no data, no predictive correlation and no known and tested algorithm.

She criticizes our tendency to keep trying to simplify complex problems. Life, she says, is complex, non-linear and fluid, but we are determined to look for cause and effect, to seek out patterns of similarities rather than differences, to accrue mountains of data that in many cases are irrelevant, and to rely on historical facts or solutions.

In our rapidly changing world, she points out, patterns are changing. New problems are arising based on complex interconnections, and subjective issues that cannot be mapped or tracked by data. To lead effectively now, she claims, requires curiosity, imagination and courage (Heffernan 2020, xviii).

## AI Phobia – The Leadership Copout

In 1985, I was asked to develop a corporate lending model for banks using the latest AI software, referred to as expert systems. I have written about my experience and my subsequent nine years of starting and running my own international AI business in a trilogy of books that explain the pros and cons of implementing AI systems.

During the 1980s one of the greatest inhibitors of the development of AI systems was the shortage of computer memory space. This is no longer an issue and is one of the reasons for the exponential growth in data analysis and AI.

All AI systems depend on algorithms. Algorithms are a logical method for the processing of rules, information or data to solve a problem or to drive an action. We use algorithms all the time in daily life.[4]

An example:

If it looks like rain
Then take a raincoat

In my corporate lending model, a simple algorithm might look like this:

If the person has a good credit record
And has a steady history with the bank
And has adequate security
Then give him/her a loan
Else . . . get more information
Or if the risk is too high
Then decline

Here you can see that to process an algorithm, data is needed.

Data such as –
What is good credit?
What is a steady history?
What is adequate security?
What makes up more information?
What defines high risk?
. . . and so on.

By defining and programming certain parameters, AI can analyze gazillions of bits of data to fulfill the definitions of good, steady, adequate and so on. One could include in our algorithm a parameter that good credit for a non-White person and a female needs to be 1.5 times higher than that of a White person. AI can also comb rapidly through zip codes and based on certain programmed parameters, establish that a house is in a declining economic area and should be downgraded in value for security purposes.

AI – if so programmed – can also look for patterns of where a person shops, what they post on Facebook, which political party they seem to belong to plus a myriad of other predetermined factors that can be made either to add or to detract from a person's creditworthiness.

An AI algorithm can also be programmed to "learn." What this means is the computer is programmed to add other inputs/data or to alter certain criteria based on the patterns of data it is analyzing. (There is more to say on this but enough for now. What must be clear is that the computer does not learn as we do as it never understands what it is doing the way we do. It simply adds and subtracts digits.) What is important to appreciate is that all algorithms depend on humanly programmed pattern definitions, parameters and data.

The expert systems I used to develop were written in a high-level language where the user could ask the computer to explain its reasoning logic; that is, the data search details, the assumptions and inferences of the algorithm were transparent.

Expert systems include the knowledge and decision-making heuristics of experts in the field. This means they can handle far more complex systems than normal AI systems such as ChatGPT. The fundamental difference between expert systems (named expert because the algorithms were developed by experts in the field) and the many AI systems currently being developed is that true expert knowledge is embedded in the system, and it is not dependent on statistically manipulating data unless it is directed by an expert guided, knowledge-based rule or algorithm.

Current AI systems are written in computer code. They do not use high-level rules but rather zeros and ones driven by statistics based on someone's rules and assumptions. In other words, the pattern matching and the inferences they draw are not transparent to the user. Remember, everything has at some level been programmed even if the machine "appears" to have a mind of its own. The big question is: Who is developing the algorithms and the rules?

In my book *Expert Systems: Strategic Implications and Applications* (1987), I spelled out clearly some of the limitations of AI, one huge one being the programmer's quality of understanding the domain that they are programming. Life is not binary. It is not a series of ones and zeros. It is full of possibles, maybes, perhapses and don't knows. The secret to an effective system is that it harnesses the best intelligence in the field, not just a series of statistically driven codes. Otherwise instead of getting "Artificial Intelligence," we will have artificial stupidity – and we do not need machines for that!

**Expert Systems as a Management Tool**

Expert systems –

- Can never include common sense
- Can never totally substitute for people
- Cannot take the place of judgment where there are qualitative emotional issues – which is nearly always the case in complex decisions
- Are only as good as the expert knowledge used to define and program the algorithms
- Are only effective in a very narrow domain area
- Should be considered as a process rather than a results-oriented tool.

Beerel, *Expert Systems: Strategic Implications and Applications* (1987, 31).

What does all this mean, and what are the consequences? To gain further insights into the status of AI and Big Data, I recommend Cathy O'Neil's astounding book *Weapons of Math Destruction* (2017).

## Lousy Data, Poor Inferences and Dumb Machines

O'Neil was a former Wall Street mathematician who became involved in auditing a variety of AI systems. Based on her extensive experience she defines the AI modelers as computer and math nerds infatuated by equations without any sensitivity or understanding of human feelings. She points out that Big Data is powered by mathematical algorithms designed by fallible human beings and should therefore be used with great caution.

Her book describes what she has found in her years of reviewing a range of AI systems.

Here is a summary of some of her major points:

- Many models are based on sloppy statistics and biased models with toxic feedback loops that reinforce racial, economic and other prejudices.
- Many algorithms perpetuate injustices and reflect a total lack of ethics or morality.
- Most models are based on historic data, or the data that is readily available whether it really is appropriate for the problem to be solved or not.
- Only data that can be measured and counted is used. Subtleties, nuances or any subjectivity is ignored or converted into some kind of data or statistic.
- Computers cannot work with uncertainty any better than we can, so they assign it a number – again programmed by some nerd based on some biased assumption.
- Algorithms are largely written based on the assumption that patterns will always repeat. As we know, in times of radical change that is not the case.
- Financial investment messes arise because we rely on computer mathematics to make human investment decisions. These work for a while until something radically changes but the model isn't changed.
- In general, there is a grievous misinterpretation of data resulting in the many, many poor decisions made by leaders and so-called professionals in all areas.
- Due to these points, predictive models are especially dangerous.

O'Neil's book provides some stark truths in the field of AI, and this barely touches the raging controversies so artfully manipulated by Sam Altman et al. on the ethical issues of AI that are currently dominating the headlines.

The critical issue here is that leaders, instead of facing uncertainty and using critical thinking skills, intuition and wisdom, are hastily, and often indiscriminately, relying on data or technological solutions to drive their decision-making. Instead of having the courage to say "I don't know, let's work this through together," they are feigning knowledge and foresight and relying on what O'Neil described as models based on sloppy statistics, inappropriate data sets, biased assumptions and lousy inferences. In my day I saw plenty of those too.

Sadly, Friedman was right, and not much has changed. Leaders have a quick fix mentality, lack clarity and decisiveness, are poor at understanding problems and lack the important ability to frame issues. Technology and especially the latest models have become the panacea to face challenging times.

## Leaders Need Strength of Character

Many people thrust into leadership positions do not understand what is expected of them other than to increase revenue, profits and, if it is a public company, the share price. Most understand that culture plays a key role, and many are not sure what that means other than plastering walls with mission statements, giving bonuses, adhering to human employment laws, having an in-house newspaper and offering performance recognition awards. Many leaders hope that Human Resources will devise an employee training plan, and nice, friendly managers will go to seminars on emotional intelligence which will assist them in inspiring employees to work hard and be loyal to the organization.

Recently, several leadership books have added courage to their titles. Few of them define courage with any rigor or discuss its elements. Many texts focus on the courage to communicate authentically and truthfully. They write about having difficult conversations, building trust and connections, and showing empathy. There is discussion of leaders having the courage to feel and show emotion and to be humble but confident. None of them get down to the hard leadership challenges that leaders face and the need to make courage the cornerstone of their existence if they wish to be effective. Just as you and I must be courageous if we wish to live a good life where we feel truly fulfilled, leaders must be courageous if they truly wish to lead.

What leaders need but many lack are the following:

- The ability to identify new realities, especially the unpalatable ones, and by taking a systemic perspective, frame what these imply for the organization. Two glaring examples are the poor way in which leaders responded to COVID and leaders' inept handling of the Israeli-Hamas crisis, how it affects their business and how it has and will impact their employees.
- The insight and tenacity to make decisions in times of uncertainty and doubt, and the ability to find perspective when everyone else is losing theirs.
- The strength of character to make wise decisions, not self-interested ones or ones motivated by the need to be liked. The ability to set aside their ego, to feel vulnerable, to face challenge and dislike, yet remain principled and hold the course.
- The ability to withstand failure and to overcome the fear of making a mistake which may lead to a loss in popularity.
- The strength to say "I don't know. I need help."
- The courage to stand alone, to be isolated and betrayed and yet to hold steadfast to their ethical principles.
- The confidence to listen to their intuition even when it counters or contradicts data, predictions and technical solutions.
- Appropriate, authentic humility.

## Your Turn

- How well are you able to deal with uncertainty and to adapt to changing reality? What examples can you provide for your answer?

- Can you make decisions during times of uncertainty, or do you always rush for data, answers, previous solutions or some guidance from someone else? Are you a quick fix person? Can you live in the zone of unknowing?
- Do you spend time during the week on meditation and reflection? Do you actively try to connect with your intuition?

## Notes

1 Book 2 of the *Aeneid*.

2 See Lynn Stout's book *The Shareholder Value Myth*, 2012. In this book Stout points out the fallacy that maximizing the firm is a legal obligation, something advocated by many followers of the neo-libertarian Milton Friedman who advocated firm maximization with messianic conviction. She points out that shareholders do not own the corporation but only own shares or stocks in the corporation and the relationship is a contractual one not one of ownership.

3 See my book *Ethical Leadership and Global Capitalism: A Guide to Good Practice* for the discussion on the unethicality of auditors and the Board or Directors.

4 While they are both problem-solving strategies, there is a difference between a heuristic and an algorithm. A heuristic is what is called a "rule of thumb." Expert systems use the rules of thumb of known experts in the field. Algorithms use step-by-step methods for arriving at solutions. They require a lot of data, and they take longer to process.

## References

Beerel, Annabel. 1987. *Expert Systems: Strategic Implications and Applications*. Chichester, UK: Ellis Horwood.

Friedman, Edwin H. 2007. *A Failure of Nerve: Leadership in the Age of the Quick Fix*. New York: Seabury Books.

Harari, Yuval Noah. 2018. 21 *Lessons for the 21st Century*. London, UK: Penguin Random House.

Heffernan, Margaret. 2020. *Uncharted: How to Navigate the Future*. New York: Simon & Schuster, Inc.

Jennings, Marianne M. 2006. *The Seven Signs of Ethical Collapse: How to Spot Moral Meltdowns in Companies Before It's too Late*. New York: St. Martin's Press.

Kay, John, and Mervyn King. 2020. *Radical Uncertainty: Decision-Making Beyond the Numbers*. New York: W.W. Norton & Company.

O'Neil, Cathy. 2017. *Weapons of Math Destruction*. New York: Crown.

Porter, Michael. 1998. *Competitive Strategy: Techniques for Analyzing Industries and Competitors*. New York: Free Press.

Stout, Lynn. 2012. *The Shareholder Value Myth*. San Francisco, CA: Berrett-Koehler Publishers, Inc.

# Chapter 3

# The Mess We Are in – How Bad Is It?

## I Will Show You How F*** Greedy You Can Be

I watched Colin as he lowered his weighty six-foot six-inch frame into the chair. Even sitting down, he towered over everyone. The three men with whom we were meeting, the future leaders of the new buyout entity, seemed to shrivel in size as he leaned forward and glared at each one of them with a condescending smile.

"Well, gentlemen, I have reviewed your numbers, and they look good but not good enough," he said in a part critical, part bantering tone. He flicked his greasy, short black hair to one side. I could never make out whether all that grease was because of too much Brylcreem or too much sordid energy oozing out of his pores. Whatever it was, it fueled my distaste for the man.

He had not reviewed the numbers. I had. I was the one who reported that they were too optimistic and that based on past performance and the state of the economy, the new management would be hard-pressed to achieve their rosy projections. I had told Colin that the planned management buyout was a stretch if ever there was one, and that we should pull out. The deal would be a flop.

Colin disagreed, snarling,

> Clearly, Annabel, you do not understand how things work. It does not matter whether they can achieve the numbers or not. The only thing that matters is that we can sell the numbers to the VCs and the banks. Let me handle the meeting. Just watch and you will see how it is done. This is about making money, lots of it. Who cares about the f*****g numbers.

DOI: 10.4324/9781003459644-4

With that he glared at me menacingly.

I had joined the firm one week previously and already hated the job. Colin's boss had wanted me, not Colin. He insisted that Colin hire me as he believed I would bring stability and different insights to the department. Of course, that was a recipe for disaster.

Try as I might to feel differently, Colin's very presence made me want to heave, and his fawning sidekick, Jonathan, who ran around pandering to Colin's needs like buying bottles of Jack Daniels for lunch and getting his suits cleaned, was more than a pain in the butt. But that is what everyone did in the financial sector in the 1980s, drink at all times of the day and engage in outrageous behavior.

I knew in my bones this job was not going to last. Would I even make the end of the week, I wondered.

Colin pulled out the business plan and began thumbing through the pages.

"If you up the revenues by thirty percent, he barked at the three men, do you realize how much more we can borrow, and how rich you will be in no time? We can leverage this baby to the hilt."

The most senior of the three men spoke up,

> Look Colin, we are not greedy people. We know our business. We just want to do this management buyout as we know we can run the company better than the current owners. We are engineers, not finance people. We know what we can do. We are relying on you for the financial advice.

Colin gave a supercilious smile and bowed his head slightly in a ridiculous attempt to feign humility.

> Well, since you are relying on my advice, I am telling you your numbers are too low. Up them by 30%. We can then borrow much more and value the shares at a much higher price. Don't you want to make some money here?

The senior engineer retorted,

"Colin, I told you, we are not greedy. If we can pull this buyout off, we will be more than satisfied."

"Well, I won't be satisfied," Colin all but yelled. "You say you aren't greedy. Trust me, let me do the numbers and I will show you how f*****g greedy you really can be."

I found my hands shaking. I tried to digest what I had just witnessed. I had recently resigned from an investment bank where everyone was lying about the numbers and now this.[1]

The late 1980s were the years of aggressive Management Buyouts (MBOs). Every management team in the universe it seemed was trying to either buy or spin off their company from a parent organization or corporate group. Of course, Old Broad

Street,[2] with its myriad brokers and growing legions of traders in every financial instrument that could be imagined, was deemed paved with gold. Whether firms could achieve their forecasts was a problem for the future. Someone else's problem. All that mattered was the fees that could be earned now, paid now and spent now. Financiers salivated at the insane commissions they were earning on cash flow projections that were often as fabricated as the Wizard of Oz.

The meeting ended as awkwardly as it had begun. Colin marched out of the room assuming he had carte blanche to create whatever financials he could manufacture the details of which only he knew. I got in my car, deciding not to go back to the office, and drove home.

That afternoon, I sat on the grass next to my patio and replayed the disgusting scenario in my mind. I will never forget those words, "I will show you how f*****g greedy you can be." I realized then and there that if I did not get out immediately, I too could get caught up in the maniacal world of showing everyone how smart I was and how many fancy deals I could close. I was already earning exceedingly well, and the truth was I loved it. But now I was at a crossroads, a decision point. I knew, and I felt in the deepest part of me, that I needed to exit rapidly before I was sucked in like Colin and thousands of others. And how tempting it all was. Would I have the courage to give up on my MBA hopes and dreams? Dreams of being a great financier, dreams of being hailed as one of the smartest women in the City of London. I stared out the window wistfully admiring my brand-new white BMW. Would I have the courage to walk away – the courage to let it all go? As I pondered my future, I was reminded of Oscar Wilde's comment that we can resist anything but temptation.

A large glass of wine later, I was satisfied with the resignation letter I had drafted. Time to quit. Time to quit SM[3] and time to quit the world of finance. I had given it my best, but it was not for me.

A month later the engineers made headline news as the latest fabulous MBO. They went to the market with ridiculously inflated numbers and the markets bought their bullshit. I was saddened. Greed is indeed infectious, and it could have been me.

Barely three years passed and there were different headlines. The new firm that had been created via the MBO went into receivership. By then Colin had switched companies twice and was a senior director at another brokerage, no doubt enthusiastically peddling greed and smiling contemptuously all the way.

## Infectious Greed

Greed was indeed infectious. I witnessed it with my own eyes. Few, if any, people had the courage to say "no." Moderation did not exist. Excess was normal and I had to combat my own inner demons who kept whispering that I should stop fighting reality and ride with the tide. After all, there were boatloads of money to be made and everyone was doing it! Young traders were selling arcane financial instruments to willing yet ignorant investors and then joyfully claimed, and were paid, six figure commissions and bonuses based on cash flows that were mere projections (another word for fabrications). I witnessed their contempt for the people they so blatantly screwed. I also witnessed how temptation, lack of accountability and distance from the people getting hurt resulted in hundreds of young men (there were very few women in the City of London in 1986) becoming obsessed with making money without any concern as to whether they came by it honestly. Distortion, lying, obfuscating, colluding and ignoring warning signals were daily fare in the service of huge salaries and outrageous bonuses. No one, not the managers, the senior leadership, the auditors, or the Bank of England regulators had the courage to challenge the system.

A decade after I left corporate life, I procured a copy of Frank Partnoy's book titled *Infectious Greed: How Deceit and Risk Corrupted the Financial Markets* (2003). I was riveted. It was like reading a biography of my own nightmare days working in the City of London. Partnoy, who did a stint as a financier himself and is now a law professor, catalogs in detail the shenanigans in the financial markets that began in full force in the 1980s and then reached what some (incorrectly) believed was their apogee in the late 1990s and early 2000s. He names many people I knew or with whom I had briefly rubbed shoulders with. At the time, I sensed things were bad, but I did not realize how dreadfully bad they were. Partnoy did that for me.

In his riveting text, Partnoy describes in alarming detail the toxic culture and brazen dishonesty that festered in every corner of the UK and US markets during that period. Stories like Colin were legion, and as more and more traders got away with their behavior, that behavior escalated at an exponential rate.

Through the pages, Partnoy tracks the development of the junk bond market, the leveraged buyout craze, the introduction of swaps and options, and currency options followed by stock options describing them in excruciating detail and naming companies and the brazen transgressors who lined their own pockets at the expense of the innocent public without remorse or afterthought. In no time, the whole system breathed corruption, involving the rating agencies, the Federal Reserve who chose to turn a blind eye, the SEC, state regulators and even Congress.

Once President Bill Clinton abolished the Glass Steagall Act in 1999 (implemented in 1933 after the mayhem created by the bankers in 1929) that prohibited commercial banks from engaging in investment banking activities to protect depositors from the risks of stock speculation, all risk containment and monitoring constraints vanished. With lightning speed banks formed investment banking arms or created subsidiaries that could engage in stock speculation and the golden path to avarice was laid.

The Savings & Loan debacle, WorldCom, Enron, Adelphia, Waste Management, Rite Aid, Barings Bank, Long-Term Capital Management and Bernie Madoff's Ponzi scheme are some prime examples of the result of poor oversight by those responsible for auditing company accounts, boards' irresponsibility of corporate governance and tepid market regulation.

Partnoy's profound understanding of the markets and their key players provides the reader with an in-depth view of how the financial system's very foundations are riven with conflicts of interest, revolving doors and an ethos of greed and selfishness. He also argues throughout his book that the "invisible hand" is one great illusion. There is no correction anywhere. Financial markets are out of control, the risk of systemwide collapse is greater than ever before, reported earnings in many cases are pure fiction, no one really understands the risks of all the fancy new instruments and both auditors and prosecutors haven't had a clue of how to audit the books or to create policies that restrict dishonesty and fraud. No one had the courage to resist. It was a free-for-all without sanction or consequences. Not one person or one agency was prepared to take on the system or to stem the flow of illegal money pouring into the hydra-like network of people making fortunes on other people's hard-earned money.

Partnoy labels the key drivers behind the deceit and greed in the large corporations to include:

- Extortionate bonuses including stock options
- No downside for financial investors or traders
- No regulation of important sectors of the market
- Inefficacy of regulators
- Collusion of public accountants
- Total focus on short-term results
- Extreme reluctance on behalf of the justice system to punish corporate executives
- Moral hazard due to financial institutions being continuously bailed out by the FED

Based on Partnoy's analysis, the 2008/2009 crash was entirely predictable as the groundwork of greed and corruption had been perfectly established but no one was prepared to stop the party and face the truth.

Even now, in 2024, nothing has changed. Thousands of people like Colin still populate the banks and brokerages, and MBAs who don't see making a fortune in technology rush to sign up for employment in the financial services sector. There was and is no courage – no courage to resist temptation anywhere.

### Corporates Fined While Individuals Escape Scot Free

According to *Violation Tracker*, the top 10 financial service companies paid $208 billion in fines since 2000. Of the $208 billion, Bank of America was responsible for a stunning $83 billion followed by JPMorgan Chase with $36 billion.

The European banks Deutsche, Credit Suisse and UBS together paid $47 billion. The US companies were responsible for $161 billion or 77% of the total.

Lest one think that Bank of America has cleaned up its act, it amassed a further $1.2 billion in expenses for litigation and regulatory investigations in 2022. Not one senior executive has been prosecuted.

Refer https://violationtracker.goodjobsfirst.org/ for details of company penalties.

## Are Humans Virtuous or Wicked?

The argument as to whether human beings are innately virtuous and benevolent or essentially selfish and individualistic has raged for centuries. Philosophers, theologians and more recently psychologists each uphold different versions of our natural dispositions.

Some put forward the alleged Darwinian argument that life is a competitive struggle. Others emphasize the significant extent of cooperation both among and between human species.

No matter how selfish humans are, the happiness of other people matters to them even though they may derive no benefit from it. They get pleasure out of seeing it. So, begins Adam Smith's tome *The Theory of Moral Sentiments* originally written in 1759. Throughout several hundred pages, Smith extolls the empathy and compassion humans have for others and claims that even ruffians and the most hardened violators of the laws of society are not without these sentiments.

Smith then goes on to explain that it is empathic imagination that results in our fellow feelings when others suffer, and the horror we feel when others are subject to traumatic events that leave them feeling wretched.

Humans, Smith writes, can only subsist in society, and that society must be a just one if it is to survive. If injustices prevail, society will crumble and this reality is what justifies the safeguards that society puts in to "protect the week, curb the violent, and chastise the guilty" (Smith, 115). He recognizes that humans face many temptations to satisfy their own ends at the expense of others, and sometimes they even behave like wild beasts, hence the need for an orderly society.

Smith also tackles the question of virtue. He begins with the question of character and like the Greeks, he upholds that a good character leads to personal health and happiness. He stresses the sentiment of sympathy which translates in our world to emotional intelligence and empathy and sums up his views on the virtues as being the personal and public expressions of prudence, justice and benevolence.

What is important to note is that Smith – the named father of the free market system known as capitalism – in his role of moral philosopher, set out these same human moral parameters to underpin his economic theories. He is quite clear that people are primarily directed by self-interest. Their feelings of sympathy derive from their imagination as to how they would feel if they were in a certain situation. He claims that in some cases we can truly empathize by placing ourselves in others' shoes not our own, but even if we do not have empathy, we always have some fellow feeling. It is on this basis that he advocated his famous free market motif that if everyone is free to act out of their own self-interest, the corrective of the market will ensure that everyone benefits. Self-interest equates to interest in the other; that is, it is in a person's self-interest to care for others with whom he works.

Even as Smith argued energetically in favor of the virtues of the free market system, he also acknowledged its limitations. He recognized that the institution of private property and the free market virtually assure inequalities and might even create enmity between the few rich and the many relatively poor. He hoped, however, that this enmity would be countered by sympathy between the parties and a sense of prevailing justice within society. He presupposed a strong sense of community that would provide the "invisible hand" of correction, as he believed there can be no justice based on prosperity alone. He also advocated a strong legal system that would enforce justice between the parties and that curbed any monopolistic powers.[4]

Our laissez-faire capitalist society has tossed Smith's guidelines aside with abandon. Instead,

- We do not have much sympathy for one another in society
- There is so little empathy between us that we must host seminars to teach people to be empathic – with minimal success
- There is a very weak justice system if one might even call it that – see the Chickenshit Justice System in a later section
- Monopolies rule the roost

Despite our lack of fellow sympathy, however, humans are prosocial by nature. We like to be together. But, even among our cooperative genes, Matt Ridley argues in his book *The Origins of Virtue* (1996) that part of our survival mechanism consists of self-interested genes that demonstrate selfish and antisocial behavior. He points out that in every group, be they animals or humans, there are always the free riders and those who choose to benefit from the cooperation of others without cooperating themselves. In fact, there are always some who will take advantage of others' prosocial and cooperative needs knowingly causing disarray and negative feelings and even creating harm.

Ridley cites studies that question the true motive of cooperative behavior. He questions whether this is truly who we are or whether we desire to escape or avoid guilt because of social sanctions or personal condemnation. He also points out that cooperative groups thrive, and selfish ones do not. Ultimately, he concludes that our societies and our minds evolved together and that it is our social instincts that result in our cooperativeness that is the very "hallmark of our humanity" (Ridley 1996, 249).

But is this true? Are we a cooperative society that willingly practices prosocial behavior in response to our developed instincts? Or are we all Machiavellian by nature, interested in achieving our own goals; manipulating; exploiting others for our own gain, caring only about our own money, power and success; and having no qualms about deceiving or lying to others? And if we don't do it ourselves, are we silently content to have others do it on our behalf? Have we all become utilitarian where the end justifies the means, any means, and where we kowtow to those in authority rather than stand up for our principles? Who are we and where is courage to be found?

**Trump University Website – 2005–2010**

> You want to be rich? I'm going to help you make so much money, your head will spin. You'll make so much money, you'll get tired of making money, okay? I'm talking more money than China, okay? So much money, crooked Hillary will be hitting you up to donate to her sleazy foundation, which by the way, that's no foundation. I know foundations. All of my buildings are built on foundations, okay? Nobody makes better foundations than I do, I can tell you that.
>
> Donald Trump

Money was taken, there were no real classes and there was even an invitation to pay $35,000 for personal tutoring from Donald Trump. Some people paid! There was no tutoring, Trump never showed up and many lost thousands. Trump University paid a $25 million dollar settlement in a class action lawsuit. Donald Trump got off free, ready to perpetuate fraud elsewhere.

https://apnews.com/article/43033e7cb9974faf879b51251c3a0d07

## Corruption Everywhere

Judging by the media coverage and the plethora of books and articles produced over the past 20 years, especially the torrent of investigative reporting into corruption since the inauguration of President Trump in 2016, according to Sarah Chayes, America is government by organized money controlled by hydra-like networks of corruption whose tentacles reach every corner of American life (Chayes 2021).

According to the recent explosion of literature on white-collar crime, some claim that the increase began after 9/11, others state that the lack of consequences for the financial sector in the aftermath of the financial crisis of 2008 was the major turning point, and yet another group assert that the major inflection point was 2019/2020 when America became awash with COVID funds. Frank Partnoy claimed that the foundation for the escalation in corruption was laid toward the end of the twentieth century. We are just seeing it play out on steroids now.

Wherever one would like to place one's thermometer, the heat of corruption has soared to a boiling point where stories of malfeasance dominate the daily headlines. The Senator Robert Menendez conflict-of-interest scandal, the brazen and defiant Sam Bankman-Friedman crypto-currency fraud, and the ignominious fall of the arrogant bankers of Silicon Valley Bank (SVB) represent just a few of the more recent egregious examples.[5]

Besides these incidents, what is most disheartening is not only corruption's pervasiveness, but that its corrosive networks extend far beyond those in power to the ordinary citizen and the everyday employee. Everyone is complicit. It is hard to find a large public or private sector organization that is not in some way tarnished with the unscrupulous brush. Regardless of industry, deceit and fraud are ubiquitous, most especially in the financial services sector, healthcare, government contracting, and the oil and extraction industries (Chayes 2021; Mueller 2019).

Credible journalists and writers, many of whom have had the personal experience of working in the financial services sector, excoriate the pervasiveness and brazenness of white-collar theft.

Today white-collar crimes affect more Americans than all other forms of crime combined resulting in a devastating ripple effect that impacts businesses, jobs, families and everyone's financial future (see statistics). So, what about this spirit of cooperativeness and mutual reciprocity?

## Recent Statistics

It is difficult to get statistics on white-collar crime largely because a high percentage of crime is not reported, and those that are reported are rarely prosecuted as the justice system has become less and less eager or interested in pursuing white-collar criminals. This has naturally added to the recent spike in crime.

Cybersecurity Ventures, a company that researches global cybercrime, expects white-collar crime to grow by 15% per year over the next five years, reaching $10.5 trillion by 2025, up from $3 trillion in 2015. This amount is exponentially larger than the damage inflicted from natural disasters in a year and is larger than the profits from the global trade of all major illegal drugs combined.

Some other white-collar crime basic statistics include:

- Since 2021, annual losses from white-collar crimes have been in the range of $426 billion to $1.7 trillion.
- Businesses lose as much as 6% of their total annual revenue to white-collar crimes committed by employees.
- US consumers lost a record $10 billion to fraud in 2023, representing a 14% increase from the previous year's reported losses.
- About 31% of external fraud cases are committed by hackers, with 28% carried out by organized crime groups.

- Fraud makes up 63% of white-collar crimes. After fraud comes embezzlement, followed by larceny/theft.
- Identity theft and fraud alone have affected over 17 million Americans.
- Executives make up 20% of crimes but they create by far the most significant damage.
- 54% of crimes are by people between 31 and 45 years of age.
- 49% of white-collar criminals have a university degree.
- Only 7% of all crimes are carried out by women.
- 80–90% of offenders are White people.
- White-collar crimes represent only 3% of federal prosecutions.
- White-collar prosecutions decreased 53.5% from 2011 to 2021.
- It is estimated that 35%–40% of all businesses are affected by criminal behavior.
- Between 5% and 10% of employees participate in crimes.
- Four in 10 of the businesses surveyed that have experienced fraud in the past 2 years said it was connected to the digital platforms they rely on.
- Very few criminals are arrested, and even fewer are convicted. Businesses try to avoid the scandal and the justice department prefers to prosecute thieves or physical offenders (see The Chickenshit Justice Department on page 61).

What is interesting to note from these statistics is the percentage of people who are educated and the small percentage of women criminals. It is also a good reminder to people with a racial bias how unfounded their prejudices are.[6]

## Theories Relating to White-Collar Crime and Why They Do It

### *Early Theories*

The term "white-collar crime" can be traced back to 1939 and Edwin Sutherland (1883–1950), one of the most influential criminologists of the twentieth century. In 1940, in a publication titled *White-Collar Criminality*, white-collar crime was defined as a "crime committed by a person of respectability and high social status in the course of his occupation."

Nowadays white-collar crime is not reserved solely for people with high social status but includes low-level employees who either are coerced by others or succumb to temptation.

It was Sutherland's contention that white-collar crime is an epidemic in American society fueled by an unholy alliance between business and politicians. He also posited that persons of the upper socioeconomic class engage in criminal behavior that differs from the lower socioeconomic classes and that their prosecution is rare due to their positions in American society. He claimed that there is a general apathy of the public with respect to embezzlement and other financial crimes (Brightman and Howard 2011).

Sutherland, a student of Thorstein Veblen, developed a *Theory of Differential Association* (1947), which states that young people develop into criminals by learning wrongful ways from bad companions and by seeing powerful and successful adults break the law.

Sutherland summarized his theory by claiming that criminal behavior is learned through the interaction with others via a process of communication within personal intimate groups. The group's definitions of legal codes influence the individual's adherence to and violation of these codes. Delinquency occurs when attitudes and justification for violating these codes outweigh adherence to them. Tutelage among the group is the overarching factor.

Sutherland also commented that few offenders consider their actions to be criminal nor do they feel any contrition but rather express anger and resentment at having been shamed (2009, 184). Their need to maintain a morally acceptable view of themselves is upheld by both Albert Bandura and Eugene Soltes's recent research (Soltes 2016).

Thorstein Veblen (1857–1929), professor of political economics and Edwin Sutherland's teacher, wrote *The Theory of the Leisure Class* (1899). Here he provided insights into the spending and purchasing patterns of the middle and upper strata of society. He explained the concept of consumerism as the evolution of conspicuous expenditure on superfluities to uphold the consumer's status in society. Regrettably an increasing number of those who can least afford it are also caught up in this same dynamic, hence society's massive credit card debt.

Greed, Veblen saw as a response behavior to the individual seeking to function "effectively" within his or her social group.

What we note from these early theories is that white-collar crime is not just about greed but about losing social status both for the individual and for his or her family. A frustrated goal of obtaining wealth to be socially "acceptable" leads to unbearable strain.[7] Other reasons cited are related to egocentricity, emotional insecurity and feelings of personal inadequacy.[8] These reasons correlate with the Kohlberg and Kegan theories that we are morally stuck at Stage 3 (see the following section).

## Recent Theories

Many of the recent books on corporate crime seek to uncover why senior executives engage in crime. Popular explanations are greed, money and fame, but these appear to be only superficial explanations.

Research shows that malfeasance often begins with small acts of deception where the executive feels in a financial corner and takes a misstep which he intends to correct (Soltes 2016). Things often move faster than anticipated and the correction is not made. Instead, the fraud gets larger and larger as he or they, in the case of collusion, try to catch up. Eventually they cease attempting to fix matters or, as in the case of Enron, they continue to knowingly perpetuate the fraud as it becomes a new way of life. Their moral justifications, if they seek any, amp up as the fraud grows in significance.

Over-confidence and opportunism seem to be key features of many of these executives. They also sense immunity from punishment as the corporation pays their fines for fiddling the books or any other malfeasance and they rarely, if ever, face any consequences.

## Motivation Theory

Saul Gellerman (1929–2004), a psychologist and professor of management, is largely known for his *HBR* article in 1986, "Why Good Managers Make Bad Ethical Choices," wherein he claims that managers engage in unethical behavior:

- Believing that the activity is not "really" illegal or immoral
- That it is in the individual or the corporation's best interest
- That the unethical activity will never be found out
- Because it helps the company, the company will condone it

Here we note again how individuals justify their behavior so as not to see themselves as being unethical.

## Entitlement

Eugene Soltes, Associate Professor at Harvard Business School, documented his correspondence and discussions with imprisoned executives in a text entitled *Why They Do It* (2016). His inquiry focused on (a) the pressures the executives faced to engage in fraud, (b) the extent to which their compensation influenced their actions and (c) what they intended to do once they were released.

Soltes detected similar themes to those mentioned earlier. Without fail, the executives refused to see themselves as criminals. They showed little moral reflection, claiming that they did not think about the crime much before they did it nor did they consider the consequences. When asked to think about their actions they commented that they didn't think they were harmful.

Many executives openly admitted in court that the testimony they provided was warped to get the greatest leniency in their sentence even if it meant implicating others rather than telling the truth. Many did not have any clear plans for after their release other than to somehow clear their name (Soltes 2016).

Soltes cites a University of Pennsylvania's Wharton School of Business research project where 500 experienced managers were asked about their willingness to engage in false financial reporting. Sixty percent claimed to be willing to deceive investors by "adjusting" the books if it achieved their aims (2016, ix).

### *Behavioral Ethics*

Recently a new field has emerged entitled behavioral ethics, which in essence is social psychology under another name. Some of the behavioral ethics theories that attempt to explain white-collar criminal behavior include:

- If senior executives engage in corruption, others will readily follow suit – conformance theory.
- If the corporate culture condones corrupt behavior, it will spread.
- Business leaders often frame immoral behavior as business decisions, not ethical ones – ascribed to lack of moral imagination.
- People engage in fraud to avoid losses at any cost even if that means compromising their values or morals – motivation of loss aversion.
- People use their roles as their defense – "I had to save the company."
- The more distanced people are from the people they impact, the less personal the issue and therefore the more abstract the consequences.
- People readily kowtow to authority for fear of losing their jobs or their status in the company. The Milgram experiments readily support this subordination to authority (Milgram 2009). (See Chapter 7 for discussion on authority.)

What we can conclude from these theories is that many people struggle to be ethical in the face of challenges to their ego such as loss of status, inability to achieve proclaimed goals and the desire to be seen as successful.

Whatever happened to the notion of virtue and the important ingredient of character to achieve enduring happiness? And what about courage to resist temptation?

## Has Corruption Increased?

The great historian Thucydides (fifth-century BC) claimed that it is in the very nature of humans to act in the future as they did in the past. Here we stand almost a quarter of a way into the twenty-first century. Was Thucydides correct? Have the forces of power and greed changed over the centuries or is it that now we have more efficient global communication channels and media coverage to bring it to our attention?

Philippe Gigantes's text *Power & Greed: A Short History of the World* (2003) tries to answer this question. His book plots the last 2500 years through key figures that influenced history either through contributing wisdom and moderation, for example, Solon, Plato, the Buddha, Jesus, or by ruthlessly manifesting power and greed and thereby radically influencing the geopolitics, and socioeconomic realities of the world. Examples include Agrippina (15–59 AD), power hungry and vengeful mother of emperor Nero, the ferocious, rampageous Ottoman Turks, the cruel conquistadores Hernan Cortes and Francisco Pizarro, and of course Adolf Hitler.

Gigantes claimed that whatever the epoch or the culture, humankind has sought to satisfy five existential desires: safety, shelter, sustenance, sex and self-expression.

To avoid chaos, society formulated rules and mores to limit the freedom of people to pursue these desires without some restraint or inhibition. Society not only was therefore a vehicle for cooperation but acted as a form of control over our selfish and greed-like tendencies.

According to Gigantes, history documents the many grand acquisitors (as he calls them) who either broke or circumvented these rules and/or social sanctions. These grand acquisitors recognized from the get-go that power is the best instrument for getting what we want. This power comes in different forms: owning more slaves, having more land to exploit, finding more subjects to tax, securing more followers who are conquered and forced to change their faith, or by having more money. Grand acquisitors "wage war" on societies' attempts to keep order by grabbing whatever power they can to satisfy their desires. And as we know, power corrupts, and absolute power corrupts absolutely (statement by Lord Acton, British historian (1834–1902)).

If we reflect on the twentieth century, there were two world wars that killed millions of people, the dropping of a nuclear bomb, a cold war, many smaller wars, mass carnage, one great depression and one smaller one (the dotcom crisis), war planes, atomic weapons, rockets in space, satellites, computers and robots. There were also new medicines, gene therapy and a multitude of scientific advancements alongside AIDS, drug addiction and surging mental health problems (Gigantes 2003).

During the past century we also saw a surgency in corporate power, the growth of multinationals and the new colonializing trend in the name of free trade. Finance became the major economic actor, far outpacing the growth in goods and services. Along with it came a resurgence of power, corruption and greed, not only by grand acquisitors who make history as did Kenneth Lay (Enron), Dennis Kozlowski (Tyco) and Bernie Madoff, but by anonymous white-collar workers in banks, peons in the vast system of government contractors, and employees of all stripes in the extractive industries, in pharmaceuticals and healthcare, and seemingly in every corner of society. People were desperately breaking the rules or violating any norms to satisfy their desires (Mueller 2019). Criminal behavior such as that demonstrated by Wells Fargo, whose employees created fake accounts in the names of its customers, and Volkswagen, whose engineers were able to create emissions-cheating software, provide two examples where a multitude of employees were complicit in fraud. People cheated and kept their jobs or received their lucrative pay rather than take the moral high road.

*The Gilded Age* was the appellation Mark Twain gave to the late 1800 post–Civil War period in America, a time when the pursuit of wealth and materialism followed industrialization, and the building of railroads along with the growth of the extractive industries swept through the country. During this era, America experienced unprecedented growth in industry and technology. But the Gilded Age had a sinister side: it was a period where greedy, corrupt industrialists, bankers and politicians enjoyed extraordinary wealth and opulence at the expense of the working class. This avarice culminated in the huge crash of 1929. Although Franklin D. Roosevelt sought to curb the rapaciousness of the new breed of industrialist and the fast-growing financial services industry not long after the crash, cycles of greed and corruption began anew. Many contemporary writers are naming the current period (2017–present) the new *Gilded Age* (Chayes 2021).

## What Is Corruption?

Before we lose ourselves further in the details of the murky world of corruption, let us take a moment to clarify the meaning of corruption.

The *Oxford Dictionary* defines corruption as morally depraved, wicked, using bribery, fraudulent activity and harm by making suspect errors or alterations.

Two US scholars, Ray Fisman and Miriam Golden, who have studied corruption internationally for many years define corruption as "the abuse of entrusted power for private gain" (Fisman and Golden 2017, 25). The power can be governmental, corporate or personal.

In their well-documented book *Corruption: What Everyone Needs to Know* (2017), which surveys multiple countries around the globe, they explain the social and economic harms that result from corruption. They point out that worldwide, even though most citizens disapprove of corruption, many feel they have no option but to participate. They also highlight that even in democracies, though people disdain corruption, they do nothing about it. Politicians win elections on anti-corruption platforms and often end up being just as and often more corrupt than their predecessors. Voters fail to vote these uncorrupt politicians out of office, and sometimes they even reelect them!

Take the case of the former president, Donald Trump, who has been charged with four criminal counts, including conspiracy to defraud the US and conspiracy against the rights of citizens along with racketeering and trying to overturn an election by destructive means. He has been found guilty of sexual abuse and falsifying business records. Currently, Trump has a following of millions who choose to overlook or rationalize his behaviors. While promising in his first term that he was going to make the US government honest again by draining the swamp, no sooner was he elected than the alligators began multiplying, Steve Bannon being one prime example.

Corporate boards, particularly in the US, retire disgraced executives with golden retirement packages without a squeak from shareholders – see story of Boeing in the next chapter – and white-collar criminals write bestselling books and have movies made about their stories. One example is Nick Leeson, a young trader who brought Barings Bank to its knees and who, since his release from prison, has been writing books, one of which is being made into a movie called *Rogue Trader.* Leeson gives talks around the globe where he earns high fees and is now a corporate corruption investigator based in Galway, Ireland.

Leeson was Barings Bank's head derivatives trader in Singapore. Over several years he raked up losses to the tune of $1.3 billion due to speculative and fraudulent trading activity. In 1993, his profits constituted almost 10% of Barings' total profits. He had developed a reputation for expertise and near-infallibility, and his superiors in London gave him little supervision. Little did they know that he was forging documents and hiding losses to such a degree that after one massive bet went against him, he brought down the bank.

Leeson claimed he wanted to stop but couldn't. He told reporters: "The word criminal is an ugly word. I don't think of myself as a criminal. It was something I fell into." He blamed Barings risk management for allowing his fraud to metastasize. As we will see, this is typical behavior of cowardly and corrupt individuals – they are not to blame, everyone else is.

Fisman and Golden also write about the negative impact of influence peddling. This is where businesses lobby and give gifts of all kinds to government employees to influence public policies in their favor. The financial services sector and the IT and extraction industries have managed to gain huge financial advantages and reduced legal oversight because of the billions they pay to regulators. (US lobbying groups paid $4.2 billion to federal lawmakers in 2023.[9])

Overall, Fisman and Goldman summarize the negative consequence of corruption which include:

- Harms economic efficiency
- Negatively impacts economic growth
- Reinforces and increases power differentials between those who have access to assets and those that do not
- Increases social inequities
- Undermines the functioning of democracy
- In the case of bribery, increases the cost of doing business
- Exacerbates racial inequality
- Often has a negative impact on the environment

They claim that the only way to curb corruption is to

- Clean up government
- Institute clear anti-corruption policies that are well monitored
- Ensure strict enforcement of rules
- Encourage citizens not to put up with it

BUT THAT TAKES COURAGE!

## Bribery and Extortion

The 2015 1MDB scandal made international headlines. The story behind the scandal is somewhat murky with the main culprits all pointing fingers at one another.

The fraud centered on the raising of $6.5 billion for the Malaysian government's economic development fund, a scheme ostensibly hatched by Malaysian businessman known as Jho Low. Goldman Sachs played a leading role in the raising and management of these funds thanks to the bribes and kickbacks made by Tim Leissner, one of Goldman's chief bankers. Prosecutors claimed over $2.7 billion was siphoned off by corrupt officials including the former Malaysian Prime Minister Najib Razak and Mr. Jho Low.

Tim Leissner pleaded guilty to conspiracy charges, violating the Foreign Corrupt Practices Act and money laundering. During his plea hearing, Leissner stated that his conspiracy was very much in line with the bank's culture to conceal facts from compliance and legal employees (Mueller 2019, 402). The bank, which made around $600 million in turn, blamed Leissner naming him to be a bad apple.

As part of his plea deal, Mr. Leissner agreed to forfeit $44 million and shares in a company worth hundreds of millions more. So far, he has avoided spending any time in jail by becoming a government witness. Goldman Sachs paid $5 billion in fines and pleaded guilty on behalf of its Asian subsidiary. Once again, the individuals got off lightly.

International attorney, Alexandra Addison Wrage, President of TRACE International, a nonprofit in the anti-bribery business, in her book *Bribery and Extortion: Undermining Business, Government and Security* (2007) provides a shocking insight into the extent of bribery, racketeering, money laundering and extortion that exists across the globe. Bribery and extortion are by no means a stereotypical Third World problem, she documents. They exist everywhere, right under our noses, and whole cultures are involved.

Wrage explains the incalculable damage wreaked by the tentacled crime that weaves bribery and extortion networks across countries and across the world. International kleptocracy, she writes, providing multiple examples, amounts to billions of dollars, and it is not just governments that participate but corporations which include employees at all levels.

Wrage documents stories of bribes and kickbacks, fraud and money laundering, embezzlement, grease payments, nepotism, extravagant gifts and tips, concealment of illegal sources of income, and the trafficking of humans. Regrettably, once again we see the collusion of thousands of employees who not only obey their bosses but participate in their own personal enrichment by corrupt means.

The US Foreign Corrupt Practices Act of 1977 (FCPA) criminalizes bribery to foreign government officials but does not criminalize private sector bribery unless there are fraud and accounting violations – which there usually are. Even so, Wrage points out that bribery enforcement resources are scarce, and the law does not prohibit payment to expedite or secure contract performance. So, there are all kinds of loopholes which organizations find to slip through.

Many businesspeople argue that bribery is part of the cost of doing business. Often a fine is way less costly than the advantages accruing due to the bribe, so they shrug and pay the fine. Some will argue that they are concerned about the impact on competitive advantage if they don't do what other firms do to secure business. Wrage cites stories of, for example, Monsanto, Lockheed and Baker Hughes, all organizations who have been guilty of significant international bribes.

Wrage points out that people overlook the huge misery, despair and violence that are associated with systemic bribery and extortion and that the global costs mount to billions. These behaviors perpetuate international criminality and negatively impact democracy. Unfortunately, she claims, there are poor governance, crooked judges, and too few resources to quell the rising tide of misdemeanors.

## Conflicts of Interest

In every sphere of life, due to people holding multiple roles, conflicts of interest abound; hence, this is a tricky topic.

To begin, a definition: "A conflict of interest is a set of circumstances that creates a risk that professional judgement or impartial actions regarding a primary interest will be unduly influenced by a secondary interest."

A primary interest refers to the principal goals of the profession or activity, such as the protection of clients, the health of patients, the integrity of research and the duties of a public officer.

A secondary interest includes personal benefit and is not limited to only financial gain but also such motives as the desire for professional advancement, or the wish to do favors for family and friends. These secondary interests are not treated as wrong in and of themselves but become objectionable when they are believed to have greater weight than the primary interests and thus vitiate attainment of the primary interest.

Alas, a great deal of the corruption that exists in the corporate world arises due to often significant and blatant conflicts of interest. Being transparent about them by completing a Conflicts of Interest form does not eliminate the conflict. This so-called transparency, if anything, provides a bizarre form of endorsement. Once one discloses, can one then play dirty?

Consider a few of the professional conflicts of interest that exist:

- Doctors and pharmaceutical firms doing medical research
- Judges and politicians
- Lawyers and the corporations they serve
- Board directors and personal connections with the CEO
- Auditors and the clients who pay them
- Employees caring for themselves versus the health of the organization

Many people deceive themselves by believing they will not be caught in the conflict-of-interest trap. Regrettably, too few of us can always place our primary interest first if the temptation is large enough to make personal benefits seem more important or even essential.

## The New Gilded Age

Sarah Chayes, who defines herself as a nonpartisan, self-proclaimed corruption fighter, has witnessed and actively engaged in anti-corruption policies and strategies in many countries including Afghanistan, Iraq, Nigeria, Uzbekistan and the Ukraine. She saw firsthand how the US government enabled corruption in Afghanistan. She helped launch the first anticorruption efforts to be adopted by the US military; however, the initiative came to nothing as it received no support from the higher ups.

She saw rigged systems throughout the world where the destitute are arrested for their petty crimes each day while the high rollers, in positions of power and influence, got away with murder.

Chayes's book is a chilling wake-up call to all of us. She tracks the path of corruption from the first so-called Gilded Age until now. She illustrates through examples and inside stories how corruption is systemic throughout American society. She likens the pervasive of corruption to a hydra-like network, the hydra being a Greek mythical predatory monster with the body of a serpent and multiple heads. It is very difficult to kill as a new head springs up each time one is cutoff. The hydra survives as long as one head remains.

Chayes explains that this is how systemic corruption works. If one gets rid of one transgressor, the next one readily takes his place. As long as one head remains, the system keeps perpetuating itself. Killing the hydra is well-nigh impossible unless, as Hercules found out, you cauterize each slayed-off head. Eradicating the network thus requires total annihilation of its constituent parts. It is clearly a Herculean task and who has the courage to take that on?

Chayes's book is filled with stories of these hydra-like networks. These include the many government-sponsored infrastructure projects where millions of funds are siphoned off to be used ostensibly for special projects that never happen or are infinitely delayed.

The military, with its massive revenue stream (a budget of $770 billion in 2023), is readily pillaged on all sides – by contractors, army personnel with special projects and overseas corruption rackets – and a blind eye is turned at the highest levels right up to Congress.

Chayes's chapters on the government and its romance with Wall Street are like reading the Who's Who of America. There is the late Madeleine Albright and her Albright Capital Management hedge fund that invested in projects around the world hand in hand with local kleptocrats, the contracts being secured through the Department of State of which Albright was secretary. Then there were relationships and deals between Jeffrey Epstein, Lawrence Summers, Alan Dershowitz, William Barr and former presidents Clinton and Donald Trump. She discusses how both the George W. Bush and Obama administrations did nothing to curb the risky behavior of banks and went so far as to support taxpayer assistance to banks that were clearly engaged in criminal behaviors. The Democratic government under Barack Obama bent over backwards to be as soft as possible on the very banks who created the 2008–2009 financial crash.

Chayes also refers to Neil Barofsky's book *Bailout* (2012), which discusses the fierce opposition he encountered when he tried to pay attention to how the $75 billion bailout funds were to be spent. The banks and their bonuses were what mattered and helping homeowners simply fell by the wayside.

During the 2008 calamity, approximately 500 banks failed, many of which were blatantly guilty of all kinds of criminal violations, yet there were no criminal referrals to the FBI, there were no prosecutions and there was no meaningful deterrence. A handful of banks were fined. The thousands of men and women engaged in selling toxic assets and lying and misleading consumers went off Scot free. In fact, while ten million people lost their homes, nine of the financial firms that were the largest recipients of the federal bailout money paid 5,000 of their traders and bankers, bonuses of more than $1 million apiece during 2008. And to add insult to injury, Lloyd Blankfein, CEO of Goldman Sachs, said he and his fellow bankers were doing God's work (Sandel, *Tyranny of Merit*, page 45).

Chayes's book claims that no one becomes a billionaire honestly. Elon Musk of Tesla is an example. Musk has received his own giant share of taxpayer money via grants meant to boost electric vehicle manufacturing, as well as a $465 million preferential loan from the US Department of Energy back in 2010. Compared to the amount of money Musk's ventures have received from the government over the years, that's chump change, she writes. SpaceX alone got a whopping $2.8 billion in government contracts in 2019, according to *The Information*, and has gotten a total of $15.3 billion from the government since 2003.

Chayes ends her sobering book by asking how American society might break its pattern of corrupt behavior. Can it get back to what it really values and what might be an alternative to a market-based morality? How might the swamps in which the hydra lives and thrives be turned around and changed into hospitable wetlands that nurture rather than destroy life?

## Bailout

In 2008, Neil Barofsky, former assistant US attorney, was appointed the special inspector general for TARP. His department named SIGTARP (Special Inspector General for the Troubled Assets Relief Program) was responsible for ensuring transparency as to how the TARP funds of $75 billion (initial amount that burgeoned to many trillion over the years) were deployed, inhibiting poor decision-making by the Treasury as well as preventing or detecting fraud.

In this damning book *Bailout* (2012), Barofsky relates in detail how he was thwarted at every turn. Timothy Geithner, then US Treasury secretary, spurned his department's attempts, lied, refused to be transparent and persisted in catering to the banks and their greed. Millions of mortgage holders never received the relief they were promised, or they were penalized heavily for it – which was not part of the bailout plan. The Obama administration feigned ignorance of the subterfuge to pander to the banks and silently gave a nod of approval.

Barofsky's comment about his time in Washington:

> The people down there don't care about justice or protecting the United States. It's all bullshit, ego, politics, turf, and credit.
>
> (Barofsky 2012, 11)

In March 2009, the Treasury authorized the insurance giant, the American International Group (AIG), to pay $168 million in bonus payments to its financial products division, the unit responsible for the company's near collapse the prior year. AIG had received more than $170 billion in federal bailout aid. Despite taxpayer outrage and a muted tut-tut from Congress, the bonuses were paid. The justifying argument put forward by the Treasury is that it was the expertise of these traders that was needed to help rescue the financial system!!! These were the very same traders that were the cause of the meltdown – go figure!

Barofsky ends his book on a somber note. The Treasury handsomely rewarded the bankers. The message the government has given is its endorsement of the too big to fail. The criminal justice system is ill-equipped to address the fundamental problems of a financial crisis. And effective regulatory reform is not wanted, nor does it exist.

Barofsky, a self-declared Democrat, writes that the American people should be angry. They should lose faith in their government. They should deplore the politicians and regulators who misspent their money. They should be revolted by a financial system that rewards failure and protects the fortunes of those who caused the collapse as they will undoubtedly do it again. They should be enraged by the unending protection of Wall Street as only with appropriate rage can there be seeds of reform that will break the system free from the corrupting grasp of the megabanks (Barofsky 2012, 214).

## Technology and Surveillance Capitalism

In 2019 I was invited to present a paper on the *Ethics of Data Profiling* at the University of Vienna. I, along with many others, gathered to explore the impact of data surveillance from every angle – the good, the bad and the ugly. What we were most interested in is whether overall heightened data surveillance, where nothing escapes the corporate or governmental sweep, advances human well-being.

One important aspect that raised its head during the conference is that according to psychological studies, people are less healthy, both physically and emotionally, if they are robbed of their privacy. Continuous lack of privacy leads to low esteem, depression and heightened anxiety. We see the impact of no privacy on increased teenage depression, distress and suicides. Psychologists also insist that being watched all the time makes people anxious and apathetic where daily states of anxiety build up. The result is that people who live under constant surveillance have more relationship difficulties, have more arguments and are more hypervigilant always scanning for threats. Of course, this evidence has scant impact on the corporations who with an apology for the damage they are doing continue their data pursuit at a rapid rate.[10]

As part of my research into the evolution and development of data surveillance, I read Shoshana Zuboff's profound book *The Age of Surveillance Capitalism* (2019). In this dense text, she documents the fascinating rise of Google as it staked its claim to the unregulated realm of cyberspace.

In 1999 Google was facing a dire threat to its business model which, at the time, excluded potential advertising revenues. While its search engine was recognized as one of the best, Google's profitability was not satisfying to investors. The critical breakthrough occurred with the recognition that the massive droves of data it was searching could be used to its financial advantage. What would advertisers not pay to target their offerings directly to a potential consumer based on his or her known behavioral patterns? Google held the gold. It could match ads with queries. The predictive power of data was Google's response to its financial emergency, and now Google instead of serving users surveils them without their knowledge and without their consent. Naturally, this opened the floodgates for other internet data behemoths like Yahoo and Amazon, who immediately followed suit.

After 9/11 all governmental and state surveillance practices were intensified. The Patriot Act (2001), with its focus on gathering warrantless information on people's personal lives, triggered a stream of legislation extending the powers of law enforcement and intelligence agencies. The internet was recognized as a great source of information and within no time the CIA and other agencies demanded partnerships with Google and others to share their trove of personal data. The agencies craved the lawlessness that firms such as Google enjoyed, and partnerships were readily established.

It was not just the government agencies that availed themselves of Google's trove, but Barack Obama partnered with Google to obtain as much data as possible to assist in his bid for election. Behind a cloak of great secrecy, Obama availed himself of the latest tech tools to peek into people's lives. Once he was appointed president, Google executives joined Obama's advisory boards and the revolving door between Google and government was put in motion (Zuboff 2019).

The ubiquitous hunt for behavioral data that is now the desire of all ecommerce businesses has opened all kinds of avenues for identity theft, wire fraud and gazillions of cyber scams. These misdemeanors are perpetrated not just by organizations but by thousands of tech savvy individuals situated anywhere in the world.

Since 9/11, the FBI has repeatedly shifted agents and other budget resources toward fighting terrorism or chasing physical criminal offenses, thus enabling white-collar crime and especially financial fraud and insider trading to run rampant (Researcher Trung Nguyen, HBR 2022). Internal FBI data reveals that cutbacks during 2021 were particularly severe for staffing of white-collar crime investigations, with a resulting decrease in prosecutions by 36% from its 2001 levels, Nguyen writes.

Further, despite attempts at tightening up regulation for white-collar crimes, especially in the financial services sector, with legislations such as Sarbanes-Oxley Act (2002) and the Dodd-Frank Wall Street Reform and Consumer Protection Act (2010), reform designed to alleviate the 2008/2009 financial crisis and prevent its recurrence, white-collar crime continues to soar as enforcement efforts get weaker. The benefits of data surveillance – such as they might be – are thus vitiated by not only white-collar crime but corporate misuse and abuse of people's privacy.

## The Chickenshit Justice System

In 2011, banking lawyer Carmen Segarra took a job with the Federal Reserve Bank of New York where she was appointed supervisor of Goldman Sachs. In her book *Noncompliant: A Lone Whistleblower Exposes the Giants of Wall Street* (2018), she documents in painstaking detail the collusion between Federal Bank employees and the executives at Goldman Sachs. During her seven months of tenure, before being laid off for refusing to alter her notes and redact her evidence of Goldman's rampant noncompliance, she discovered that Goldman blatantly ignored banking rules and regulations, failed on many risk assessment ratings, had no conflict-of-interest policy, ignored rules relating to foreign transactions, and did not have safety nets in place to protect people's investments, to mention a few transgressions.

These failings were known to the Fed and they jokingly would poke at Goldman using the motto, we will "let them hurt, but not too much." Time and again when Segarra tried to make progress on any compliance matter, the employees at Goldman stalled and she, Segarra, was cautioned by her superiors to go lightly.

After being laid off in 2012, Segarra sued the Fed for wrongful dismissal and due to some small technicality, her case was dismissed. Since being laid off, nothing has changed. The same people run Goldman Sachs and some of the players Segarra wrestled with have been promoted. She has some interesting reflections on You Tube.[11]

In *The Chickenshit Club*, (2017) Pulitzer Prize–winning journalist Jesse Eisinger describes the loss of integrity of the US Department of Justice. He points out that the justice system has become a revolving door for lawyers wanting to land lucrative careers in large corporations and who are therefore reluctant to investigate their executives' misdemeanors. These chickenshit lawyers want to brag of their high successes in closing cases, so they go after easier targets such as the small fry engaged in street crime.

The situation deteriorated after 9/11 when many in the justice system including the FBI were reoriented to seeking out terrorists. Further, in the wake of the 2008/2009 crisis, as pointed out earlier, not one of the top bankers went to jail.

Worse still, President Obama selected several of these top bankers in firms that needed the largest bailouts due to their fraudulent sale of subprime mortgages as advisors to his cabinet.

This reluctance to take on large corporations has led to a loss of skills by lawyers to persecute complex cases. White-collar crime investigations, which can range from Ponzi schemes to accounting fraud, can take months, if not years, before they lead to a potential prosecution. These cases require agents to sift through vast amounts of data and sometimes physically surveil suspects. These are costly and time-intensive efforts and require great skills which many in the justice department do not have. So, instead of going after individuals, the chickenshit types go after the corporations for money, for example, AIG, Google, JP Morgan Chase, Pfizer, who have paid billions in penalty monies through negotiated deals not indictments (see Violation Tracker noted earlier). This strategy adds to the moral hazard factor in that executives can act with impunity, confident they will not be sued, and that the fines and penalties will be paid with other people's money, namely that of the shareholders.

Statistics show that over 50% of the most serious fraud and larceny culprits are recidivists, repeat offenders, which makes the lame justice department even more complicit in turning a blind eye to white-collar crime.

## The Honest Truth about Dishonesty

The once highly acclaimed behavioral economics researcher and writer Dan Ariely has confessed that more than one of his studies has been based on false data.

Ariely was a Duke University professor of psychology and behavioral economics and author of best-selling books including *The Honest Truth About Dishonesty: How We Lie to Everyone – Especially Ourselves* (2013).

Ariely undoubtedly needs to look deeply into his own insights about lying to oneself. Recently several of Ariely's studies, as well as his methods, have come under question. Experts have examined some of his data and have found without doubt some of it has been faked. His response was "I made a mistake."

It has also come to light that Ariely was suspended from MIT after he conducted an experiment using electric shocks without proper approval from the ethics committee.

In a 2010 interview on NPR, he cited data from a dental company that the company said had not been collected and did not exist. The network later said that "Ariely's unsubstantiated assertion unfairly hurt the reputation of many honest dentists and planted a seed of distrust with patients." (NPR, 2010).

Several of Ariely's other studies have also come under scrutiny, with external researchers later unable to replicate the results. Ariely, however, remains at large – no consequences and no prosecution.

## Where Is the Courage to Be Who We Are?

INSTITUTIONS DO NOT COMMIT CRIMES
ORGANIZATIONS DO NOT COMMIT CRIMES
THE ONLY CRIMINALS ARE PEOPLE
AND THERE ARE HUNDREDS OF THOUSANDS OF THEM
ARE WE ONE OF THEM?

In 2006, Lisa Newton, Philosophy Professor of Fairfield University, penned a brief but penetratingly scathing text attacking the US economic system, titled *Permission to Steal.*

In her book, Newton excoriates the behaviors that led to WorldCom, HealthSouth, Enron and others, by pointing an accusing finger at "the evil perpetuated by the privileged at the expense of the trusting."

She also attacks the notion that the system is at fault by asking "who is the system?" The system doesn't cheat – it's the people who cheat. Where do our sinfulness, violence and greed come from? she asks. In response, she claims it arises due to the lethal marriage of ideology and opportunity. What happened to the virtues, the excellences of honesty, stewardship and responsibility? she asks. When did the public stop holding those in power to account, and how have we managed to create the illusion that a healthy society can be organized around the pursuit of wealth?

Liberalism, she writes, needs vigilance. We need a mindful society that upholds the virtues of self-awareness, moderation and the civic virtues of compassion for others – the fellow feeling and sympathy advocated by Adam Smith. We need a sense of responsibility and accountability, and we need a return to the noble virtues of courage and justice.

The face of corruption is an ugly one. Sadly, in some way we are all implicated; however, that is not our true nature. Somewhere we lost our way, and the mess we are in is bad.

Most people long to live noble lives and to express the courage that Tillich claimed so assuredly that lies at the root of our very existence. Being courageous is by no means easy – to which most of us can attest. In the chapters that follow we explore the many barriers we need to overcome, and we discuss steps in overcoming them.

But before we do that, let us look at what it means to stand up and stand out by being a whistleblower – a brave act to be sure.

## Your Turn

- Did you find the research and statistics provided in this chapter surprising? Did they challenge your views of well-known organizations?
- Can you think of instances in your own professional experience when financial greed prevailed over ethical behavior? Did you or others have the courage to voice concern in these situations?
- Can you think of any ways in which you turn a blind eye to other's corruption?
- Are there things you can do as a consumer, as a member of society or as an individual contributor within your organization to prevent or to safeguard against greed and corruption?

## Notes

1 See Annabel Beerel, *Ethical Leadership and Global Capitalism: A Guide to Good Practice* (Abingdon, Oxon: Routledge, 2020).
2 Old Broad Street is one of the main streets in the Financial Center of London marked by its towers of financial institutions.
3 This is an acronym for the name of the company.
4 Refer Adam Smith, *An Inquiry into the Nature and Causes of the Wealth of Nations* (Chicago, IL: University of Chicago Press, 1976).
5 Silicon Valley Bank workers were paid annual bonuses just hours before the bank collapsed, according to a report by CNBC. The payments were for 2022, unnamed sources told the outlet, and had been processed before regulators shut the bank down on March 12, 2023.
6 Sources: Proclaimed fact checked websites:
https://www.zippia.com/advice/white-collar-crime-statistics/; https://www.embroker.com/blog/white-collar-crime-statistics/
https://techreport.com/statistics/white-collar-crime-statistics/
https://www.financierworldwide.com/white-collar-crime-in-the-post-covid-19-landscape#:~:text=Certain%20types%20of%20white%2Dcollar,adapt%20quickly%20to%20new%20threats.
7 See discussion on a *Tyranny of Merit* in Chapter 11.
8 See discussion on greed in Chapter 9.
9 https://www.nbcnews.com/investigations/lobbyists-spent-record-42-billion-2023-federal-lawmakers-rcna135943.
10 In early February 2024, several CEOs were grilled on Capitol Hill about the proliferation of child abuse on their platforms. Much of the questioning from Senators was reserved for Meta's Mark Zuckerberg who gave online abuse victims sitting behind him in the audience, an awkward, almost dismissive apology.
11 https://www.youtube.com/watch?v=0FYITqxW4BY.

## References

Ariely, Dan. 2013. *The Honest Truth About Dishonesty: How We Lie to Everyone – Especially Ourselves*. New York: Harper Perennial.

Bandura, Albert. 2016. *Moral Disengagement: How People Do Harm and Live with Themselves*. New York: Worth Publishers.

Barofsky, Neil. 2012. Bailout: *How Washington Abandoned Main Street While Rescuing Wall Street*. New York: Free Press.

Brightman, Hank J., and Lindsey W. Howard. 2011. *Today's White Collar Crime: Legal, Investigative, and Theoretical Perspectives*. Oxon, UK: Routledge.

Chayes, Sarah. 2021. *On Corruption in America: And What Is at Stake*. New York: Vintage Books.

Eisinger, Jesse. 2017. *The Chickenshit Club: Why the Justice Department Fails to Prosecute Executives*. New York: Simon & Schuster, Inc.

Fisman, Ray, and Miriam A. Golden. 2017. *Corruption: What Everyone Needs to Know*. Oxford, UK: Oxford University Press.

Gigantes, Philippe. 2003. *Power & Greed: A Short History of the World*. London, UK: Constable & Robinson, Ltd.

Milgram, Stanley. 2009. *Obedience to Authority*. New York: Harper Perennial Modern Classics.

Mueller, Tom. 2019. *Crisis of Conscience: Whistleblowing in the Age of Fraud*. New York: Riverhead Books.

Newton, Lisa H. 2006. *Permission to Steal*. Malden, MA: Blackwell Publishing.

Partnoy, Frank. 2003. *Infectious Greed: How Deceit and Risk Corrupted the Financial Markets*. New York: Times Books.

Ridley, Matt. 1996. *The Origins of Virtue: Human Instincts and the Evolution of Cooperation*. New York: Penguin Books.

Sandel, Michael J. 2020. *The Tyranny of Merit*. New York: Picador.

Segarra, Carmen. 2018. *Non-Compliant: A Lone Whistleblower Exposes the Giants of Wall Street*. New York: Bold Type Books.

Shepard, Alicia C. 2010. 'Should you be Suspicious of your Dentist or NPR's Source'? *NPR Public Editor*. November 8.

Smith, Adam. 1817. *Theory of Moral Sentiments*. Boston, MA: Wells and Lilly.

Soltes, Eugene. 2016. *Why They Do It: Inside the Mind of the White-Collar Criminal*. New York: Public Affairs.

Veblen, Thorstein. 2009. *The Theory of the Leisure Class*. Oxford, UK: Oxford University Press.

Wrage, Alexandra Addison. 2007. *Bribery and Extortion*. Westport, CT: Praeger Security International.

Zuboff, Shoshanna. 2019. *The Age of Surveillance Capitalism: The Fight for a Human Future at the New Frontier of Power*. New York: Public Affairs.

## Recommended Reading

Mayer, Jane. 2017. *Dark Money*. New York: Anchor Books.

# Chapter 4

# The Courage to Blow the Whistle

## Is It Worth It?

It is 2011. You work at Halifax Hospital, Daytona Beach, Florida. Halifax is a non-profit hospital with 764 beds, 500 physicians, and 46 medical specialties.

Recently you attended a meeting orchestrated for all staff by Arvin Lewis, VP of Patient Business and Financial Services. The purpose of the meeting was to make everyone aware of the importance of the bottom line.

Arvin began the meeting by playing music and swaying to a tune while singing "show me the money." Fellow employees clapped and joined in the song and other rituals he had devised to remind everyone of the significance of billing everything in sight. His repeated motto was that the only thing that was better than cash was lots of it.

You were astounded by both his behavior and your colleagues' participation.

Three months ago, you were appointed the director of physician services. You are very proud that you have this important role. You worked your way up from being the food manager to the compliance department in 2005. You attended night school so that you could get an MBA, and now you have the important role of overseeing everything related to physician services. You are extremely thorough and very committed to Halifax.

One day, while reviewing the EMR (electronic medical records) and physician billing records, you discovered that Halifax was overbilling Medicare and giving kickbacks to the doctors via incentives linked to the organization's profitability. This is illegal according to the Stark Law. You also noticed that a significant number of Medicare claims referred to medical procedures that had never been performed.

DOI: 10.4324/9781003459644-5

Further probing led to your discovery that inpatients were being admitted for ailments that should have been handled as outpatients. Improper admissions amounted to a $2.2 million overcharge. Digging even deeper, to your consternation, you found that there were a vast number of unnecessary spinal infusions, which are a high reimbursement procedure resulting in a further several million-dollar dishonest claims. You know from your in-depth studies that many physician errors occur with these procedures, especially when they are not needed and thus done hastily. There are also added dangers to being an admitted patient. Statistics show that thousands of people die every year in hospitals due to poor infection protection and physician errors.

You alerted several high-level managers to your findings. In response, your own boss told you to pick your loyalty or get out. You went to the hospital's general council and discussed what you had detected. You pointed out that your own reputation was on the line. He said not to worry, no one would be sued under the False Claims Act or the Stark Law as he had friends in the Department of Justice (DOJ) who knew how to handle these cases.

You have noticed in the past few days how you have been snubbed. Somehow it has leaked out that you are a whistleblower. As a result, one of your colleagues snarled at you that you were morally obscene. Another said you should be ashamed of yourself for ruining it for everyone. No one sits next to you at lunch anymore and when you enter the elevator others get out. You have become a pariah in your own community and even among your supposed friends.

Your spouse has been with you all the way but is very concerned about your stress levels and keeps asking whether you are up for this fight. You know you can rely on your spouse's support whatever you do.

## What Should You Do?

- Escalate the problems by going public as people's lives are at stake and theft is taking place?
- Negotiate some kind of compromise with senior management?
- Quit while you can and get another job because once you are a public whistleblower no one will hire you. It will be the end of your career and you need to work to help support the family.

Adapted from Tom Mueller, *Crisis of Conscience* (2019)

In this true story, described in detail in Tom Meuller's book *Crisis of Conscience* (2019), Elin Baklid-Kunz, a brave whistleblower, was blamed for harming the hospital for having to spend more than $120 million in legal fees and settlements under the False Claims Act. To finance these expenses, the hospital took on debts, announced layoffs and defunded the employee pension plan. The executive pension plan, however, remained intact, and many of those complicit in the fraud have since been promoted to executive positions.

This is a typical whistleblower story. The whistleblower pays a huge price to reveal the truth and instead of being hailed as a hero is persecuted, demeaned and attacked not only by the organization, but by colleagues and friends, and in some cases, even by the family. He or she becomes an outcast who is usually forced to leave the firm and then struggles to get another job. The price is high. Is it worth it?

Is it worth losing everything which is how some whistleblowers describe their experience? To any heartfelt reader, their tales are devastating. Try as they might to alert their bosses, management or co-workers to fraud and corruption, they are invariably abandoned and left to carry the torch of truth on their own. Worse than how they are treated by the higher-ups is the treatment by their very own colleagues and friends who are terrified that they may be associated with the now labeled traitor. What about courage? What about character and the principles of excellence we claim to live by on our resumes and CVs?

Even if one argues that people have always been like that and that nothing ever really changes, does that justify our cowardly behavior? Why can't things change? How dare we talk about being more civilized, more progressive, more liberal if we wallow in unprincipled behavior wrapped up in cowardice.

Tom Mueller's book, *Crisis of Conscience*, is not only a compelling read, but kept me up at night. I found myself asking whether I too slink away from the truth and busy myself when others were doing the important work of caring for customers, employees and the environment.

## The Price of Whistleblowing

In writing about whistleblowers, it would be remiss to exclude reference to Daniel Ellsberg (1931–2023), arguably the first formally named whistleblower known for leaking the Pentagon Papers beginning in 1971.

The Pentagon Papers revealed that the US had secretly enlarged the scope of its actions in the Vietnam War with coastal raids on North Vietnam and Marine Corps attacks – none of which were reported in the mainstream media. Most important, however, the highly classified study revealed that administrations from Harry S. Truman through Lyndon B. Johnson's had willingly deceived the American people about the nation's involvement in Vietnam.

In 1964, Daniel Ellsberg joined the Department of Defense, where he was tasked with analyzing the expanding US military effort in Vietnam. The following year he transferred to the State Department. His headquarters were at the US embassy in Saigon (now Ho Chi Minh City). During that time, Ellsberg reached the opinion that the war was unwinnable and that certain things did not stack up. He returned to the US in June 1967 and worked on a top-secret report commissioned by Secretary of Defense Robert McNamara entitled "U.S. Decision-Making in Vietnam, 1945–68." Its contents strengthened Ellsberg's opposition to the war, and in October 1969 he and a former colleague, Anthony Russo, after trying in vain to get various people to agree to make the report public, began photocopying the document with the intention of making it public themselves if they continued to be rebuffed. Over the next 18 months, Ellsberg offered the document to several members of Congress. None chose to act on it. He then leaked parts of the document to the *New York Times*.

Ellsberg and Anthony Russo were soon charged under the Espionage Act of 1917 along with other charges including theft and conspiracy. Instead of being hailed as heroes they were denounced as traitors. Despite various nefarious attempts to discredit them, the charges against Ellsberg and Russo were ultimately dismissed. Ellsberg claimed all his long life that he had no regrets about what he did.

Besides Daniel Ellsberg, Mueller documents the shocking details of corruption and cowardice in some of the governments' most significant departments, especially those with huge budgets such as the Department of Defense, Department of Justice, the Environmental Protection Agency and the State Department. He also tells many private sector stories that include the automobile industry, pharmaceuticals and insurance.

One particularly appalling story is that of the Hanford nuclear site in Washington, which is no longer active (decommissioned in 1989), but is still trying to clean up its nuclear waste.

Hanford, according to Mueller, has had more whistleblowers than any other site on earth (Mueller 2019, 274). The problems are many. These include 56 million gallons of radioactive waste held in underground tanks and solid waste buried throughout the site. By the site's own admission, innumerable spills and solid waste burials were never accurately recorded and 60 square miles of groundwater remains contaminated above federal standards. The environmental and health effects have been devastating and have largely been ignored. Toxicity for workers and vapor injury have affected hundreds if not thousands. Safety measures remain inadequate, and the threat of explosions persists.

Currently, 10,000 people still work on the site providing salaries and jobs for the community. Without the site, the community would not be able to exist. "The leaking tanks and the threat of explosions all fade into the background," claimed one worker. "You just gotta keep on the blinders, pop in the mouthpiece and focus on certain things, and certainly don't say the wrong things, and you're gonna be just fine" (Mueller 2019, 287).

Mueller describes the devastating tales of several of the Hanford whistleblowers who, among other things, received death threats, had their records falsified, were identified as psychologically impaired, and were discredited in every way possible. No significant action was ever taken, and mismanagement continues. Added to the toxic waste problem is also the issue of corrupt contractors. They put in false invoices, charge exorbitant fees for work that rarely gets done, put in continuous change orders so that budgets are always radically overstretched and everyone in the system is on the take.

One of the worst offenders is the Department of the Environment. They are known for corruption, overspending, working on projects that demand creating budgets that don't exist, and a very poor safety record. Again, everyone knows, and no one does a thing.

## An Open Secret

Thirty years ago, Madeleine Albright, then secretary of state, asked General Powell: What's the point of having this superb military that you're always talking about if we can't use it?

The truthful answer would have been: It serves as a job creation scheme, virility symbol, stimulus package for politically powerful regions, and a state subsidy for arms companies.

The unfortunate reality, writes Mueller, is that whistleblowers are not liked by the politicians nor the Department of Justice who treat them with disdain and rarely give them the opportunity to present their case most effectively – if at all. President Obama was noted for decrying whistleblowers. He refused to deal with disclosures relating to the intelligence or the military and immediately named the whistleblowers as traitors who had betrayed the country (2019, 461). According to Mueller, the extent of his efforts to clamp down on leaks and to control information have not been seen since the Nixon administration (2019, 508). He attacked both relentlessly and viciously the few national security insiders who questioned the betrayals of the constitution and many whistleblowers during his tenure got short shrift where they were dismissed and not allowed to publicly voice their concerns (2019, 256).

## Manipulating the Truth – Trump's Truth Social

"I knew the risks," claimed Will Wilkerson, former vice president of Truth Social, a social media platform created by the Trump Media & Technology Group, run by Donald Trump. Wilkerson, who was also co-founder, turned whistleblower when he handed over 150,000 internal documents, contracts and emails to the Securities and Exchange Commission and federal and state investigators.

Wilkerson's high-paying job, with stock options, had the potential to make him a millionaire, but he decided to distance himself from the Truth Social platform after he became concerned that investors in the company might be at risk of losing their investments.

He told the *Washington Post*:

> I made the conscious decision. I knew the risks . . . especially regarding retaliation. But I don't think I could have sat back and stayed quiet, even

> if I was compensated handsomely for doing so. I'm here and I'm not going away.
>
> Ultimately, you know, I just want to do what's right.

Wilkerson was fired after having been accused by the company of concocting psychodramas. He now works as a Starbucks barista for $16 an hour under a federally protected whistleblower program. After applying for other jobs, only Starbucks called him back.

The SEC took no action and instead recently approved a merger between Truth Social and a "blank-check acquisition vehicle" in a deal that currently values the parent of his social media app Truth Social at as much as $10 billion. Mysterious? Perhaps not!

## Whatever Happened to Johnson & Johnson?

Johnson & Johnson (J&J) once stood out for its integrity and consumer care. Its famous credo, which sets outs its values, was hailed as the forerunner of positive culture creation.

When I began to study business ethics in the early 1990s, J&J was cited everywhere as the company that set the ethical standard for others. This misty-eyed view was reinforced when J&J responded with alacrity to the Tylenol tampering scandal, recalling millions of dollars' worth of Tylenol to ensure consumer safety. What has happened since then? Like Boeing – see page 75 – it appears as if greed and the bottom line are now what matter most.

Mueller cites an alarming tale about a state investigator, Allen Jones, at the state office of the inspector general in Harrisburg, Pennsylvania. Jones discovered that the supposed impartial research carried out to convince the FDA and medical community of the efficacy of certain medicines was ghost-written by certain pharmaceutical companies, and that major research had revealed the side effects of the drugs were downplayed, and, in some cases, concealed. Misleading clinical trials were created, and doctors were receiving honoraria to spread the gospel as to the medicine's effectiveness. Dangerous side effects were ignored.

Jones also discovered that people working in state agencies were receiving pharma money to close their eyes to what was taking place. Jones sent letters to the DOJ and the Department of Health and Human Services and to attorneys in the states where one of the main offenders, J&J, was operating. He was effectively ignored. His own bosses told him to go easy and when he refused, he was relieved of his investigative duties. His office mates and former friends avoided him. Then he was placed on administrative leave and shortly thereafter fired for insubordination.

Mueller claims that the defense contract fraud is in the billions and money lost under false claims nears the trillion-dollar mark.

## What We Do to Whistleblowers

Whistleblower retaliation knows no bounds. People are threatened and even shot at. Their private premises are ransacked. Fake documents are created to discredit them. Bosses and co-workers fabricate stories to demean and disenfranchise them. They are humiliated for being traitors and turnkeys and are ostracized both at work and in their communities.

Companies often deploy tactics that place them under intense psychological stress whereafter they are sent for psychological assessment and invariably pronounced as deranged, unfit, paranoid or psychologically disturbed. The whistleblower is turned into a patient who has a flawed perception of reality and who needs reform and remediation.

Whistleblowers are also often transferred out of their jobs into one where they do not have the needed skills and are then fired for their inadequacies. Every possible ruse is used to demoralize them and make them feel as if they are the problem. Colleagues are recruited to help denounce their ineptness, and regrettably most of them comply.

Organizations are wily in the strategies they use to disconnect the act of whistleblowing from their actions of retaliation. Organizations hire coaches (I have been one of them) to ostensibly help the person reach new levels of performance when in fact they are expecting the coach to "agree" that the person is inept, unsuitable or difficult to work with. Sometimes, the organization is explicit, asking that the person be "coached out" under any pretense possible. In my case, I refused and quit the assignment. I found out later that the organization's leadership had branded me as incompetent and that HR was told that I was never, under any circumstances, to be hired again.

C. Fred Alford's book *Whistleblowers: Broken Lives and Organizational Power* (2001) focuses on how whistleblowers try to make sense of the world and their lives after they have blown the whistle and then been tormented and punished for keeping the world safe.

Alford claims to take a psychological approach to the many whistleblower stories he has heard and discussions that he has held. What stands out, he writes, is that most whistleblowers feel compelled to tell the truth at any cost. In return, they claim that their lives have been ruined and that they will never do it again. They have lost not only their jobs, but in many cases their house, their family, their friends and their community. Most of them struggled to get work as potential employers would shun them once they did any background checks. They are branded for life.

Alford describes how the whistleblowers try to reconcile themselves to accept the terrible truths about the world. They realize the organization they worked for will usually not become better for their brave actions and people will not become more virtuous. It was all for nought other than to satisfy the inner voice that commanded them to do the right thing. They had to do what they did because otherwise they could not live with themselves, yet they do not know how to make meaning out of it. They keep retelling their story in the vain hope that some light will break through, and they will experience some redemption. Any satisfaction, however, remains elusive. They find that they must forsake what they understood about matters relating to society, law and justice, and the loyalty of friends. They try to reassure themselves that somewhere, someone knows and cares. But all in vain. They see how the world really works and are left confused and embittered. Their families think they were selfish for taking the risk and their friends think they were out of their minds.

Once you report on the boss you get fried. Reporting on subordinates is usually not quite as dire. According to Alford, whistleblowers feel they pay for other people's injustices who do not have the courage to look at their complicity and many of them are left living between paranoia and despair.

The whistleblower's story reminds one of George Orwell's *1984*, where the key protagonist, Winston Smith, sacrifices everything as he tries to take on the totalitarian system. The result is that he loses not only everything, but himself. In this dystopian novel, totalitarianism wins over humanity; Winston is one of the masses who end up putting his real self aside for the Party, for Big Brother. As a destroyed and lost soul, beaten senseless, he finally admits he "Loves Big Brother."

**1984**

O'Brien to Winston Smith

> The face will always be there to be stamped upon. The heretic, the enemy of society, will always be there, so that he can be defeated and humiliated over again. Everything that you have undergone since you have been in our hands – all that will continue, and worse.
>
> *1984* – George Orwell.

Totalitarian organizations are the enemy of ethics and morality. Fred argues, as does Hannah Arendt, that many large organizations, especially bureaucracies, are totalitarian. They operate like a system of government that is centralized and dictatorial and demands complete subservience to the state. To run against the organization, just as in a totalitarian state, is to risk annihilation.

Added to the danger of taking on the corporation, as mentioned, the DOJ has little respect for whistleblowers which makes it difficult for them to get a fair hearing, if any at all. Their motivation is deemed suspect. When they are eligible for a percentage of corporations' penalty funds, they are categorized as the bounty hunters of old. For most people, supporting them is far too dangerous.

The whistleblower's psychological load (see Boeing in the following section), as they are demeaned from every quarter and publicly and blatantly ostracized, is huge, so is it worth it? And yet, we, the public, depend on whistleblowers for our safety and well-being. The service they provide to society is immeasurable.

## Boeing's Disgrace

According to *Business Insider*, 2024, Boeing is a quintessential example of America's rotting business culture. Over several decades the company relentlessly disgorged cash onto shareholders when it could have spent it on building a better (and safer) product. Instead, Boeing focused on pleasing Wall Street and lining its senior executives' pockets.

For decades Boeing was hailed as the pinnacle of American engineering. This changed in the late 1980s when T.A. Wilson, the last Boeing CEO with an engineering background, was replaced by Frank Shrontz, an attorney and businessman. The new choice of CEO was a signal to Wall Street that engineering would now take second place in favor of cost-cutting and investor rewards. Boeing undertook a program of billions of dollars in share buybacks to pump up its stock price and paid out further billions in dividends. While shareholders basked in funds the employees were made to penny-pinch.

The 737 Max 8 was supposed to be the most efficient, cost-effective, environmentally friendly plane on the market. Instead, the plane exposed the rot at the core of the company's culture. In his book *Flying Blind: The 737 Max Tragedy and the Fall of Boeing*, journalist Peter Robison describes how when the new model was being built, managers asked for a detailed accounting of every test flight and resisted making any engineering changes. One manager apparently lamented that people would "have to die" before Boeing made changes to the aircraft. And die they did: two crashes, due to the company's attempt to work around a technical failure, claimed the lives of more than 300 people and grounded the 737 Max 8 for about 20 months.

The crashes, which happened in Indonesia in 2018 and in Ethiopia in 2019, killed a total of 346 people. After the second one, the Justice Department investigated how Boeing had convinced the Federal Aviation Administration (FAA) to certify the 737 Max. Prosecutors determined that Boeing committed fraud against the US by deceiving the FAA about elements of a key flight-control system that was later implicated in the crashes. None of the Boeing executives were called to account. Instead, the company and the Justice Department secretly negotiated a settlement – called a deferred prosecution agreement – in which Boeing blamed the deception on two low-level employees and agreed to pay $2.5 billion, mostly to its airline customers. In exchange, the government agreed to drop the criminal count of fraud if Boeing kept clean for three years.

The Alaska Airlines Max 9 door blowout heightened Boeing's problems with communication, supply chain and overall quality control failures.

Boeing is one of the largest recipients of government aerospace and military contracts. It has a long history of whistleblowers reporting fraud in the areas of accounting and under the False Claims Act. In recent years, Boeing has been involved in numerous whistleblower investigations relating to its financial reporting process, and its reports of plane sales.

One of the many whistleblowers, John Barnett worked for Boeing for more than 30 years before retiring in 2017. In the days prior to his death (suicide) on March 9,

2024, he had been giving evidence in a whistleblower lawsuit against the company. In 2019, he reported to the BBC that under pressure workers had been deliberately fitting substandard parts to aircraft on the production line. He also claimed to have discovered serious problems with oxygen systems, which could mean one in four breathing masks would not work in an emergency. He later told the BBC that workers had failed to follow procedures intended to track components through the factory, allowing defective components to go missing. In some cases, substandard parts had even been removed from scrap bins and fitted to planes that were being built to prevent delays on the production line.

Boeing quality engineer Sam Salehpour and former Boeing engineer Ed Pierson recently slammed Boeing for allegedly knowing about defective parts and other serious assembly problems and choosing to ignore or even conceal them. Salehpour said he had gone up high in the chain of command at Boeing to alert them of his concerns, having written "many memos, time after time." Yet he says his warnings went unheeded – and he was punished for bringing them up.

"I was sidelined. I was told to shut up. I received physical threats," he said. "My boss said, 'I would have killed someone who said what you said in the meeting.'"

Salehpour, who has worked at Boeing since 2007, came forward again in early April 2024 warning that more than 1,000 Boeing planes in the skies were in danger of structural failure due to premature fatigue. In the 787-line, tiny gaps between plane parts hadn't been properly filled, he said. "I found gaps exceeding the specification that were not properly addressed 98.7 percent of the time."

On the 777s, he found "severe misalignment" of airplane parts. "I literally saw people jumping on the pieces of the airplane to get them to align," he said. Salehpour urged Boeing to ground all 787 Dreamliner planes ahead of his testimony. Boeing, for its part, has denied Salehpour's assertions, saying that "claims about the structural integrity of the 787 are inaccurate" and noting further that it had tested the 787 line many more times than the jet would take off or land in its lifespan, and had found no evidence of fatigue.

For all the mistakes and safety problems Boeing has suffered under CEO Dave Calhoun's watch since 2020, resulting in a dozen corporate whistleblowers, multiple groundings and a chunk of a plane's fuselage literally blowing off in midair, he has not been held to account. On the contrary, Boeing's board of directors has lavished him with salary and stock options worth more than $20 million a year, plus a $45 million golden parachute when he retires later this year.

How does one make sense of that?

## Providing a Whistleblower Hotline

During one of my careers, I was an organization's designated Ethics Officer. Having an ethics officer was then in vogue. The Enron, WorldCom and Tyco scandals were still being unraveled and everyone was talking about the necessity of an ethics officer responsible for establishing in-house ethics policies and a whistleblowing hotline.

In 1991, an Ethics and Compliance Officer's Association (ECOA) had been founded that went into full gear after the financial scandals came to light. The ECOA provides training, seminars, consultancy and certification. By 2004, nearly every large company was shamed into appointing an ethics officer who was trained by the ECOA. Without an ethics officer, organizations were warned, their company was sure to become the next Enron or Tyco. As usual, a whole new field of consultancy was born. People were hurriedly appointed as ethics officers – usually some lower level or close to retirement employee – and ethics compliance and whistleblower policies were drafted. Policies had to be posted where employees could readily access them, and in-house seminars and ethics sessions became mandatory – just as we do now with Diversity and Inclusion. Has it made a whit of difference? In my opinion – nope!

My experience as an ethics officer and as someone responsible for the whistleblower hotline was like that of many others. Most people in organizations were disgruntled about having to attend ethics courses. They felt they were honest citizens and that this was all a waste of time. Few people used the hotline and then it was for the wrong reasons such as being denied FMLA by their Boss – clearly a Human Resources department issue. Many scoffed at the idea because they claimed the working classes were subject to "all this ethics stuff" while the elite leadership were the ones pilfering, defrauding or being dishonest. Why weren't the CEO and his or her executive team part of the training? And was the whistleblower hotline truly confidential?

In general, the term "whistleblower" carries a negative connotation that also carries with it the idea of being branded a tattletale, and we know how we feel about tattletales. Retaliation is swift and brutal. Judging by the continued pervasive corruption and the lack of consequences for the perpetrators, fewer and fewer people are standing up for honesty and the truth. (For more information refer to the National Whistleblower's Center – https://www.whistleblowers.org/.)

We all know that rather than having ethics officers that police the organization and whistleblower hotlines, the CEO and his leadership team should lead with character and courage. They should shape an ethical culture where people feel comfortable to call one another out when things are questionable or when the slippery slope is beckoning. Clearly, these organizational efforts, particularly in the large public organizations that are motivated by how the stock market sees them, are wanting.

## Courage in Whistleblowing

Are whistleblowers courageous? That depends on, among other things, the circumstances, and their motivation. The next chapter discusses courage in detail and provides us with a framework for evaluating courageous behavior. What we note is that motivation is a critical element in defining a courageous act. For example, if a whistleblower is motivated by compensatory dollars, then his or her actions would not qualify as being courageous. Similarly, if the whistleblowing act were one of revenge, or irrational anger and compulsion, this too would nullify it being deemed a courageous act. Motivations of self-righteousness or actions that are bound up in projections of an ideal self who takes the high road also muddy the waters as to the whistleblower's courageousness.

True courage is always an act motivated by goodness; that is, the conscious desire to promote well-being, flourishing and harmony, we could say to promote life in all its forms. Courage is not a response to shame, nor is it an act of defiance. More on this in Chapter 5.

## See No Evil, Hear No Evil, Speak No Evil

What leads people in positions of power and authority to use their power for no good – one might say for evil? And why do we put up with it, put the blinders on and shut up? What led us to be such cowards? How do we go to bed at night knowing that people are being defrauded, lied to and abused so that we can keep our jobs, our medical insurance and our treasured 401(k)s?

How many of us are like the Hanford worker who says to themselves, "You just gotta keep on the blinders, pop in the mouthpiece and focus on certain things, and certainly don't say the wrong things, and you're gonna be just fine."?

What happens to us that makes us check our personal ethics at the door, put on the blinders and see, hear and speak no evil? Why have so many of us become like T.S. Eliot's *Hollow Men* stuffed with straw, spiritually and morally empty?

Albert Bandura (see Chapter 7) referred to bureaucracy as the rule of the living dead where we kill part of ourselves to be part of the system. We become dead to ourselves or to others. The system owns us. People are no longer agents in their lives. They have ceded their will and their ability to make choices to "Big Brother" the Party or some charismatic demagogue. Is this what has happened to us?

Why do we succumb so readily to willful blindness and self-deception when in truth what we long for and desire are honor, justice, virtue and truth.

Maybe the next chapters can help us out.

## Your Turn

- Have you ever been a whistleblower? How were you received?
- Have you ever supported a whistleblower who is trying to make an inconvenient truth known?
- What are your honest feelings about whistleblowers? Are they tattletales? Or do you admire and respect them? Would you be willing to align with them?
- Do you ever wish that you had the courage to speak truth to those in power?

## References

Alford, C. Fred. 2001. *Whistleblowers: Broken Lives and Organizational Power*. Ithaca, NY: Cornell University Press.
Mueller, Tom. 2019. *Crisis of Conscience: Whistleblowing in the Age of Fraud*. New York: Riverhead Books.
Orwell, George. 2023. *1984*. New York: Signet Classic.
Robison, Peter. 2022. *Flying Blind: The 737 Max Tragedy and the Fall of Boeing*. New York: Knopf Doubleday Publishing Group.

# Chapter 5

# Courage

## The Foundation of Character

### A Personal Reflection

What does courage mean to you? What visions or ideas does the word "courage" conjure up in your mind? Are you reminded of daring action shots with John Wayne or Clint Eastwood? Do you have visions of Florence Nightingale, Mother Teresa or Susan B. Anthony helping those in need or standing up for justice? Or do you envision fighting soldiers or images of a person jumping in a stream to save a child?

Is your image of the courageous person predominantly male or female? Is it mostly related to physical feats? What about moral courage?

How about corporate leaders? Do any corporate leaders stand out as role models of courage? What makes them notable?

These reflections, among others which we shall entertain throughout this chapter, give us a sense of how we understand courage.

Let us begin by being clear right up front that courage is not the absence of fear. Courage is, however, about the appropriateness of what we fear. Also, a common vision of courage is one of soldiers at war or the achievement of some major physical feat usually performed by men. This is unsurprising in that the idea of courage was first formulated by the early Greek philosophers around the time of the much written about and mythologized Greek wars that took place between 600 and 400 BC. These early philosophers extolled war heroes as exemplars of supreme courage, the type of courage that should be emulated if one wanted to live a good life.[1] However,

DOI: 10.4324/9781003459644-6

despite our tendency to associate courage with war heroes, courage is not simply about war nor is it the preserve of men.

In Latin the word "courage" derives from Cor, where *Cor* means heart. In French we have the word for heart as *Coeur* which has resulted in our English word "courage." The idea is that courage is an activity of the heart, and it is only the heart that makes us brave enough to act in times of danger, even at the risk of our lives. Think of the blockbuster movie Braveheart!

Today, we use many words as synonyms for courage such as heroic, valiant, daring, fortitude, steadfast, bold, fearless, brave and pluck. This plethora of synonyms does not help us to understand what it means to be courageous and why courage is the basis of a good life and happiness.

In the next pages, we roll up our proverbial sleeves and dive into the deep meaning of courage and its relevance to happiness and a good life. We also examine whether any of our courage synonyms are fitting or appropriate. You might ask why we are going back over 2500 years to the Greek philosophers to provide us with insights and a framework of courage, after all, don't we have plenty of wise people who have talked and written about courage since then? My answer is fourfold:

- First, in our Western history, the Greeks, as far as we know, were the first to develop the concept of virtue and courage. Since then, philosophers, sages and new age wisdom teachers have adapted their thoughts and writing from this original source by interpreting, translating, summarizing, diluting and even distorting the original Greek teachings.
- Second, the Greeks provided a comprehensive framework around the virtues and courage. Each part is dependent on the other. Many interpreters since then have stripped the meaning of courage, from its context of virtue and character. They rarely connect happiness with inner freedom and courage in a way that we can see how these ideas support one another. There is no happiness without freedom, and no freedom without courage.
- Third, the Greeks provided a rigorous framework for defining what makes a courageous action. That framework is rarely, if ever, referred to in modern texts. Further, they sought to encourage people to be courageous and not just to do courageous things. In our day, the prime focus is on courageous acts omitting the essential ingredient of the character of the person.
- Fourth, the Greek philosophers were very specific about language, whereas in modern times we have disposed of the discipline of using precise vocabulary to convey our thoughts. We randomly generate synonyms without realizing how they detract or distort an original meaning.

So, while reading about happiness and courage you might say "Well, that is old hat." Yes, it is, thanks to the Greeks!

Before we proceed, let us remind ourselves of Pericles's great phrase which is highly relevant to our discussions.

## The Secret to Happiness is Freedom and the Secret to Freedom is a Brave Heart

### *Happiness and a Good Life*

According to the annals of Western history, it was the Greek philosophers, notably Socrates, Plato and Aristotle,[2] who were the first to question what it means to live a good life.[3] Their starting point was that humans, contrary to other animals, can reason. Since we have reason, what kind of conscious (reasoning) behaviors, they asked, would result in a good life? What kind of person should we be, and what kind of choices should we make to live a good life? And then, what is a good life?

Let us begin with what is meant by "good." What are the defining elements of goodness and how can goodness be measured or evaluated?

For guidance on these questions, we turn to Aristotle (Plato's pupil), and his famous text known as the *Nicomachean Ethics* (1999), where he tackles the issue of a good life and the meaning of goodness in detail.

Aristotle's foundational premise is that we humans are goal driven. We are always seeking to achieve some end (goal), the ultimate one being happiness (Greek – *eudaimonia*). Everything we do – get a job, buy a car, marry, save money – is a means to achieving our ultimate goal of being happy (NE 1097b). For Aristotle, this purposiveness of life (known as *teleology*[4]), namely seeking happiness, is what makes life meaningful. All our actions are in the service of achieving this end. There is nothing beyond happiness. There is no answer to the question "Why do you want to be happy?"

Now we must be clear here that Aristotle's happiness does not refer to a contented state of mind but to an admirable state of *being*. This type of happiness is achieved by practicing wisdom and virtue; it arises because of one's character. It is not found in worldly goods.

Aristotle also says that the best good is something that is complete, stands on its own, is pursued for its own sake, and has ultimate value. Happiness fits the bill and therefore happiness, he concludes, is the highest good (NE 1097b21). Our first question is thus answered – to live a good life is to live a happy one. Now we might say that is a no brainer. We did not need Aristotle to tell us this. But wait, it is not quite as simple as that.

How is one to measure (evaluate) this happiness since different people are happy based on different things? Some say their happiness lies in having a large family, others prefer wealth, or power, or leisure or a life of exotic travel. Will any form of happiness do? Not so according to Aristotle. There is a great qualifier!

Aristotle explains that everything has a function. A chopper's function is to chop wood. A good chopper gets the chopping job done effectively. A pair of glasses is there to improve one's vision. Good glasses perfect one's capacity to see.

In the case of humans, Aristotle claims that a human being's function is directed by his or her soul. All living things have a soul. It is what makes a being a living being. The soul is the animating principle of life that guides a human being in reaching his or her full potential, that is, living out his or her destined blueprint. In ancient times it was believed that the soul holds the blueprint for our lives and only by being connected to our souls can we live out our true potential according to this blueprint.

For Aristotle, therefore, what makes a human being function optimally is a life of activity directed by the soul in accordance with reason (NE 1098a9). The key points to note are direction by the soul, active living and reason. What Aristotle is getting at is that firstly, a good and happy life depends upon one heeding one's soul for inner guidance in living life. Secondly, one must engage in active living not just in theorizing about what is good or what is happiness. And thirdly, behaving rationally in all things is paramount. Impetuous, irrational behaviors detract from our true happiness. A human who lives by functioning optimally, insisted Aristotle, achieves true, deep, soulful happiness that is the ultimate good (the *summum bonum*). It is only this type of happiness that qualifies for the best life for the individual and for society.[5]

Now how does one go about living this life directed toward our optimal humanness and happiness? Aristotle explains that our soul has both rational and nonrational elements; that is, we have both rational and nonrational desires[6] in our striving for happiness, and we need guidance in how to manage these desires so that we do not stray from achieving our true potential. The guidance lies in what Aristotle refers to as the "virtues."[7] He divides virtues into two classes. The intellectual virtues which deal with our rational desires, and the virtues of character, that is, the moral virtues, these being the ones which guide our nonrational desires in cooperating with reason (NE 1102 xv).[8]

It is the moral virtues that are needed for achieving true, quality happiness. Being virtuous is the best life for a human being. This brings us to the important concept of virtue and the role of courage.

**Summary of the Good Life**

- A good life is a life of well-being where we live out our full potential as directed/guided by our souls.
- When we live this good life, we achieve deep abiding happiness. Happiness becomes who we are.
- To live a good life, we must practice the virtues as directed by our capacity to reason.

## Virtue and the Role of Courage

So far, so good. Now to the question of virtue. What is virtue? And where is courage in all this?

Virtue is a special type of excellence that is part of someone's character. As I mentioned earlier, there are two types of virtue, the intellectual and the moral or character virtue.

Intellectual virtues include truth, knowledge, understanding and wisdom. The intellectually virtuous person is motivated to live a life in pursuit of these virtues acquired from learning and teaching.

Moral virtues, by contrast, are pivotal in forming our character. They guide us in dealing with our passions and desires. They are excellences developed through the practice of self-mastery, self-discipline and principled behavior. What makes these behaviors desirable is that they redound in advancing goodness, well-being and harmony. They do not have to prove themselves by claiming to achieve beneficial consequences. Virtuous actions are inherently beneficent in that their aim and their execution are to do something good.

Plato (Aristotle's teacher) named four distinctive virtues called cardinal virtues. These four virtues, he claimed, determine all others. They are wisdom, justice, fortitude (courage) and temperance (self-restraint or moderation).

Aristotle also named four central virtues, these being prudence (*phronesis* or practical reason), justice, courage and temperance.

Here we note that courage is a premier virtue. It is an excellence of character that aims at achieving goodness and well-being. But, once again there is much more.

Virtuous people are those that exhibit virtues in daily life. They consciously choose to act virtuously because they know it advances well-being and flourishing. This means that virtue is a consistent state of being rather than a capricious choice depending on one's mood, the situation or the day (NE 1105b34). Virtuous actions are not one-offs or flukes nor are they the result of an impetuous desire (NE 1105a31). Truly courageous acts, for example, are not isolated responses. One isn't courageous today and not tomorrow, or in this instant and not that. One does not cherry pick when it suits or pays one to be courageous or just or wise. You either are or you are not. For example, you cannot be courageous at home but not at work. Fickle people are not virtuous.

## Developing a Virtuous Character

How does one develop this virtuous character? According to Aristotle, through habitual action. We are our habits. What we regularly do and to what we give regular attention shape us – our thoughts, our feelings and our behaviors. To be a virtuous character – someone who aims at the good life and at achieving good ends – means practicing virtue. You want to become an excellent tennis player, you practice tennis. You live, breathe, eat everything to do with tennis. Similarly with character development and the virtues. Practice, practice, practice. Developing a virtuous character is where life is one of intentional and attentional living of the virtues choice by choice by choice. Virtue is an ingrained habit of choosing, and over time, it becomes a trait of one's character.

Is being virtuous a skill? No, in that it is not something one can totally master. It is a never-ending quest. There is no goal to be achieved. It is a way of intentional and attentional living that is transformative in that it alters one's being.

Aristotle is also known for his articulation of the golden mean – the mean being the intermediate point between excess and deficiency. For example, courage is the mean between brashness and cowardice, and generosity is the mean between miserliness and profligacy (NE1106a26).

A virtue is thus acting from this intermediate point which is never static; all situations are always in dynamic movement and interplay. Being able to choose this "mean" – or intermediary point – which is always relative to time and circumstance, requires prudence (practical reason) (NE 1107a3).

For Aristotle then, a courageous man – women get short shrift in his world – is someone who thinks before they act. Justice or courage is not impulsive reaction. They are rationally based, deliberate, prudent actions performed at the right time and right place for the right reason. And are always appropriate to the circumstance (NE 1106b23).

One might challenge the idea of thinking before we act by asking whether jumping into a raging river to save a child from drowning first requires rational deliberation. Aristotle would answer that a person of character has internalized courage through habitual practice. Courage has become part of who one is. Therefore, what might appear as impetuous or impromptu is far more reasoned and deliberate than it seems. Of course, too much deliberation, as in the case of Shakespeare's poor Hamlet, can result in paralysis rather than action. So, here again we can apply the golden mean between rash and risky unmeditated action and paralysis.

We might ask whether there is a preference of virtues. Plato argued that courage was the prime virtue as without courage, it is not possible to practice the others. For him, courage is the primary condition to being wise, just or self-restrained. Being courageous is inherently both noble and just. Courage also contains a certain wisdom that is reflected in its appropriateness, steadfastness and perseverance.

Aristotle argued that prudence – practical reasoning – comes first. Without prudence, he argued, there can be no appropriate courage. Prudence gives one the ability to see what is really there – the truth.

By now you might feel that your own courage has been tested. We are not quite there yet, but with a little more patience and fortitude, we will arrive at a definition of courage, and we will understand what makes for true courageous behavior.

### Summary of the Principles of Virtue

- There are two classes of virtues – the intellectual and the moral.
- A virtue is an intermediate point between excess and deficiency.
- Moral virtues are traits of a person's character that exhibit moral excellence in that they guide our irrational passions and desires.
- A morally virtuous person lives according to the cardinal virtues of wisdom, prudence, courage, justice and temperance.

- Virtues are good in and of themselves. They stand alone without being dependent on their attainments or achievements.
- Virtuous behavior advances goodness; that is, it enhances flourishing, harmony and well-being.
- Virtuous actions are not erratic or thoughtless. They have been honed and integrated into one's character through practice. They define who one is.
- Virtues are rationally based, deliberate and well-chosen actions performed at the right time and place for the right reason.
- Being virtuous is a state of being that leads to ultimate happiness.

## Understanding Courage – Plato

Staying with our Greek philosophers, we find that two of Plato's dialogues – *Laches* and the *Republic* – tackle the concept of courage in some detail.[9]

In *Laches*, Socrates (Plato's mouthpiece) stresses that courage is a virtue in that it has the capacity to endure extreme pains and fears and to exhibit steadfastness (Scarre 2010). He also points out that courage is wisdom; that is, it is inherently wise. He explains that what distinguishes the courageous individual from the coward is not that the former is willing to "go toward" what he fears while the latter is not, but rather that the courageous individual, unlike the coward, knows what is truly deserving of fear. All cases of cowardice, according to Plato, are cases in which the agent is ignorant or mistaken (at least temporarily) about what is truly fearful and bad. Courage, by contrast, is wisdom about what is and is not to be feared.

Socrates goes onto claim that courage, being a virtue, is a good in itself (Rabieh 2006, 50, 53). He points out that by acting courageously, man exercises the most important part of himself, his soul, something we stressed earlier (2006, 64), and is reiterated by Paul Tillich who we met in the Introduction.

In the *Republic*, one of the most well-known of Plato's dialogues, Plato discusses the nature of spiritedness, something we refer to as boldness or as daring. This state, he claims, makes a person feel fearless and invincible in the face of everything. Because this is not a rational response but an emotional and impetuous one, it is not courage. Courage is where one is in control of one's actions. One is not angry or seeking glory or combatting shame (Miller 2000). Neither is one self-righteous. These states blind one. Courage is rational and honorable, not tempestuous, nor is it about amassing glory, honors or accolades.

Plato also points out that courage is not the result of passion or anger. It is a clear-headed response motivated by an autonomous agent who is not slave to external or internal emotional pressures. So, a person who is hesitant to act due to his or her fear, and who, because of encouragement or coaxing screws up the courage to dare to act, is not a truly courageous person. The reason being that one emotion, namely fear, is being overcome by another, daring, an emotional or spirited action that incites boldness and defiance. The role of the autonomous agent has been lost as he or she has succumbed to one or other emotion.

*The Republic* includes Plato's famous analogy of the cave. He claims that most of us are like people tied up in a cave with our only reality being the shadows thrown on its walls. If we break loose and are brave enough to leave the cave and emerge into the sunlight, we find the light blinding. Few can endure the illumination of the truth when confronted with the illusions they have been living. Courage is the psychic strength not to flee the truth and return to more familiar things (Rabieh 2006, 149, Republic 518 c). Courage challenges us to face reality head on – something we discussed in Chapter 1 and shall return to again.

## Summary of Plato and Courage

- Courage is the ability to endure extreme pain and fear with steadfastness.
- Courage is inherently wise. It appreciates what truly deserves fear.
- Courage is a virtue which means its aim and execution are to advance goodness.
- Courage is an exercise of the soul.
- To be courageous requires being an autonomous agent not under the sway of emotion, for example, anger, daring or glory seeking.
- Courage is the ability to face the truth.

## Understanding Courage – Aristotle

Now, let us return to Aristotle, who as usual has a lot to say.

Aristotle confirms that courage is a virtue, and virtues, as we know, are directed at achieving good ends (NE111a20). The first criterion of courage is that it is aimed at advancing goodness, flourishing and well-being.

Along with Plato, Aristotle insists that courage is not fearlessness. On the contrary, courage is about knowing one's fears and being able to make difficult choices, hold steady, persevere and act in the face of those fears. Someone without fear is neither courageous nor brave. On the contrary, as Aristotle pointed out, the fearless person is more dangerous to have around than the coward. What he did stress, however, is that there are some things we fear that we should not and there are ways we act out our fears that are often not constructive. Knowing what to fear and when is part of being courageous. Like Socrates/Plato, he links courage and wisdom.

As mentioned earlier, brave acts, according to Aristotle, are fearing the right things, for the right reason, in the right way, at the right time and according to the merits of each case (NE 1115a16–19). A brave person is someone who holds fear in the right perspective and acts accordingly. And a brave person takes his or her fear into account when pursuing any action. In other words, the courageous person is in touch with his or her fear but is not overwhelmed by it.

Now what actions can we call courageous? Will any seemingly brave action qualify? Aristotle refers to the person who is courageous as being someone who performs brave acts that make supreme demands on them that may result in his or her "death" (NE 1115a34–35). Courage is not just the mastery of fear of physical death but the mastery of fear of different kinds of deaths. These may be physical, emotional, psychological, economic or spiritual. Courage is needed just as much to face feelings of doubt, alienation, isolation and hopelessness as it is to meet any enemy on the physical battlefield (Scarre 2010, 142). What is important is that the threat of "death" must be real, significant and unavoidable. Whistleblowers most often face devastating derision, ostracism, demotion and loss of a livelihood for taking a courageous stance. For many this is an experience of "death" (discussed in Chapter 4).

Courage is also needed to face our fears of not only our mortality but our fear of abusive authority, fear of uncertainty, fear that we will not fit in and fear of loneliness. All these fears hold the terror of emotional and psychological death. Facing these fears and acting courageously despite the terror they might hold require courage.

Contrary to popular sentiment of the day, Aristotle argued that in general soldiers are not courageous. They fight and sometimes die in battle because they are following orders. They would be punished, shunned by their comrades or dismissed if they failed to obey, so their actions are motivated by fear rather than by their inner compass or their hearts. However, the soldier who throws himself on a hand grenade to prevent it from blowing up his companions is performing a courageous act (Scarre 2010). People who voluntarily got onto their ships and who were ready to do battle to save their fellow soldiers at Dunkirk during World War II were undoubtedly courageous.

Flamboyant risk-taking does not qualify as a courageous act, nor does killing a mouse with a hatchet or setting a house alight and then saving the residents from burning. Further, according to Aristotle, someone who is trained to perform certain dangerous acts, for example, a firefighter, who expects these dangers (possible death because of a fire), is also not courageous. The danger must be out of the ordinary and unpredictable (Scarre 2010).

Can courage be a quality that someone displays in the performance of a bad act? For example, are suicide bombers courageous? Afterall, they die for their principles. The answer is a clear "no!" Courage may mean risking death but not seeking it. We know by now too that acts of courage attain good ends. They are not only about getting an extraordinary thing done but about getting a "good" thing done.

Courageous acts are also not one's undertaken when a person is on strong tranquilizers, inebriated or otherwise not of a clear mind. And according to Socrates, a person who cannot swim and dives into deep water to save someone is not courageous but stupid.

Brene Brown, the Texan professor, author, and shame and vulnerability researcher, has pounded out a series of "daring books" aimed at inspiring people to fight their fears and be courageous. Brown equates daring with courage.

She begins the book *Daring Greatly*, by quoting a 1910 speech by Theodore Roosevelt that describes good citizenship in a republic as being akin to being a gladiator fighting in a dusty, bloody, sweaty arena and who strives valiantly to prevail. He may triumph, but if he doesn't at least he "dared greatly."

While Roosevelt's speech is rousing, the daring he promotes does not fall within our Greek sages' guidelines. Alas, it is true that in our society courage is mostly deemed a male trait where the hero is fighting valiantly for or against something, but courage is not the preserve of men only, and it does not only occur in physical battles.

The analogy of the dusty, bloody sweaty arena evokes an image of bloodthirsty crowds screaming enthusiasm for the gore they are witnessing. Courage is thus depicted as a show for the crowds, who, for the most part, are enthralled and delightfully entertained whether the gladiator triumphs or doesn't. His compensation is that he can at least say or feel "I dared greatly." While this is great political rhetoric, and reflects the heroic images of ancient days, it is not in keeping with the true spirit of courage. The courageous person is not engaged in putting on a show for anyone. As both Plato and Aristotle insisted, courage is not about defiance or daring, boldness or pluck.

Courage rests in rationality (NE 1916b4). Daring, defiance, boldness or any form of emotional or irrational compulsion are not acts of true courage but are acts of bravado or rashness.

A whistleblower who feels compelled after a certain time or a certain event to spill the beans about unethical behaviors is courageous, provided he or she is not motivated by anger or revenge or compensatory dollars. The motivation needs to be purely to promote goodness and well-being. Courage is noble risk-taking where there is no desire for self-gain (NE1115b20–24).

Now what about fortitude? While courage and fortitude used to be synonymous, nowadays fortitude has a narrower meaning than courage. Fortitude as it is currently understood means endurance with composure. It includes a certain patience during adversity. One might say that fortitude is a steadfastness, an unwavering dedication to standing one's ground in the face of danger or evil. Fortitude or steadfastness is not passive or submissive. It is a recognition that at a certain time, holding steady in the face of hardship or suffering is the more prudent and courageous choice. It demonstrates firmness of character, dignity or self-possession when we are in a tight spot. Practicing fortitude, patience and steadfastness develops a greater capacity for courage; however, it may mask the courage to act.

Courage is not motivated by victory and defeat but rather by confronting a challenge or conflict that is nonlife-giving and seeking to give it life. True courage has an inherent poise and serenity. Despite heart pounding fear it is not done to prove anything to anyone.

Courageous actions aim at the most exalted goals, and in striving for these exalted goals courageous people affirm their essential nature and bring their own perfection closer. "It is part of the beauty of courage, that the good and the beautiful are actualized in it" (Tillich 2000, 4–5). There is a self-transcendence in courage where one is called to act from one's highest self.

## What Courage Is and Is Not

**What courage is:**

- A state in which one is in control of one's actions
- A soul-directed act
- A good in itself
- A capacity to endure extreme pains and fears and even death
- An ability to exhibit steadfastness
- Wisdom in knowing what is truly deserving of fear
- A clear-headed response motivated by an autonomous agent who is not slave to external or internal emotional pressures
- Noble risk-taking
- The psychic strength to face the truth
- Something that is consistently practiced and can be relied upon

**What courage is not:**

- Fearlessness
- An action motivated by anger
- A response out of self-righteousness
- The result of passion or emotion, for example, anger or revenge
- About seeking glory or recognition
- A reaction out of shame or to counter shame
- Boldness or daring
- An action that deliberately results in harm to prove or support an idea or belief

Based on the key components of courage à la Socrates, Plato and Aristotle, we can compile a working framework as our guide.

## Courage Framework

- Courage is a moral virtue and, as such, is an end in itself. It is not done for the sake of anything else other than to advance goodness, flourishing and well-being. It is a selfless act.
- Courage lies in its wisdom, not its bravado. It is a choice resulting from a discernment guided by wisdom and prudence.

- Courage is not fickle and impetuous – it is the act of a person with a courageous character.
- Courage is the willingness and a commitment to act in the face of extreme danger.
- It is the mean between cowardice and over-confidence.
- Courage is not fearlessness, bravado or daring.
- Courage is always mediated by reason.
- Courage exhibits fortitude and endurance and often patience.
- There is a nobility and beauty about courage in that it is about facing the truth of a situation.
- Courage means confronting a challenge or conflict that is nonlife-giving and seeking to give it life.
- There is a self-transcendence in courage where one is called to act from one's highest self. It is a call from the soul.

## Examples of Courageous Acts

- Encountering physical danger to save a life
- Facing realities or truths that are unpalatable and are threatening or challenging
- Resisting social pressure to be nice or accommodating at the risk of being ostracized and being made to stand alone
- Being a principled whistleblower
- Speaking truth to power
- Standing for one's principles in the face of challenge and unpopularity
- Fighting injustice
- Making difficult decisions where there is a lot at stake and holding steady against resistance
- Being open, honest and candid without worrying about whether one is liked, admired or conforming with group expectations
- Wrestling with one's own inner demons despite the challenge and seeming death of one's ego

## The Stoics

When discussing the ancient Greek idea of courage, it would be remiss to omit the Stoics.

Stoicism is a school of philosophy that was founded in Athens in the early third-century BC by Zeno of Citium, Cyprus. Well-known Stoics are Seneca, Epictetus and the Roman Emperor Marcus Aurelius known for his book titled *Meditations* (2006).

The Stoics were great followers of Socrates. They too held that the life of virtue is a happy life and that the Platonic virtues of wisdom, courage, justice and temperance were the path to happiness. They argued that it is our perceptions and attitudes that lead us astray. They focused on our ability to reason and to choose how we categorize and respond to events. They viewed courage as part of daily living and held that it brings true joy as it is the experience of our self-fulfillment.

Stoicism takes a highly practical approach to daily living. People are nudged to watch their perceptions and attitudes and to accept the unpredictable nature of everyday life. Stoicism encourages self-awareness, practicing fortitude and developing mental clarity by controlling one's thought processes. For more on Stoicism, see Recommended Reading.

## Final Word

It is time now to attempt a definition of courage that includes some of the defining characteristics mentioned earlier. I offer the following:

> Courage is a trait of character that motivates and guides a willingness to rationally, selflessly and actively confront danger, adversity, severe hardship, or radical uncertainty despite great personal risk in the service of advancing goodness and well-being.

One important thing to note regarding our discussions is that there is a significant difference between physical and moral courage. Attaining physical courage is far easier than attaining moral courage in that we would rather face physical death than the dictates of our conscience, something we discuss in the chapters to come. Putting it simplistically, more people would jump into the river to save a child or animal than stand up against authority or the system to fight for injustice.

A distinctive focus on moral courage as distinct from physical courage only began in the early nineteenth century with the beginning of the Victorian era; however, in the twentieth century we shrugged off all Victorian virtues as being prudish and inhibitive. Alas, this dismissal of attention to moral courage has cost us dearly.

In his challenging book *After Virtue* (1984), Alistair Macintyre critiques modern society claiming that morality, like everything else, has become fragmented and is no longer part of the coherent conceptual scheme so thoroughly developed by the Greeks. As a result, he claims, we have lost our comprehension of both the theoretical and practical elements of morality. Further, Macintyre argues, we have lost our ability for rational arguments where instead everything succumbs to emotivism. We reject objective principles and truths preferring to claim and express our personal preferences, attitudes and feelings. (See my discussion on inspiring people to speak up – Chapter 9, page 160)

In support of Macintyre's assertions, what is revealed in the following chapters is that our contemporary understanding of courage and the rigor of its principles is pitiful. The survey results discussed in Chapter 10 highlight how much courage and the idea of virtue have almost disappeared from our vocabulary and our mental frames. As I have pointed out several times, courage is also barely mentioned in either leadership or ethics texts nor is it part of most leadership and advanced education training programs. Children are not taught courage in schools and adults are largely unaware of the essentiality of courage if one is to uphold a democratic society. Too bad and too sad!

## Your Turn

- Has your view of courage altered since reading this chapter? If so, how?
- What element of courage speaks to you the most?
- List the courageous actions you have engaged in over the last week or month. What can you learn about yourself from reviewing this list?
- Based on the framework of courage, which business leader/s do you think demonstrate/s courage?
- How can you apply the Courage Framework to enhance your own leadership practice?
- How could implementing the Courage Framework increase the freedom and happiness you experience personally and professionally?
- Where in your life do you see a further opportunity to act courageously?

## Notes

1 In Greek, the word "courage" derives from the word *andreia*, which means manliness. This bias no doubt arose, as mentioned previously, due to the development of the virtues during the time when Greece was at war and heroic courage in battle was lauded as a supreme virtue.
2 Plato was a student/follower of Socrates and Aristotle was a student of Plato. While all three support the same basic concepts and apply the same principles, each of them adds their own nuances.
3 The term "Western" draws on an affiliation with, and/or a perception of, a shared philosophy, worldview, political and religious heritage grounded in the Greco-Roman world, the legacy of the Roman Empire and medieval concepts of Christendom.
4 Teleology comes from the Greek – *telos* means end/purpose or goal and *logos* means reason.
5 How many books are now written on the importance of being in touch with our souls?
6 Examples of nonrational desires include greed, envy and lustfulness.
7 Virtue ethics began with Socrates, and was subsequently developed further by Plato, Aristotle and the Stoics.

8 We will not pay much attention to the intellectual virtues in this text as we are more interested in the moral virtues and the role of courage. Aristotle, however, placed great store in the intellectual virtues and the benefits of living an intellectual life.
9 Plato wrote approximately 35 dialogues where Socrates, his teacher, is the main character. The dialogues are constructed so that Socrates, the interlocuter, through the technique of penetrating dialogue reveals how little most people know about the many things they think they know a lot about. The dialogue is also a method for Socrates and Plato (the author) to articulate their own views.

## References

Aristotle. 1999. *Nicomachean Ethics*. 2nd ed. Translated by T. Irwin. Indianapolis, IN: Hackett Publishing Company, Inc.
Aurelius, Marcus. 2006. *Meditations*. New York: Penguin Books.
MacIntyre, Alasdair. 1984. *After Virtue*. 2nd ed. Notre Dame, IN: Notre Dame Press.
Miller, William Ian. 2000. *The Mystery of Courage*. Cambridge, MA: Harvard University Press.
Rabieh, Linda R. 2006. *Plato and the Virtue of Courage*. Baltimore, MD: John Hopkins University Press.
Scarre, Geoffrey. 2010. *On Courage*. Abingdon, Oxon: Routledge.
Tillich, Paul. 2000. *The Courage to Be*. New Haven, CT: Yale University Press.

## Recommended Reading

Aurelius, Marcus. 2006. *Meditations*. New York: Penguin Books.
Holiday, Ryan. 2021. *Courage Is Calling*. New York: Penguin Books.
Sandbach, F.H. 1989. *The Stoics*. London, UK: Gerald Duckworth & Co., Ltd.

# Chapter 6

# Courage – Freedom – Happiness

## The Fight for Freedom

Once upon a time, thousands of years ago, during the warring states period in China, a young warrior went to seek out the wise man who lived in the mountains. He wanted to know how his clan could defeat the enemy, once and for all. For years, throughout the country, raiding clans would arrive and burn homes, steal livestock, rape the women and run off with the children. People lived in terror, never knowing when the next raid would occur.

For years the young warrior and his clan had responded by doing the same to the neighboring clans warning them that they were strong and would fight back. To no avail. Everyone kept fighting and the wars continued. The young warrior wanted to know from the old man what they should do. How could they win and end this never-ending war.

The old man listened carefully to the young man's tales of fighting, woe, sadness and revenge. He saw the anger and frustration in the warrior's eyes as he wrung his hands and clutched his sword.

The old man pulled at his long beard that nearly touched his knees and sat silently after the young man ended. After several minutes the old man spoke:

> You can never defeat your outer enemy if you have not defeated your inner one. Once you have made peace with your inner enemy you will easily overcome your outer one.

DOI: 10.4324/9781003459644-7

> You are trying to beat your outer enemy by thinking like him, acting like him, and in no time, you become like him. You become your own worst enemy and you never know it.

The old man paused, and after a deep breath continued:

> But if you sit quietly and meditate and look deeply into your own fears and angers you will become the true you. Your fears and anger will dissipate. There will be no inner enemy. You will gain mental clarity and you will drop into your own wisdom that will defeat the enemy by its very existence. Calm, grounded energy, inner confidence and peace is the hallmark of the true warrior; the warrior that does not need to fight to win.

"Remember," said the old man, true courage is self-conquest, and that is our most important task. The heart of the warrior is filled with this courage that gives us inner freedom, real freedom.

Have you thought about how much of life is spent fighting and defending? Our lives are filled with fighting. We are continuously fighting something. It could be a reality we don't want to face; it could be for more money, more recognition, more status, more opportunities to get our own way or more things to satisfy our desires. And then we are always defending ourselves against something, or someone, or some truth we would rather not hear about or deal with, justifying what we did or said or what we believe or support. Fighting and defending is what we all do, male and female alike, all day, almost every day. We are the everyday warriors of our lives. We are always reacting to some external event or encounter armed for battle, ready for either offense or defense. The problem is, so is everyone else. So, much of our lives is that of the warring states: fight, defend and then counterattack.

In the previous chapter we took a deep dive into the origins and structure of courage and its significance for living a good and happy life. We noted that courage is a state of being and that it is not an emotional event or experience. Its aim is not to prove anything, to acquire any accolades or create feelings of self-aggrandizement.

Courage comes from our souls, that deepest part of ourselves that aspires to goodness and transcendence. It is a manifestation of one of the excellences as a human being.

Courage means acting despite our fear, not out of bravado or daring, but as a prudent and measured approach to advance goodness, wholeness and well-being – our own as much as anyone else's.

What we learn from the old man in the story is that we need the courage to face our inner enemy as much as our outer one. In fact, facing our inner enemy, that is, those fears and shackles that inhibit our freedom, takes precedence over tackling the outer ones and is usually the far harder battle. We would rather tackle something outside of us that we can objectify than deal with our own subjective, messy inner world.

Our human ideal is to be inwardly free. While total external independence is not possible, inner independence is the secret to inner freedom and the happiness we all long for. Aristotle said, there is nothing more admirable than when one has achieved self-conquest. Immanuel Kant claimed there is no more noble person than someone who is inwardly free, and Hannah Arendt, the well-known twentieth-century philosopher, stated that only when we give ourselves to our principles are we free. Pericles, of course, reminds us that attaining freedom takes a brave heart.

## Understanding Freedom

Freedom is most often understood as freedom from oppression, injustice and so on; that is, our freedom is dependent on things external to us. Rarely do we dwell on the notion of inner freedom, that is, freedom from our conditioning, our reactivity and our mechanical ego defenses.

In truth, we don't really think much about what it means to be free, not only free from whom or what, but free for what purpose? What is it that we want to do with our freedom once we have it, once the fight is over? Once we have demolished all our external enemies and given up on our attachments, desires, expectations and need to be in control? Once we realize there is no one to fight or to blame and that the buck truly does stop right here at our very own door?

We know what it means to live enslaved, but do we know or truly want to be free? Can we live in total freedom?

The reality is that nobody can make us unfree. We can only do it to ourselves. Finding the courage to free ourselves from our inner chains takes work and is the self-conquest the old warrior was talking about, and self-conquest lies at the root of the age-old saying of "know yourself."

## External Freedom

Freedom is commonly understood as being free to do as one pleases. This means being free from oppression, having the right to experience civic liberty, entitlement to freedom of speech and religious practice, and the right to determine our future free from other influences. Freedom thus implies free choice as to how we live our lives. External freedom removes all exterior handcuffs.[1]

In general, we understand that some constraints are necessary so that we do not exercise our freedom at the expense of others. That is why we have governments, laws and the police to keep us in check.

Often, however, we confuse freedom with independence. Freedom does not mean being able to do just as one please. Young children wanting to grow up quickly make this mistake, people who long to be independently wealthy make this mistake, and once again politicians perpetuate this confusion. Freedom does not mean independence. We will never be totally independent. As human beings we thrive on relationships, and relationships require inter-dependence. We are also part of interdependent systems; independence does not exist. Even our so-called independently wealthy businessman or woman is dependent on the financial system, the financial advisor, the stock market or whatever to ensure his or her wealth remains intact.

There is also no nation state, country, province, community or group that can ever claim independence as they will never have all the resources they need to survive and flourish. Healthy interdependence contributes to happiness. Independence at the external level does not exist, and even if it did, it would not provide freedom but isolation and eventual death.

What about freedom from authority? Theoretically if we were to be totally free to make any choices or to take any actions we desired, we would not want any forms of authority in our lives. However, as we live with others in society, we need certain norms and rules to maintain order. Some would argue that we also need "authorities" who ensure that we make certain decisions deemed in our best interest, for example, that we wear a seat belt or that we are deterred from taking drugs. Others argue that authorities interfering in our lives curb our freedom and our liberties. So, we do not all agree on what external freedom means.

Freedom also surfaces several contradictions, a major one being that while we want the freedom to choose, we also want to be able to relinquish that freedom in favor of being told what to do. Frequently, we do not want responsibility for our actions that come with having freedom. It is useful to have others to blame.

Now to the real stumbling block – internal freedom.

## Internal Freedom – Combatting the Enemy Within

As in this chapter's opening story, most of us know, whether we admit it or not, that our greatest enemy lies within. This is the enemy we must conquer before we try to conquer anything without. Our lifelong challenge lies in facing this inner enemy which has many faces and many weapons of personal destruction. This inner enemy shows up in the form of envy, guilt, shame and anger, emotions we thought we had stuffed into a dark room with the door firmly shut and locked. Unfortunately, this wily enemy has a way of slipping through the keyhole and showing up at the most inopportune times.

This enemy within consists of all our undealt-with emotions regarding our fears: our fear regarding safety and security; our fear of uncertainty and impermanence; our fear that we won't be liked; our fear that we are not worthwhile, our fear that we will fail to achieve our ambitions and be seen as failures; our fear of change and transition and whether we will be able to keep up; the fear that we cannot handle what life might bring us; our fear of living and our fear of dying. Deep inside we have one huge, cavernous room full of fears!

The enemy called "fear" that is jammed into the dark room inside readily sabotages our creative spirits by beating us up about our mistakes, our bad decisions, our incompetency, our failures and worst of all our fears. It tells us how inept we are for having lost our jobs, how no-one will hire us again, and how we will never be able to stand a chance against the young-something or others who know more than we do and are cheaper to hire.

The enemy within blames us for our bad marriage, for the excessive mortgage and the diminished savings. The enemy within encourages us to cry victim, and to feel sad and sorry for ourselves and the troubles we are experiencing. The enemy within encourages us to be angry and fearful and to find someone to blame for our troubles. The enemy within does not encourage us to celebrate how courageous and brave we can be. It prefers to keep us in fear, and it works hard to inhibit our freedom.

The inner enemy, by definition, is not our friend, yet paradoxically it holds the key to our inner freedom, and it can be one of our greatest teachers.

Buddhists claim that desire and freedom are incompatible. Once we have desires, we become attached to the results, and attachment is the greatest inhibitor to freedom of both the mind and the heart. The moment we want to be something, avoid something, grab hold of something or achieve a particular outcome, we are no longer free. As long as we are dependent on others for safety, esteem, affirmation, appreciation, comfort or happiness we have given our freedom away. Any desire whatsoever inhibits our freedom, as our eyes are focused on getting the result we want. Consequently, our perceived options become increasingly limited, and our decision-making becomes increasingly narrow too.

Let us now unpack some of these attachments one by one and see how they inhibit our inner freedom. As we will notice, these attachments are not mutually exclusive in that they are inter-related and reinforce one another.

## *Facing Our Fears*

The big one that underpins them all is – FEAR. We all have fears. No one is without fear. Those who claim they are, as Aristotle would say, are inhumane and dangerous people, or simply liars. Fear is an existential condition. It comes with our humanity. It is not a bad thing. It is essential for life.

Now it takes great courage to look at what lies behind our fears and to understand what causes them. And it is by facing both the fear itself and what creates that fear that we learn whether it is an appropriate fear or something that in truth does not deserve to be feared. (Remember Socrates and Aristotle and the wisdom of knowing the appropriateness of what we fear.) It is only by facing our fear head on, something that is often painful, that people are motivated to act courageously and be brave, because the fear has become a known. What is known is far less frightening than the unknown.

Courage involves "pushing" through to understanding our fear, and bravery is acting in the face of that fear. Courage means actively working with one's fear; not denying it, avoiding it or suppressing it, but by facing it head on.

Fear is our emotional response to our vulnerability as human beings. We are vulnerable to an infinite number of things – many of which are manufactured by our ego minds.

As human beings we are all physically vulnerable – a reality we cannot escape or avoid. We will all die. We all get sick. We all make mistakes; no one is perfect. We hurt one another, undermine one another, steal from one another, lie to one another and the list goes on.

Ira Progoff wrote a wonderful book titled *The Dynamics of Hope: Perspectives of Process in Anxiety and Creativity, Imagery and Dreams* (1985). According to Progoff, anxiety is an existential condition. It comes with being human and mortal. Because anxiety is something free-floating, it is always there without anything to define it, so we create fear projects that give us something to cling to, to fight, to conquer and to blame in our effort to manage this existential anxiety. We use fear projects to manage our anxiety, and it is these fear projects that inhibit our freedom.

Most of us are embarrassed and even ashamed of the long list of fear projects we have accumulated over the years. We do our best to conceal these from ourselves and of course from others. We are frequently unaware of how obvious our fears are to an observant person and how much better off we might be if we owned rather than disowned them. Disowning our fears makes it difficult for us to be authentic, and the more authentic we can be the greater the freedom we experience.

By facing our fears head on and naming them we claim them. They no longer claim us. We expose them to the light. This does not mean we immediately resolve them or that they will miraculously go away. But facing them gives us power over them; they no longer have power over us. They cannot sabotage our actions unsuspectingly and we can make decisions by working with them and through them, rather than ignoring them or denying their existence. One of the hallmarks of courage is knowing our fears and acting despite their existence.

## Safety and Security

We all have a huge desire for safety and security – remember Maslow – it is a basic need. Alas, as long as we have the compulsion to seek safety and security, we will not be free. Freedom lies in accepting what is and what will be. There is no guarantee of safety and security ever! When we cling to the notion that safety and security is a permanent possibility, freedom of self-determination is immediately compromised. We will forever chase this elusive goal exhausting ourselves in the process.

Recognizing there is no guaranteed safety or security does not mean being negligent, ignorant or foolish. It does not mean avoiding appropriate precautions and weighing up circumstances and options. Once the desire for assured safety and security is the main driver in a decision, however, the quality of the decision will be adversely affected as its source is no longer that of acceptance of reality which is the source of inner freedom.

## Certainty and Permanence

Linked to our desire for safety and security is our desire for certainty and permanence. We desperately desire to secure a good thing forever. We want to know where we stand and that we can control anything that comes up. We don't want unpleasant surprises. We want certainty, and we want permanence. Once we have taken an action we want to depend on its lasting effect – be it love, marriage, a job, investment in a new house or the stock market. If only things could be certain and permanent. After all, we believe we did our part, why can't the universe – or whatever – do its part? Why can't we have lasting health, happiness, gratification, security and certainty?

Certainty and permanence do not exist. That is reality. Everything is in continuous motion, and change. Nothing is certain, nothing lasts forever. Everything is possible and many things are highly probable. That is the best hand we are dealt with – all of us! No one has an inside track. Some people appear to have more good fortune than others, and there is no real explanation for that. Luck invariably plays some part. Our task is to find equanimity in going with the flow as best we can. Life is in continuous transition. There is nothing we can do but accept this truth. Our acceptance needs to be as agents riding the waves of possibility rather than as lamenting victims who bury their heads in the sand. Once we try to base our decisions on securing certainty and permanence, we are not only in a fantasy land, but we are forgoing our inner freedom. We are trapped in a cage of our own making.

## Courage to Face the Truth

As I discussed in both the Introduction and Chapter 1, one of our biggest challenges is to face unpalatable realities. We fight or flee from truths that place us in situations of perceived danger, discomfort or uncertainty. We tend to defer, deny, defend, distract or obfuscate rather than face these truths and we make whatever physical or mental accommodations are required to deal with our discomfort.

The ancient adage "the truth is what sets us free" refers to this ability to face and integrate the truth. If we fail to face the truth, whatever it may be, we are not free. We live in a world of self-deception and illusion. And because the truth, which is always the unvarnished reality, will always persist, our illusions will inevitably be torn to shreds. It is just a matter of time.

The first truth we all must face is that we are vulnerable. We can be harmed, destroyed and killed, physically, emotionally, psychologically or spiritually. As human beings, vulnerability is part of the package. We can protect ourselves up to a point, but we will never be totally invulnerable. That is for the movies. We can make ourselves unnecessarily vulnerable by making poor decisions or taking imprudent actions, but invincibility is an impossibility. That is the truth, and facing it takes great courage and is part of what Tillich names as our self-affirmation. The more we can make facing the truth our life's practice, the greater our inner freedom.

## *I Had No Choice*

There is no such a thing as "I had no choice." We always have a choice! Whether we can live with the consequences of a difficult choice is another matter. The worst place for our ego or self-esteem to be is in the place of the victim. This puts us in a position of being powerless, and that is really frightening! Being a victim, we lose any sense of significance we might have.

Saying "I had no choice," is the coward's way out. Now let's be clear; sometimes we are caught in a difficult situation where our freedom (and happiness) is at stake. We make what we consider to be the best choice at the time. Maybe this is an instance where the best we can do is to muddle through. Even so, we must be aware of the decisions we make, the fears that influence them and the resulting impact on our freedom. We must own them. And every moment, every day, every week or every month, we must strive consciously to make a few more decisions from a place of inner freedom. Finding this courage is a journey, a quest. It is not a one-off. It is about setting a new intention, a new mindfulness and a new agenda for making our life's choices.

## *Self-Worth and Being Liked*

Another shackle that inhibits our inner freedom is our need for self-assurance that we are worthwhile. We all want to be appreciated and seen as worthy. Our ego and self-esteem have been trained since we were young to focus on being someone – someone special, someone respected. Many of our decisions are influenced by how we believe others will perceive us: whether our decisions will reinforce our good name, whether they will enhance others' respect for us and so on. Making decisions that are dependent on others' responses radically inhibits our inner freedom.

Why do we care so much about what others think? One big reason is because we are afraid of isolation or of standing alone. Another is that we have been programmed to believe that our self-worth is dependent on what others think of us. This is all at a great cost to our freedom to be.

## *Loneliness*

Loneliness. Who is not afraid of loneliness? It is one thing to be alone, and another to be lonely: deeply, personally, lonely. The great psychologist of the twentieth century, Carl Rogers, claimed that in his consulting experience one of the existential fears that appeared to plague modern people was the feeling of deep loneliness and their fear of how to overcome it.

Along with the other inhibitors to our freedom of choices, the fear of loneliness is a big one for many. When it comes to close relationships, we can fall into the trap of "hanging in there" for fear of the alternative of being alone. We can hold onto ailing friendships because we are afraid of not having friends. But this fear of loneliness can never be removed by having other people in our lives or engaging in distracting activities.

Many people depend on others for affirmation of their existence and their self-definition. Being alone they are not sure of who they are and whether they can stand alone. Being highly identified with one's social roles is an indicator of this lack of a sense of self. It is this inner lack of a "Who am I without my family or friends?" that feeds an inner loneliness.

Being lonely is something we must tackle with our inner selves – no one else will do. If we avoid this work, we may be inclined to make choices that once again inhibit our inner freedom.

In his sobering book *Together: The Healing Power of Human Connection in a Sometimes Lonely World* (2023), Vivek H. Murthy, MD, the nineteenth surgeon general of the US, claims there is a new epidemic, namely loneliness. What can we gain by sailing to the moon if we are not able to cross the abyss that separates us from ourselves? he asks.

Loneliness is best treated by getting to know oneself, and that requires spending time alone. We need to gain insight and acceptance of who we are, and we must find a balance between time with others and time alone. Only by spending time with ourselves can we come to terms with our loneliness.

From a leadership perspective, we discussed the need to be able to stand alone, and to experience being abandoned by others who disagree with us or who do not like the new realities we are holding up. Leadership is inherently a lonely business, and if we do not have the mettle to be isolated and alone – and as Friedman says, to even welcome it – then we will likely be ineffective leaders (more on this in Chapter 9).

## Desire to Please

The desire to please is one huge shackle that weighs many of us down. How often don't we suppress our own needs so as to please someone else? – or so we think or tell ourselves. Too many of us live our lives ostensibly pleasing others – husbands, wives, children, parents and bosses. We tell ourselves it is our duty; it is no big deal; we would feel guilty if we did not. And so, we don the mantle of martyrdom! Soon it becomes we "had" to do it; there was no choice. Now we have assumed the cloaks of both martyr and victim. Freedom is gone and so is happiness. All we are left with is our infantile fear of not being liked. Fear! (This fear, American psychologists claim, is a significant one that plagues American society. See Chapter 7, Why Can't We Be Courageous?)

## Ambition

For many, ambition is the greatest inhibitor to personal freedom. When we are ambitious, we make our decisions based on our need to be "someone." We strive for titles, position and knowledge so that we can climb the corporate or some other ladder. Our decisions are no longer made from inner freedom but based on a drive to get ahead. We compromise or reprioritize our values simply to attain the next goal. We are no longer free but shackled. If we fail, we feel like failures. We flagellate ourselves and we challenge our self-esteem. Often, we tell ourselves we did the wrong things, or we did not do enough. So, we strive and strain some more. Both freedom and happiness disappear as we reassure ourselves that we are doing what we really want to do. By this stage we know no other way. More chains. Fear strikes again!

## The Courage to Stay True

> This above all: to thine own self be true,
> And it must follow, as the night the day,
> Thou canst not then be false to any man.
>
> *Shakespeare – Hamlet Act 1 sc.3.*

Sometimes our fear prevents us from being true to our authentic selves. We say "yes" when we mean "no." We agree with others when our hearts disagree. We acquiesce to doing things we do not believe in or find unethical. We silence ourselves so that we do not stand apart from the crowd. We feign ignorance or claim "that is none of my business" when we know the system of which we are a part is corrupt or deceptive. At times we even co-operate and participate in unethical behavior telling ourselves everyone else is doing it. We pander to our boss, feigning respect, or admiration, while talking disparagingly about him or her out of earshot. We smile and lie, and inside our stomach churns.

Often, we get caught up in these inauthentic behaviors because we fear doing otherwise. We fear losing our jobs, our raises, our friends (if you can call them that) or our popularity. We fear not being part of the in group and we fear being isolated.

Now, there is nothing that hurts us more than when someone betrays us. We despise betrayers. Betrayal cuts deep, destroying close friendships and severing what might have been strong bonds of trust. It is very difficult to repair an act of betrayal and the scars we carry hurt us to our very core. Despite this knowledge, why do we so readily betray ourselves?

Every act of self-betrayal is an act of disempowerment. The more lies we live; the more frequently we dissemble and avoid the truth; the more often we create another Faustian bargain to get through today or to solve our short-term economic or emotional challenges; the more deeply we erode the authentic self, with its infinite potential for creativity, vitality and energy, the greater the cost to our true selves. And that cost is huge as it dims the force field of light that is the real us, the you and me whose very existence is the courage to be.

### *Our Habits*

And now a final shackle – our habits. These are our habitual programmed choices and actions that limit our freedom.

Every moment of every day presents us with new opportunities. By repeatedly responding in the same way to life's invitations with the same thoughts and the same actions, we are not open to and often not even aware of the other possibilities available to us. Habits shut down options. Habits make our decisions rote. Habits dull our self-awareness. Habits curb inner freedom. We hold onto our habits because they give us a pseudo sense of the safety and security we crave. Giving them up can be scary.

The problem with habits is that they are like silent thieves. Without us realizing it, habits steal from our freedom to see and explore other possibilities. The more ingrained our habits become, the more myopic we become, and the more our range of vision gets narrower and narrower. Eventually we have no peripheral vision left and the world becomes a very small place indeed. We cling to our habits largely because of fear of change. Here we have it again – fear!

## The Courage to Resist Temptation

There is a well-known prayer that goes like this: "Lord please do not lead me into temptation, I can easily find it for myself."

As we know, temptation lurks at every corner. There are overt, direct temptations such as joining others in acts of deception, malfeasance, theft or other types of corruption, and covert, indirect ones, where we turn a blind eye to unethical behavior.

Succumbing to temptation sometimes begins with small things like altering records, backdating or predating invoices, adjusting inventory amounts or claiming expenses that did not exist. We tell ourselves this is special, a one-off; the Boss told me to, if I don't, I will probably lose my job.

And sometimes the temptation is big. The reward is lucrative. The likelihood of getting caught is small. One would be a fool not to do it. If one is caught, one is in good company. And we tell ourselves: I am doing it for the kids' schooling, for my family, to pay the medical bills, to help us get out of debt. We find all the rationalizations we can muster to help us avoid our inner critic that is calling out "no!" And the more we succumb, the easier it becomes and soon cheating, and corruption become a way of life.

Then there are the more passive and indirect temptations such as turning a blind eye to wrongdoing or feigning one does not know. A favorite argument is "It is not my business," or "I don't want to get involved, it is not really my problem."

You may recall our discussion on willful blindness in Chapter 1, and the heinous acts that are perpetrated under the cloak of "I did not realize," or "if that is what the leaders want, then so be it." None of this excuses us. And much as we may protest outwardly, in the deep recesses of our minds and hearts we know we are enabling evil.

When we reflect on why we submit to temptation, we soon recognize it is because of one or other of the inner shackles we discussed earlier. We fear losing our jobs. We fear standing out as being different or difficult. We want to please the higher-ups by being obedient. We do not want to create personal insecurity. We had no choice but to go along with what everyone else is doing. The rewards we gain from cheating, for example, more money, will enhance our sense of self-worth, and so on.

This is where we need courage.

## The Challenge of Courage and Inner Freedom

It is not easy to live in a world of uncertainty and clashing opinions. It is not easy to stand up and stand out for our principles. It is not easy to refuse the attraction of dogmatism and the call to take sides, and instead to hold steady and expose our ideas to challenges and critique. It is not easy not to concern ourselves with public disfavor and to maintain our principles in a world where nothing but the opinion *de jour* matters. It is not easy to stand apart, alone, not trying to please others, not looking for affirmation, not letting our ambition erode our principles and not succumbing to the temptation to "go along."

Finding our inner freedom requires courage, great courage. At times, this entails not only speaking up and taking risks but being willing to die. Yes die! That's how we might experience it – emotional or psychological death. What that really translates to is a defeat of our ego – the structures of our minds which determine our sense of identity.

The challenge here is that courage and freedom are intertwined. We need inner freedom to exercise our courage and it is courage that gives us the inner freedom to do so. Yet, despite how challenging this can be, we can do it. Often, sometimes unexpectedly, we rise to it; our courage comes up from our deepest existence. While we may not manage to live from this place all the time, we long to do so; we just need to make this an intentional quest in our lives.

Courage gives us an inner serenity. Despite heart-pounding fear we know that above all else our actions will advance goodness, wholesomeness and life. And every courageous act, no matter how small, advances our own wholeness which adds immensely to the well-being of the world. Courageous acts give life, whereas cowardly acts, like the story of Jack and Piggy in Chapter 1, kill life.

Each one of us by virtue of our very existence has the inherent power to give life – it is one of our greatest gifts. When we do stand up for ourselves, and when we act from our best principles, that is when we experience deep happiness. The more often we do it, the more we become that happiness.

## Courage for Organizational Leaders

Organizational leaders' challenges are magnified. They need courage to be truly effective. They need the courage to face unpalatable new realities and to wrestle with them and not defer or deny them. They need courage to take risks, to take the high road in the face of opposition, to stand apart from the group and break the pact of collusion, and to create new precedents, new norms and new conventions. They need courage to hold their own ground and they need to be able to take on a group and challenge its behavior, its ethics, and individuals' complicity in corrupt behaviors.

Leaders need courage to have difficult conversations around ethical and moral matters. They need courage to face organizational troubles and to make thoughtful, nonreactive decisions during troubled times. And they need huge courage to face failure and to say "I got it wrong; I need help."

Leaders especially need to make decisions from a place of inner freedom. Some might claim that is not possible and there are too many countervailing issues. There is always a reason not to try, not to work at it, not to make it a principle one strives for, but it IS possible.

In our hearts, and in our souls, inner freedom is what all of us want. We know it is the source of wisdom, peace and abiding happiness, the fountainhead of life. The choice is ours.

## Your Turn

- To what extent do you live a life of inner freedom?
- Which major decisions in your life have been influenced by the challenges to your inner freedom – positively or negatively?
- Which of the various shackles mentioned earlier is most relevant to you?
- Which attachment is your greatest inhibitor?
- What are you afraid of losing when you act with courage?

## Note

1 Liberty means freedom from arbitrary and unreasonable restraint upon an individual. Freedom from restraint refers to more than just physical restraint, but also the freedom to act according to one's own will.

## References

Murphy, Vivek H. 2023. *Together: The Healing Power of Human Connection in a Sometimes Lonely World.* New York: Harper Paperbacks.

Ouspemsky, P.D. 2001. *In Search of the Miraculous*. New York: Harper Paperbacks.
Progoff, Ira. 1985. *The Dynamics of Hope: Perspectives of Process in Anxiety and Creativity, Imagery and Dreams*. New York: Dialogue House Library.

## Recommended Reading

May, Rollo. 2009. *Man's Search for Himself*. New York: W.W. Norton & Company.

# Chapter 7

# Why Can't We Be Courageous?

## The Allegory of the Cave

Let us imagine human beings in a cave where they have been since childhood, bound in such a way that they can only look in front of themselves. Behind them burns a fire, and between them and the fire is a raised parapet, like that used in a puppet show. Behind the parapet people are carrying various artificial objects such as figures of men and animals made of wood and stone.

The human beings who have been bound since birth are positioned such that they can see only the shadows cast by the fire of the objects parading on the parapet on the wall of the cave in front of them. They also hear sounds which they assume are made by these shadow objects. The shadows constitute their entire reality.

The bound-up people converse among one another about these shadows. Some of them become quite adept at distinguishing among the various shapes and noises, and honors, praises, and prizes are awarded to those who are the sharpest at making out the things that go by.

Consider what would happen if a person were to be released, and suddenly compelled to stand up, turn his neck around, and to walk looking towards the light emanating from the front of the cave. The turning would be painful as it is a turning away from the familiar world. Initially the light would be blinding and would hurt the person's eyes. Gradually he would see what he perceived as shadows before as he looked towards the light. He will struggle not to see the shadows as the truer reality

DOI: 10.4324/9781003459644-8

> while considering the real objects he now sees as mere illusions. As the light hurts his eyes, he will continue to try to turn back to take refuge with what he is accustomed to.
>
> Then let us suppose the person is forced to step outside of the cave along the rough steep path into the sunlight, and even then, it will take a long time before he can look directly into the sun. He will initially be pained and irritated and at first, as in the glare of the sunlight, he will not be able to see anything at all. Bit by bit he will be able to see people and objects for what they are. Eventually he will be able to see the sun and to contemplate its nature. In time, he will conclude that the sun produces the seasons and directs the course of the year and that it controls everything in the visible world.
>
> The full light represents the truth, and this only comes with the turning towards the light. (Turning being the Greek word metanoia.) Now if the man went back into the cave to tell his fellow prisoners of his new understanding he would struggle with the lack of light and the darkness. They would laugh at him and say he had gone up only to come back with his sight ruined. And if he tried to set them free and lead them to the light, they would kill him. Yes, they would.
>
> And so, I, Plato, have come to the realization that the last thing that is to be seen (apprehended) is the good (i.e. the light). For once it is seen it points us to the conclusion that it is the cause of all things that are right and beautiful, and that it provides the root cause of all wise action. But seeing the good takes a great deal of effort and requires firstly new eyes that then must stimulate a new mindset.
>
> (Hamilton, Plato, *Republic*)

This allegory (previously referred to in Chapter 5) is perhaps Plato's best-known story. It is included in his great book *Republic* which is filled with poignant dialogues on how to create the ideal state. Its prime message is how conditioned we are to live with our illusions and to consider them reality. Even when we have an opportunity to step out of our bondage and claim our freedom, often we elect to remain in our shadow world. The world dominated by the inner enemy that keeps us hooked to our fears and that generates justifications for side-stepping the courage which is calling us. We denounce those Cassandras who try to dispel our illusions, and we find an external enemy to fight as the foil for the inner one.

As we know, "looking into the light" is blinding, just as it feels blinding to look directly at the naked, frank, undiluted truth. The truth that shows us how to untie our shackles and set us free. The truth that we can indeed be free if we choose to make the effort.

In Chapter 5 we explored the roots of courage and how it is a fundamental character trait. We saw that courage is no simple matter. It calls on all of us. It challenges us right to the very essence of who we are. And we were reminded that when we act courageously, we feel good about ourselves. We experience a deep sense of worthiness, that self-affirmation Paul Tillich wrote about.

Alas, often we do not act courageously. We shut ourselves down. We cling to our shackles, we cry victim, we say we had no choice, we blame, we deny and we succumb to temptation. Frequently, we hide behind order and authority, or we are simply thoughtless, distracted, caught up with ourselves and don't even register what we are really doing.

Why are we so afraid to be free, free to choose who we wish to be?

## Thoughtlessness and the Loss of Moral Imagination

In 1961, The New Yorker commissioned the German Jewish historian and philosopher, Hannah Arendt (1906–1975), to cover the trial of Adolf Eichmann, a key figure in organizing the transportation of millions of Jews across Europe to the Nazi concentration camps in compliance with Adolf Hitler's Final Solution.

Two years later, Arendt published her book *Eichmann in Jerusalem: A Report on the Banality of Evil*, wherein she covers Eichmann's trial and tackles many questions. One is how one explains that ordinary folk can become unrestrained criminals, and more centrally, can commit evil deeds without being innately evil.

Arendt used the phrase "banality of evil" to describe the evil that results when people stop thinking, and when thoughtlessness is fostered by everyone else complying unquestioningly. It is a thoughtlessness that arises when the truth becomes empty and trivialized (Young-Bruehl 2006).

According to Arendt, one of the biggest inhibitors of ethical behavior is an inability to think critically or to take the standpoint of someone else, that is, to practice empathy. She saw in Eichmann particularly, a shallowness and this "thoughtlessness." He had an intense desire to please his superiors and to cooperate. He claimed to be proud that he had done his duty and obeyed orders, saying he would have felt guilty if he had not done so. He was impressed with Hitler and saw that so were others proving to him that he should subordinate himself to the man (Arendt 2006, 126). One must wonder whether this is how people felt about Charles Keating of the Savings & Loan crisis, or Kenneth Lay and Jeffrey Skilling of Enron or Richard Scrushy of HealthSouth or Lloyd Blankfein of Goldman Sachs.

According to Arendt, Eichmann and similarly afflicted people lack any moral imagination as to the consequences of their actions. Eichmann claimed he did not feel guilty because he was not personally killing any Jews even though he was directly responsible for the transport of between 6,000 and 12,000 people to the gas chambers each day. Similarly, how many bankers do not feel guilty selling toxic assets to innocent customers? The fact that this might impact their livelihood is of no interest to them whatsoever.

Arendt stressed how authority, routinization and dehumanization, a feature of bureaucrats, can destroy a whole people, while they are sitting at their desks. The bureaucratic, industrialized cultures supply lack of personal accountability where people can comfortably either be ignorant or feign ignorance. Bureaucracy destroys the thinking process of its subjects transforming human beings into automatic and banal receivers of orders. The new criminal, she argued, is the ordinary, so-called law-abiding citizen who is emotionally disengaged and acts out of blind obedience to superiors (see Bandura 2016, 9; Milgram 2009, 15).

What stands out in the Eichmann trial and is a feature of almost all white-collar criminals is their lack of personal accountability or recognition that they have done an evil deed. They refute any wrong-doing and are unrepentant criminals.

Arendt believed that every human has the potential to eradicate evil and has the moral responsibility to do so. The essential moral question, she claimed, is: Could I live with myself if I did this deed? But without moral imagination, there is no reflection and no personal questioning. How long, she wondered, and what does it take for the average person to overcome his innate repugnance toward crime? And what happens to the person then?

Arendt held that a new type of criminal came into the world in the mid-twentieth century, this being the blind bureaucrat, unconcerned about the world or alienated from it. Rare courage is needed to resist being caught up in the spread of such banal people and their thoughtless evil deeds.

This motif of terribly normal people who are either perpetrators or bystanders observing dreadfully inhumane and evil deeds repeats itself endlessly throughout history, no less so in our so-called liberal progressive world. The bankers and their contempt for others as they knowingly destroyed their wealth to serve their own interests are no better than the train attendants who drove the Jews to Auschwitz and who scrawled "perishable goods" on the side of the carriages.

The famous Italian poet Dante (1265–1321) is known to have said, "The hottest places in Hell are reserved for those who in times of great moral crisis, maintain their neutrality." Alas, terribly normal people exist everywhere feigning either ignorance or impotence as helpless bystanders.

In his powerful book *Humanity: A Moral History of the Twentieth Century* (2012), Jonathan Glover mentions, among others, Joseph Stalin and how he ordered the deaths of millions in the gulags. He describes some of the horrific torture carried out by ordinary people. How does one explain this? he asks. What can we make of our brutality, cruelty and dismissal of other human beings? Will we do anything at all to ensure our own survival? This was so contrary to Pericles's idea that there is nothing more noble than to die a courageous life fighting for our freedom. But we cannot even do that for our external freedom, no less for our inner one.

Glover provides some reasons for our erosion of moral identity. He claims that where there is division of labor, such as in the military or bureaucracies, this makes the evasion of personal responsibility easier. He also claims that psychological denial of what is really going on – something we discuss more of later – provides a defense and obscures the horror of our brutality and cruelty. Because everyone is complicit there is a lack of a climate of criticism and all fear of embarrassment can be concealed.

In this environment people create a new identity and try to mentally shut out the old (Glover 2012).

If we consider the engineers that allow toxic waste sites to kill hundreds of people, bankers who speculate with peoples' lifesavings, executives in the pharmaceutical companies that forge or misrepresent the effects of their drugs, account officials at Wells Fargo who participated in faking accounts to save their jobs and their bonuses, and the Boeing engineers who allow faulty planes to fly, are they any the less evil, less cowardly? Are some of them "terribly normal people?"

**The Madness of Groups**

> Every man is, in a certain sense, unconsciously a worse man when he is in society than when acting alone. . . . Any large company of wholly admirable persons has the morality and intelligence of an unwieldy, stupid, and violent animal. The bigger the organization, the more unavoidable is its immorality and blind stupidity. . . . Society, by automatically stressing all the collective qualities in its individual representatives, puts a premium on mediocrity, on everything that settles down to vegetate in an easy, irresponsible way. Individuality will inevitably be driven to the wall.
>
> C. G. Jung, *The Archetypes and the Collective Unconscious* (New York: Princeton University Press, 1959, 240).

## Stage 3 Thinking

The Harvard psychologist Robert Kegan in his signature book, *The Evolving Self* (1982), reinforced several significant findings of Lawrence Kohlberg's research into people's moral development. Both Kegan and Kohlberg found that a high percentage (greater than 80%) of adults remain stuck in "Stage 3" thinking; that is, they are fixated on fusing with others or into the crowd.[1]

Robert Kegan' s psychological development model has six stages that plot an individual's growth in maturity, reflection and meaning-making. His Stage 3, titled the interpersonal stage, describes the stage where people do not have an independent self; their reality is wholly dependent on other people's existence and approval. Other people bring them into being (recall our loneliness discussion in the previous chapter).

According to Kegan, individuals in Stage 3 cannot reflect on emotions, feelings and situations. Everything experienced is part of a reality that is embedded in their relationship with others (Kegan 1982).

People in Stage 3 are unable to express genuine anger as that might risk interpersonal relations and would amount to a declaration that the person is a self apart from the relationship. With Stage 3 the person is always attentive to the external world, where there is no possibility of critical reflection on personal obligation, satisfactions or purposes in life. Individual choice or moral conscience are totally repressed or denied in the service of the collective. Stage 3 people have no moral values apart from those of the group. Conforming, belonging and affiliating with the group are their only reality. All cognitive or emotional conflict is totally intolerable. Fear of loss of belonging is the main motivator or drive. Moral courage is not possible at this stage.

Lawrence Kohlberg's "stages of moral development" outlines six stages that define increasing levels of maturity and complexity in moral reasoning.[2]

Of the six stages, Stage 3 refers to the huge transition of a person from being a child into his or her teenage years where fitting in and belonging to the group become paramount factors that influence all moral decision-making. Stage 3 thinking is where the individual is preoccupied with being loyal to the group, conforming to their norms and being accepted by others. At this time, the person has a limited appreciation of situations as viewed by others and assumes that everyone has a similar outlook. Approval by the group is essential regardless of the consequences. The individual readily subordinates his or her own needs to those of the group (Kohlberg 1981).

Clearly both Kegan and Kolberg arrive at the same point – one through a psychological lens and the other through an ethical one. Kegan argues that the situation has become exacerbated by the intensity, greater complexity and freneticism of our lives. He explains that only a small percentage of the population can cope adequately in this new world and that we are "in over our heads" (Kegan 1982).

Does the fact that most of us are stuck in Stage 3 explain why we collude and comply with evil deeds? Is belonging to others more important to us than belonging to ourselves?

Let us consider some recent research.

## Collective Illusions

*Collective Illusions* is the name of educator and researcher Todd Rose's (2022) best-selling book that spells out in unnerving detail how mistaken our individual perceptions are, especially vis-à-vis the group. He defines collective illusions as social lies that occur in a situation where the majority of individuals in a group privately reject a particular opinion but go along with it because they incorrectly assume that most other people support it (Rose 2022, xv).

Rose names this tendency to conform to what we falsely believe others expect of us as Conformity Bias. His book is filled with real-life experiments that show how many of our actions are dependent on what others are doing or how we interpret or project their actions. We readily go along with the crowd, colluding and not realizing that everyone else is colluding too. In these challenging times, Rose states, there is enormous pressure to get along and to stay silent about our private beliefs. We think that since norms exist, and most people follow them, everyone agrees with them.

This can lead to an entire society participating in destructive behaviors that people do in fact not condone – but they have sold themselves out.

The Conformity Trap, as Rose names it, is reinforced by our lack of information, our fear of embarrassment, lack of confidence in our own beliefs and conviction that the crowd (the herd) cannot be wrong. We also defer to authority and prestige and to those who claim to have expertise without really checking out whether their credentials are valid.

Rose claims we look for affinity with others even when the basis for doing so is tenuous or trivial. Our personal identity is so intertwined with our social identity that we cannot tell them apart. We have an irresistible need to belong. The pain of any social rejection causes huge distress and even immeasurable despair. We would rather compromise our personal integrity for the sake of belonging. We will lie for our team, personally support things we don't like, and become complicit in harming others if we believe it will improve our social bonds. We tell ourselves that if this many people are doing it, it must be okay. We should play it safe and stick to the crowd.

Rose insists that we are biologically wired to be attached to the group and have a dreadful fear of social isolation. He refers to this as the Consensus Trap which is akin to the well-known bandwagon effect. When actions are either right or wrong, we want company. Over time we are not sure what our true personal beliefs are, and we come to believe our own lies.

Rose also discusses the bystander predicament, where we observe wrongdoing and fail to speak up or become involved. We hope someone else will do it.

In the corporate world, where the pressure to conform is great, silence is the norm. Peer pressure not to break ranks is high. Think of the Challenger disaster, Volkswagen *Dieselgate*, Wells Fargo and Theranos. As a result of a fear of disconnection or retaliation, people practice self-censorship. They forgo their self-esteem and self-worth to remain an insider and be part of the group. Social media magnifies this collusive behavior by amplifying the loudest and most extreme voices regardless of their credentials. This is part of the mess we are in.

While Todd Rose's research supports and expands on the findings by Kohlberg and Kegan, do these findings help us understand what happens to "terribly normal people?" Does it explain why millions of people go along with performing heinous deeds because they believe that most other people support it, that this behavior is the accepted norm? Does it explain the emotional and moral disengagement, the thoughtlessness and the loss of moral imagination exhibited by so many? Do they just shut down or shut out? Does it answer the question as to why people lack personal accountability, are not reflective and don't engage in self-questioning? Can we truly just put it down to our DNA?

How does that explain the many who do not conform, who challenge heinous norms, who stand up to corruption and evil? What about those that put their lives on the line – physically, economically, emotionally and psychologically – to save others or to combat unscrupulousness?

Kohlberg and Kegan indicate that greater than 80% of people are stuck in Stage 3, which allows for a possible 10%–15% not being trapped in that psychological and emotional state. Are we truly facing a reality that only one in ten or 15 of us are self-defining, self-determining and courageous enough to stand up for our principles? Surely, we can do better than that.

## Moral Disengagement

Psychologist Albert Bandura explains the mechanisms of moral disengagement in his book titled *Moral Disengagement: How People Do Harm and Live with Themselves* (2016).

Bandura states that in the development of the moral self, individuals adopt standards of right or wrong that serve as guides and deterrents for their conduct. In general, people tend to do things that give them a sense of moral worth and refrain from conduct that will result in self-condemnation. However, they often face pressures to engage in harmful activities that provide welcome benefits but that violate their moral standards. To engage in these activities and to live with themselves without self-condemnation they morally disengage. With moral disengagement people's self-sanctioning mechanisms fail, and people assign righteous ends to justify harmful means.

Bandura explains how people go to great lengths to achieve self-exoneration. He names eight psychosocial mechanisms by which people selectively disengage, and it is these selective strategies where their morality is suspended that allows them to retain their positive self-regard. The eight mechanisms are as follows:

1. Moral justification – Righteous ends are used to justify harmful means.
2. Palliative comparison – The argument is advanced that harmful actions will prevent more human suffering than they cause: the utilitarian argument.
3. Euphemistic labeling – Convoluted and innocuous language cloaks true behavior, such as in the phrase "collateral damage."
4. Displacing moral responsibility to others as in the boss told me to do it.
5. Dispersing responsibility so widely that no one is responsible – typical of bureaucracies.
6. Efforts are made to minimize, distort, deny and dispute injurious effects of immoral actions. Harmful effects are out of sight, out of mind – for example, cheating online banking customers.
7. Excluding people harmed from the category of humanity by divesting them of human qualities, dehumanizing them. Racism and antisemitism are examples.
8. Blaming the victim for bringing the maltreatment on themselves; that is, the perpetrator claims he or she had no choice but to do what they did.

Bandura explains using his Social Cognitive Agentic Theory that to be an agent (someone who takes an active role in something) is to exert intentional influence over one's actions. This means one must experience one's functioning as making a difference. The ability to achieve goals promotes purposeful and foresightful behavior. Unless people believe they can produce the desired effects by their actions, they have little incentive to persevere or to take a moral agentic interest. This explains both the lack of courage and the bystander effect, where people stand by and observe unethical behavior and do nothing citing that they don't have the power to do or to influence anything. Further, they fear retaliation by those engaged.

Bandura mentions three types of moral sanctions: legal, social and self-evaluative, of which self-evaluative sanctions are the most potent. It is not moral principles but investment in one's own self-regard that governs moral motivation and self-regulation. Meeting one's moral standards affirms one's positive self-regard, while violating them causes self-chastisement. Because individuals have to live with themselves, they strive to preserve the self-view that they are decent people. There is nothing more damaging than a person's self-loathing and people will do anything to avoid this state. They will engage in a variety of forms of self-deception where they are aware of the reality they are trying to deny. They often try to create a public appearance that they have naively misjudged the circumstances and make efforts to convince others that it was all a mistake. For example, during the 2008/2009 economic crisis, Jamie Dimon, head of J.P. Morgan Chase, claimed "So we made a stupid error. If an airplane crashes, should we stop flying all planes?" (Bandura 2016, 221). J.P. Morgan received $25 billion under the US government's Troubled Asset Relief Program (TARP).

When harmful means are sanctified as "worthy purposes," wrongdoers take pride in doing harm well and when harm is ignored there is no need for moral self-sanctions or recrimination (note the bankers in Chapter 3).

Bandura also delves into moral disengagement in the corporate world. He emphasizes that people are swayed by the high payoffs that result from the crimes they commit and the ineffective legal system where the chances of being caught and prosecuted are minimal. The higher ups in firms often feign ignorance as to what their peons are up to and the distancing of responsibility results in zero personal accountability.

A further incentive for moral disengagement is that not only is the whole culture embroiled in unethical behavior, but the company ends up paying the fine, that is, the shareholders, while the perpetrators walk away scot-free with the gains. Legislative reforms are unable to keep up with the creativity of the ambitious who are eager to make their fortunes at any cost.

The lure of the finance and technology industries is wealth and status and by now, after the multitude of scandals that were never prosecuted, any social sanctions and stigma associated with transgressive behavior have evaporated. People believe they can outsmart the system – and do. Regrettably, the public condones it.

## The Criminal Mind

Stanton E. Samenow (1941–2023), the well-known American psychologist, who spent over 40 years researching criminal behavior and interviewing criminals of all stripes, claimed that he never met a single felon who would admit they were wrong. They all practice self-deception.

In his book *The Criminal Mind* (2014), he claims that it is a fascinating fact that white-collar criminals refuse to see themselves as criminals. They have every excuse on the planet for their behaviors and most often claim to be a victim of forces over which they have no control.

Samenow insists that the many excuses we make for people's delinquent or criminal behavior do not hold. Their behavior is by and large not the result of a bad environment, poverty, bad parenting or peer pressure. Criminal personalities exist. Parents don't turn children into criminals, he insists, and they are often the victims and the children the victimizers. The person might say they fell into the wrong crowd, or they were bullied into doing wrong. Samenow says, these people are drawn like a magnet to others with criminal intent.

Those with criminal minds typically view honest work as something for slaves and suckers. The people who they can manipulate, cheat or steal from deserve it because they are the fools and the suckers. This confirms the contempt that was rife in the Financial Services Sector in the 1980s and persists to this day.

Samenow claims that the criminally minded feel as if they never have enough power, control and excitement. They are continuously looking for opportunities at almost any cost or any risk. They have no concept of obligation as obligation renders them powerless. They need to continuously feel success.

Having worked with dozens of criminals over his 40 years, Samenow claims that every offender regards themselves as a decent human being (recall Nick Leeson and Barings Bank in Chapter 3). The only wrongfulness or regret they recognize is being caught. They have gigantic egos, are masterful at deception and have no empathy. Many are narcissistic psychopaths.

One disturbing fact that Samenow presents us with is that there are way more criminally minded people than we realize, and many white-collar criminals fall under this banner. He insists that some people have a valence for criminal behavior and that it is their patterns of thought that lie at the root cause of their behavior. Changing these patterns of thought, he claims, is extremely difficult and is exacerbated as the criminal refuses to see himself as doing something wrong. Moral disengagement and self-deception reign supreme.

In the Preface, I described the Day of Reconnaissance and how often we would discover frauds due to this technique. At the time, I never ceased to be amazed how the friendly, smiling CEO, CFO or VP of Sales, with pictures of his happy family all over his desk, was actively siphoning off funds, and was invariably annoyed at having been caught. I never witnessed regret or even embarrassment for their unethical behavior. It is hard to believe that these supposedly normal people are "terribly normal people" or are narcissistic psychopaths. Alas, whatever statistics one turns to, it seems that approximately 10% of the population fall into this category.

## Self-Deception Revisited

In Chapter 1 we discussed self-deception and how we do not see what we do not want to see.

In *Vital Lies, Simple Truths*, psychologist Daniel Goleman of Emotional Intelligence renown describes the psychology of self-deception. He details how we use it to sink into obliviousness rather than face threatening facts and how we lack the courage to seek the truth by breaking through the narcotic of self-deception.

Goleman claims that self-deception operates at both the individual and the group level. Membership of the group is based on the tacit agreement not to notice one's own feelings of uneasiness and certainly not to question the group's way of doing things. The group dynamic squelches any courage to seek the truth. We trade off a distorted sense of awareness for a sense of security with the group, he claims. Our dimmed attention soothes the pain in the brain. Our anxiety interferes with our normal cognition, resulting in numbness, a flattened response, the dimming of attention, being in a daze, having constricted thought and fantasizing.

According to Goleman, to repress our feelings of shock or discomfort we engage in a variety of strategies. These include:

- Repression
- Denial
- Projection
- Rationalization
- Selective inattention
- Automatism where we don't notice what we do

In sum, according to Goleman, to avoid anxiety we close off crucial points of awareness creating blind spots.

### Fear, Self-Deception and Lethargy

#### *Co-worker Discussions*

I don't want to know!
You don't want to know what?
What is going on? Leave me out of it.
Why don't you want to know?
Because if there is anything fishy going on, the less I know the better.
So, you are afraid you suspect something?
I told you it is not my concern. I have lots of other things to worry about.
Do you think that suspecting something but not knowing for sure leaves you blameless?
Yes – I don't want to be involved. Leave me out of it!

Beerel, *Ethical Leadership and Global Capitalism*, 2021, 35.

Max Bazerman and Ann Tenbrunsel in their book *Blind Spots* (2011) focus on the theme of blind spots as providing reasons why "we fail to do what is right." They discuss the psychological ploy of bounded awareness where deliberately "we exclude important and relevant information from our decisions by placing arbitrary and dysfunctional bounds around the definition of a problem" (Bazerman and Tenbrunsel 2011, 7).

Bounded awareness is a feature of the term bounded ethicality where we engage in ethically questionable behavior that is contrary to our own personal ethics. These strategies place constraints on our morality that favor our own self-interest at the expense of others. The result is that we overlook the obvious and we become blind to factors we clearly should see.

Another factor Bazerman and Tenbrunsel raise is that businesspeople tend to turn everything into a business problem. If it pays to cheat, to break the law, to allow people to drive in faulty vehicles as the penalty and insurance for any accidents are calculated to be less than the cost of recalling the vehicles and fixing the problem, they will select the choice that is least costly or generates the highest return (recall the Ford Pinto scandal). In other words, they do not frame the problem as an ethical one but simply a business one.

The strategies of self-deception and creating blind spots are further explanations as to why we do not make the effort to be courageous and tackle our inner enemy.

Alas, there is more. Let us consider how we kowtow to authority.

## Fear of Authority

Early childhood lessons taught us to obey authority as those in authority are "right." The person in authority knows the "right" thing to do and the "right" thing for us to do is to obey. Those in power define reality. They make the rules! To obey equals moral rightness. Obedience to authority, the boss, the president or the Fuehrer is considered by many as doing one's moral duty. Authority also counts as rules or the law.

But do those in authority really know better than we do? Are their ideas and their principles superior to ours? Does their version of reality align with the truth? Are the rules and laws they advocate and support just? Do we submit to authority because we have tested these things out or because it is just easier? Do we prefer not to be accountable and to have someone else to blame?

Two famous experiments that have been written about and analyzed extensively are known as the Milgram (Stanley) and Zimbardo (Philip) experiments.

Briefly, the Milgram experiments invited members of the public to participate in what they called a study of memory and learning. Some of the participants were designated "teachers" and some as "learners." The experimenter (the authority dressed in a white coat) explained to participants that the study is concerned with the effects of punishment on learning.

In the experiment, the teacher (member of the public) administered shocks of increasing intensity to the learner any time the learner made an error. The shocks ranged from 15 volts to 450 volts, in 15-volt increments.

The teacher is a naïve participant in the experiment – a volunteer off the street. The learner is an actor who does not receive any shock at all. The goal of the experiment is to see how far a person will proceed in administering pain to a protesting victim when he or she is ordered to do so.

The results of the Milgram experiments (several hundred people participated in a variety of similar experiments to that described) are literally "shocking." Many "teachers" obeyed the experimenter no matter how vehemently the person being shocked pleaded, and no matter how painful or dangerous the shocks seemed to be. A significant percentage of participants (in some cases 65% of subjects) administered the highest level of shock possible (450 volts!). Few if any people did not agree to participate in the experiment once they learned that shocks had to be administered.

What is more alarming is that similar "authority" experiments have been carried out in recent years, and the results are similar and, in some cases, worse than those presented by the initial studies. People are nowadays even more inclined to succumb to authority than in the 1960s.

The results of the Zimbardo or Stanford Prison Experiment are perhaps even more alarming. The experiment was set up to explore the psychology of prison life and how specific situations affect people's behavior. Twenty-four out of 70 college-aged men were picked and randomly assigned to be either a guard or a prisoner. The experiment lasted only six days out of a planned two weeks when Zimbardo had to pull the plug. The mistreatment of the prisoners and the disturbing behavior of the guards escalated so alarmingly that the experiment had to be terminated.

For six days, half the study's participants endured cruel and dehumanizing abuse at the hands of their peers. At various times, they were taunted, stripped naked, deprived of sleep and forced to use plastic buckets as toilets. Some of them rebelled violently; others became hysterical or withdrew into despair. As the situation descended into chaos, the researchers stood by and watched. Like the fake guards, Zimbardo himself got caught up in the study, and started embodying the role of the prison's warden. It was thanks largely to his wife that he snapped out of it and ended the experiment.

In Zimbardo's book on his 40-year study of evil, he writes with regret not only about this experiment, but about the enormous power of systems (discussed in Chapter 9, pages 158–159), and the unpredictable human response to situations they elicit (Zimbardo 2008).

How do we explain evil? What happens to us that we lose all sense of humanity and become violent? How is it possible that as adults we cede our personal authority and our personal integrity so readily to our boss or someone in charge? Is our job, money, status, belonging to the group more valuable than ourselves? Is committing evil better than standing alone? Is evil truly part of our human nature? The philosopher Thomas Hobbes believed so. He argued that life was nasty, brutish and short and that we are like wild animals, hence the need for government, laws and a strong police force. In his world, courage was rarely if ever found.[3]

## Conclusion

What conclusions can we draw from these insights? The psychologists conveniently provide us with the rationale and the rationalizations of why we lack courage. They describe the psychological and emotional inhibitors that prevent us from getting out of the cave of illusions to see and embrace the light.

But, as we have discussed before, explanations do not excuse us, nor in our deepest selves do we want to be excused. The reason we do anything to avoid self-condemnation is that we care about how we feel about ourselves. We care a whole lot! When most of us know that we have done an unkind or unethical deed, or when we feel caught up in complying with actions that violate our own principles, we experience an inner disquiet, a deep discontent. Collusion and deception are tiring. They seep right into our very marrow. Courage, by contrast, is energizing. It is life-giving. It puts us in touch with our self-worth and infuses us with hope.

There are times when we lose touch with our courage, the courage that is part of our existence. And at times we don't know how to access it and activate its transformative power. But we need to remind ourselves, our courage is always there, waiting for expression. It just needs a nudge. For that, let's turn to the next chapter.

## Your Turn

- Have you ever found that you have behaved thoughtlessly and missed an important cue that would have made you react with greater courage?
- How important is it for you to be liked or to be popular?
- Do you ever find yourself saying "Well, the boss told me to do it?"
- Do you care about the welfare of your customers or clients or are they just people who avail themselves of your goods and services?
- Do you find yourself repressing your disagreement with the way things are handled at work?
- Thinking of the last time you were part of a decision-making process, and your views were different from those of the majority of the group, was your first reaction to comply or to courageously challenge the group's thinking?
- Referring to the eight mechanisms of moral disengagement, can you think of an instance where you justified your own behavior or that of others based on these principles?
- Is there a situation you are currently involved in where increased courage on your part, or the part of others, could significantly impact the outcome for individuals or an organization?

## Notes

1. See more on "fusing" in Chapter 9, Courage for the Leadership Team.
2. Lawrence Kohlberg was a Harvard professor renowned for his research into the moral development of children into adulthood. His work was largely influenced by that of psychologist Jean Piaget (1896–1980).
3. Hobbes sees men always in a power struggle with one another. This means that in a state of nature men will always be at war with one another. A reasonable man would give up his right to invade others if they would do the same. This requires an enforceable contract. It would also mean conferring some of their power to a person or body to make the agreement stick. In order to live a peaceful life, men would have to agree to leave the state of nature (Thomas Hobbes, *Leviathan*, 1985).

## References

Arendt, Hannah. 2006. *Eichmann in Jerusalem: A Report on the Banality of Evil.* New York: Penguin Books.

Bandura, Albert. 2016. *Moral Disengagement: How People Do Harm and Live with Themselves.* New York: Worth Publishers.

Bazerman, Max H., and Ann E. Tenbrunsel. 2011. *Blind Spots: Why We Fail to Do What's Right and What to Do About It.* Princeton, NJ: Princeton University Press.

Beerel, Annabel. 2021. *Ethical Leadership and Global Capitalism: A Guide to Good Practice.* Abingdon, Oxon: Routledge.

Glover, Jonathan. 2012. *Humanity: A Moral History of the 20th Century.* New Haven, CT: Yale University Press.

Goleman, Daniel. 1985. *Vital Lies, Simple Truths: The Psychology of Self-Deception.* New York: Simon & Schuster Paperbacks.

Hobbes, Thomas. 1985. *Leviathan.* New York: Penguin Classics.

Kegan, Robert. 1982. *The Evolving Self.* Boston, MA: Harvard University Press.

Kohlberg, Lawrence. 1981. *The Philosophy of Moral Development: Moral Stages and the Idea of Justice.* New York: Harper & Row.

Milgram, Stanley. 2009. *Obedience to Authority.* New York: Harper Perennial Modern Classics.

Rose, Todd. 2022. *Collective Illusions: Conformity, Complicity, and the Science of Why We Make Bad Decisions.* New York: Hatchette Books.

Samenow, Stanton E. 2014. *Inside the Criminal Mind.* New York: Broadway Books.

Young-Bruehl, Elizabeth. 2006. *Why Arendt Matters.* New Haven, CT: Yale University Press.

Zimbardo, Philip. 2008. *The Lucifer Effect.* New York: Random House Trade Paperbacks.

# Chapter 8

# Cultivating Courage

## The Courage to Die

It was 1992. The dot-com boom was beginning to froth. Rick Stevens had recently been appointed Vice President of Marketing and Sales of the UK Division of Company X, one of the largest computer companies in the world. He was tall and wiry with boyish good looks that belied the fact that he was well into his sixties.

Over 20 years, Rick had worked his way up the ranks from being a "box" salesman as they used to call it, to now being head of a vast international network of thousands of staff in at least 30 different countries.

Rick was gregarious, exceedingly ambitious, who loved lavish dinner parties but who could get nasty if things did not go well. As a result, people would conceal their mess-ups. Anyone in the vicinity of any hiccup to Rick's plans would collude to ensure that things did not bubble up and render them within proximity of the firing line. If Rick got wind of things going awry, he would get icy cold, sarcastic and demeaning and would threaten people with layoffs. "Perform your best all the time" was his motto. If you didn't or couldn't you didn't belong on his team, and you were out before you knew it.

Rick prided himself on having increased the organization's sales by a consistent 15%–20% over the past ten years. He loved travelling the world and would regale everyone with his adeptness at clinching intricate deals with what he described as demanding and difficult customers in far-flung territories.

The head office of Company X was in London. My position was that of senior strategic planner. My responsibilities included tracking the arrival of shipments of parts from East Asia to where they would be assembled at the organization's huge assembly plant on the city outskirts. I would also match completed orders delivered to the customer with the original sales forecasts. Timing was everything! Sales were recorded and reported daily. The late arrival of parts or delays in assembly could

DOI: 10.4324/9781003459644-9

threaten all forecasts which would result in dreadful ranting and raving from Rick and other members of the senior management team.

My most important task was to ensure that sales forecasts were accurate and achieved. This required reviewing a gazillion spreadsheets, calling people, asking for clarification, querying why things did not stack up and redirecting shipments that had been sent to the wrong countries or customers. It was a painstakingly detailed job, and I hated it. My intense dislike for the tedious detail was fueled by being repeatedly told untruths and never being able to find anyone I could trust.

At the time, both semiconductor companies and original equipment manufacturers (OEMs) were experiencing a radical shortage of chips and parts due to the soaring demand for computers. Rather than be honest, they fabricated all kinds of stories to assure me that chips and/or parts would arrive on time. These contrived stories were reinforced by people in the assembly plants and further lies were concocted by the salespeople. I never knew who was being honest or who was fabricating. But what I could see quite clearly is that the numbers did not add up. Everyone shirked the realty that we were not going to meet our sacred forecasts in the coming quarter and even the next. Commissions on sales were paid quarterly and people had come to expect tidy bonus checks. No one was going to rock that boat!

In our weekly meetings, Rick kept asking the seven members of his planning and sales team of which I was the only female, whether our sales forecasts were on track. Everyone would nod their heads vigorously, producing slides with fictitious numbers to assure Rick that we would meet our goals. My slides showed a different story. In an effort not to lose his temper, Rick would sarcastically deride me saying I was a naysayer, overly perfectionistic, difficult and clearly still needed to learn the ropes. Things were often "off," he would insist, but they always would correct themselves just in time. I did not see how on earth any adjustment, no matter how humungous, was going to change the reality that there were not enough chips or parts in the world to go round. This was not just about being "off."

I recall that last quarterly meeting as if it were yesterday. We were in Rick's office, as usual, with one exception, everyone, barring Rick, knew we had missed the forecasts significantly. He began his usual check-in, going round the room asking people to show their PowerPoint slides detailing the quarter's results. The truth was out. Every one of Rick's sales territories had fallen significantly short of its targets: the Americas, Europe, Africa, Australasia and of course East Asia.

Rick began to rant that we were all f******g imbeciles, that he could never trust anyone, that no one told him the truth, that to a person we were hopelessly incompetent and that everyone was just taking care of themselves. Breathing heavily and red in the face, he swore we were all going to be fired on the spot. We were a disgrace to the hallowed firm and on and on.

Suddenly, Rick stopped, looked at each one of us in turn, sighed, took a step back and sank into his chair, his hands covering his face. He began to sob.

> It's me, isn't it? You don't tell me the truth because I don't listen, I don't give you a chance. Some of you try, but I always fight you. I have made

> you afraid of telling the truth. I wanted to believe we were on track and refused to accept anything else. I got caught up. Oh God, I have made you afraid of me. What have I done? What have I done? This is all my screw up!

Rick sat in his chair sobbing into his hands while the seven of us sat and shuffled in silence, not daring to move or make eye contact.

Rick's secretary, who must have been eavesdropping, calmly walked in and handed him a large handkerchief. After several large nose blows, Rick slowly sat upright and looked at us.

In a soft voice, he said:

> I am sorry. It is my fault. I am sorry. I have made this mess. And it is a mess. My mess. I need you to help me fix it. Can we work together on this? What shall we do? Where shall we begin? I need your help.

I could never figure out what cataclysmic epiphany Rick had that made him see reality so suddenly. What part of him rose in rebellion against his inner demons and gave him the courage to face the truth? It made a huge impression on me – as you can tell.

I left the company a month later pressured by a headhunter to accept a more challenging and responsible position elsewhere. I was not sad to go, but I carried deep inside me the huge lesson I had learned from Rick who, after that courageous act, was a changed man. Months later, I learned from a colleague that he had revolutionized his leadership style and that his team was doing exceptionally well and had come to love him.

What exactly initiated Rick's metamorphosis remains a mystery but somehow his courage was aroused. He doubtlessly faced the public death of his then "ego," which must have been a terrifying experience.

What inspired Rick to emerge from the cave of illusions and face the blinding light, the naked truth that he was the biggest problem of all, and that he had to change? Where did he get the courage to humble himself before the group and own that he was caught up in fear and defensiveness? What made him suddenly realize that he was in the grip of his ambition and a need to prove his self-worth? What made him see that he was overcompensating for a sense of inadequacy? (see Alfred Adler, page 133).

In that pivotal moment, Rick realized that as an authority figure he wielded a great deal of power. He recognized that he intimidated his staff and as a result they lost their moral compass and their courage.

Rick also realized in that epiphanous moment that he was living in a world of self-deception, a life of moral disengagement. He repressed what he feared and did not want to hear, and he denied, rationalized and used selective attention to bully his way to the finish line which was always his own self-aggrandizement.

How did he do it? The answer is that in his heart of hearts he knew he was not passing ethical muster. His own self-sanctioning mechanisms kicked in and his true self-regard was at stake. The veil was ripped off and he realized he could no longer live with himself unless something changed. Acknowledging all this and acting on it took great courage.

So, what lessons can we take from Rick's story? How can we find the courage to fight our inner demons and gain our inner freedom which makes the deep happiness and self-worth we long for possible? How can we cultivate our courage? Here are some ideas.

## Freedom Means Acceptance

The very first courageous step toward claiming our inner freedom is the acceptance so perfectly articulated in Reinhold Niebuhr's *Serenity Prayer.*

> God, grant me the serenity to accept the things I cannot change, the courage to change the things I can, and the wisdom to know the difference.

Three important words stand out in this prayer, namely *accept*, *courage* and *wisdom*.

We need serenity to accept the reality that we are vulnerable, that we can be hurt, that we might get ill and that we will certainly die. We must accept these realities that underpin all our fears, with equanimity. Life means vulnerability. We can deny, distort, deceive all we want but nothing will change that eternal truth.

Acceptance does not mean renouncing who we are, or our ability to influence how or when we are hurt or sick. We can take steps to mitigate or diminish the impact of these experiences. We cannot, however, change the reality that we will die physically. We can also not escape the reality that a life of development and growth means a continuous challenge to our ego and that this ego (our conscious psychological and emotional self) is destined to die several times throughout our life span. But each death of the ego makes space for the structuring of a new one, as we saw in Rick's case above. And each new ego reflects greater maturity and inner growth.

We must also accept that things always change. Nothing is static. The seasons change. People come and go. Institutions grow and fail. Jobs open and close. Circumstances alter. New tides of culture and behaviors challenge our existing value systems. That is the reality we cannot change. There is no permanence and no guaranteed safety and security in anything or anyone. We must accept that truth.

In the *Serenity Prayer*, there is the distinct request to have courage to change what can be changed, and what can be changed through acceptance is our attitude. We can shift our attitude toward reality and practice becoming more adaptive to change. We can practice becoming more courageous in our relationships and in living according to our principles. By accepting what is true, even if we do not like it or it does not suit us, we find the courage to affirm ourselves as self-determining human beings. And Tillich reminded us that self-affirmation is what gives us the capacity to love.

The *Serenity Prayer* also asks that we have the *wisdom* to know what is ours to change. That we take responsibility for discerning what it is we can in fact control and then our acting on it.

Wisdom requires reflection, questioning and mindful presence. This requires courage. We need the courage to reflect on and question honestly, without dissembling, what our responsibilities are and how we can take them up and live our true selves. And we need to be both present and take the time to do this and not hurtle from one distraction to the next – something we are inclined to do, especially when we are anxious.

The *Serenity Prayer* is also an act of humility. We are asking for help to have serenity, to carry ourselves with dignity, to be able to accept and to be able to act with wisdom and courage. Asking for help acknowledges that we are not omnipotent. We need help from something beyond us, however we name it, which means there is a transcendence to our request. In doing so, we recognize that we need to rise above our usual, mundane, ego selves to a higher level of existence. That is our inner courage calling – calling us to reach toward a truer way of being. Calling us to hear the soul.

## Courage to Confront Our Ego

The concept of the ego was first formulated by Sigmund Freud in his book *The Ego and the Id* (Freud 1990). Here he explains his theory of the structure of the psyche as comprising a system made up of the id, the ego and the superego.

The id is the instinctive part of the mind that is unconscious and feeds our most basic needs and drives. The ego develops as we develop and are conditioned by our environment. It is in continuous tension between the realities we encounter and the demands of the id. The superego is the internalization of the codes of conduct, moral prohibitions, commands and rules from parental figures. It adds further tensions to the ego that is trying to balance the pleasure-seeking, pain-avoiding demands of the id, the challenges of the real world and the superego's internalized proscriptions of authority figures. In working with these tensions, the ego becomes the organizing personality structure within the psyche.

In our Western culture, since birth, most people have been encouraged to develop a strong, independent, separate sense of self or ego. From early on, we were assured that a strong ego would help us to survive the "jungle" of life. Growing up involved a series of psychic transitions that helped form and craft the many contours and barriers that have shaped our egos. The conditioning of our families and cultures has pressured us into defining what is us, and what is not us. The infinite potential with which we arrived at the portal of birth is soon radically narrowed into a socially constructed "me" who fits in, fits in at home, fits in at school and fits in in society. Not fitting in invariably exacts a high price (Beerel 2021).

The ego is the limited self that arises due to our conditioning in the world. It shapes the structure of our consciousness and as such defines our universe. As we grow up, the ego structure solidifies, becoming a prison where we see the world through its barred windows. Unless we focus on personal growth, especially with some spiritual dimension, our prison begins to totally define us. The ego controls our feelings, thoughts and behaviors that we have so carefully constructed to make ourselves feel secure.

The ego serves as our conscious identity. It circumscribes the way we see and understand ourselves. It includes a vast array of inner proscriptions and defensive behaviors that form an armory against life's ups and downs. It is the ego that fights impermanence, uncertainty, unpalatable truths and our sense of vulnerability and inadequacy. Think of Rick and his weak, unworthy-feeling ego.

By early adulthood, the egoic structure of the separate defined self, fighting for survival against both inner and outer tensions, is all but solidified. The ego perceives challenges to itself as potential "death threats," and will fight to the "death" to ensure psychological, emotional and certainly physical survival. The ego's central concern is taking care of number one – me!

To rise above the ego, and to challenge its structure, its dos and don'ts, and its projected image of ourselves, is the great inner battle the old warrior was alluding to at the beginning of Chapter 6. "Killing" the old ego structure that is not serving us well, and transcending to a place where a new one is constructed, takes huge courage. Tackling the existing ego head on is invariably experienced as a "dying" of oneself – which in some ways it is. It is dying of the conditioned self that requires recalibration. And, based on our serenity prayer, it is one of the things we can control and can change. It is our work to do.

Rick must have been in a ferocious inner turmoil to have been able to challenge his ego so bluntly and so publicly. Often it requires a great shock in one's life for one to be faced with no alternative but to change one's self-understanding, criteria of self-worth and identity. Somehow, Rick experienced that shock.

There is no greater growth than when one confronts one's ego and develops the ability to transcend it and move to a higher plane of consciousness. Ego maturation means that we are not shackled or imprisoned by our egos, but we are free to come and go. We can remove the ego filters. We recognize the ego as servant and not master. But all of this is not easy to do as the ego does not like to examine itself and challenges us when we threaten its supremacy. This is where we need self-mastery and attention to personal growth and development.

People with strong and healthy egos are those who have a sense of self. They are self-determining and do not depend on the approval of others. (See the next chapter for a further development of this theme.) They are the people willing to be transformed by experience and who understand the importance of self-regulation. They can be vulnerable and know when to take a stand (recall Edwin Friedman in Chapter 1).

By contrast, people who are excessively identified by their egos to the point of being unable to have any other reference point than themselves, usually defined as narcissists, are unlikely to attain the transcendent experience. They are imprisoned, they are tyrants, and they are insecure and behave as insecure people do. There is little shortage of public examples, and sadly, many of those who head up our major corporations suffer from this affliction.

To cultivate our courage is to grow in self-awareness, and to continually ask ourselves to what extent our egos are running the show. We must be open to candid feedback from others, and even more importantly, from our inner selves. Reflection, deliberation and a regular mindfulness practice can take one a long way in developing our ego maturity.

## Courage to Face Our Vulnerabilities

Vulnerability is part and parcel of life. We don't like this truth. No one likes to be vulnerable. It strips us of our can-do adulthood and throws us back into the place of being an infant.

The well-known psychologist Alfred Adler (1870–1937) claimed that all infants have a feeling of inferiority and inadequacy immediately they begin to experience the world. These early experiences, such as the need to gain their parents' attention, get approval, and feel loved, influence the child's goals throughout his or her life.

Adler believed that all infants, by virtue of their innate vulnerability to everything in life, develop an inferiority complex and that the residue of this complex lasts throughout their lives – the degree varies. To counter this feeling of inferiority and inadequacy, Adler claims, we create a unique set of goals or a self-deal toward which we strive. These goals and self-ideal influence our personality structure and inform the opinion we have of ourselves.

A natural and healthy reaction to our sense of inferiority, says Adler, is what he terms "compensation." These are our efforts to overcome a real or imagined inferiority by developing our abilities. If, however, we cannot compensate adequately for these natural feelings of inferiority through achieving some of our goals or attaining part of our self-ideal, we are left with an enduring inferiority complex.

At times, says Adler, our efforts of compensation go awry. One way in which this happens is that our feelings of inferiority become overly intense, and we strive so strenuously for compensation that even when we achieve it, it is no longer satisfactory. This, Adler claims, culminates in a state of overcompensation, where our focus on meeting our goals is exaggerated and can even become pathological.

A significant part of this process is unconscious and is the key to understanding the person. The striving for superiority, call it power, perfectionism, status, being admired, is often evidenced by aggression. This aggression masks the inner anxiety of never being good enough. Think of Rick, his overcompensation and his aggression intended to mask his fear of failing to reach his goals which were so tied up with his sense of inadequacy and self-worth.

Like Rick, for many, the innate sense of inferiority feeds a chronic anxiety about what we have made of ourselves. Often this culminates in a continuous inner voice that is critical, condemnatory and self-rejecting. It feeds a sense of inadequacy and guilt for our failures which are magnified. Consider those inner demons of self-criticism, our fear of failure, plus the continuous need for reassurance about our self-worth, the desire to please and the sense of shame.

Think about how we tend to focus on setbacks rather than on progress. Consider the huge negative emotions that are generated when receiving criticism and how any criticism, no matter how small, has a far stronger impact than any affirmation, such as receiving praise.

Daniel Kahneman in his book *Thinking, Fast and Slow*, 2013, discusses our loss aversion which he claims is rooted in our fear of failure of not achieving our goals. We are more upset about losing $10 than we are happy about finding $10. Roughly speaking, he writes, losses hurt about twice as much as gains make you feel good (Kahneman 2013). Regret and disappointment weigh far more heavily on us than the pleasure of satisfaction.

Loss aversion, says Kahneman, reflects a general bias in human psychology that makes people resistant to change. A bad status quo is often favored over the risk of something new and promising. When we think about change, we focus more on what we might lose rather than on what we might gain. This reflects our fear of inadequacy and loss of confidence in our ability to adapt and achieve our desired goals or make new ones. These are all old hauntings of our sense of inferiority.

How can we find the courage to take positive steps in the face of our feelings of vulnerability and inadequacy? Self-awareness is always the first step. Confronting the truth of ourselves and our behaviors with an open and nonjudgmental stance goes a long way toward finding one's courage to make changes. We must also understand that we do not have to "fix" everything at once. One step at a time, consistently taking the next step forward, and the next, and appreciating every step of progress that we make. Simply being true to yourself in terms of your values and ethics, being honest about who you are with all your fears and perceived failings, and taking responsibility for how you think and feel make a huge difference. Cease seeking perfection, because it does not exist and appreciate yourself for all the things you do rather than what you fail to do. Take up a mindful practice – it will make all the difference – see page 139.

## Courage to Face the Truth

Along with the *Serenity Prayer*, having the courage to face our vulnerabilities is an important step. It helps us to face the arrival of new truths or new realities. Instead of engaging in willful blindness by ignoring, denying, deferring or fabricating an alternate reality, we find the courage to face inconvenient truths by recognizing and acknowledging that they exist.

As we saw in our story, Rick had not dealt with his inferiority complex, and was caught up in overcompensating, and therefore he could not allow himself to see any truths that might shake the illusion of the self-ideal he had created.

As we know, unpalatable truths are arriving all the time, and courage means cultivating the ability to face them. What indeed are these truths that we need to face? How do we describe them to ourselves? What language do we use? Do we always look at the glass half-empty where things appear dire or frightening? What is it about a particular new reality that makes us uncomfortable? Is it about being out of control, of having to give up something we are attached to? Does it appear to threaten our livelihood, our health, our ability to do things? What is it that makes it inconvenient, or frightening?

Now, how might we reframe this new reality? The way one frames a question, or a problem, always determines the range of answers. For example, if our company is rapidly losing market share and profitability can we shift from "Oh my God, I will be out of a job and destitute?" to "This is a chance to reinvent myself and perhaps make myself less vulnerable to employers in the future." Reframing does not mean eliminating or denying the truth. However, with a change of attitude, we can transition from being a victim to someone who has options.

Once we have acknowledged the inconvenient truth, we can explore our realistic options by looking at the "good, the bad, and the ugly." We will find that by taking an unpalatable or harsh truth by the horns, and facing our anxiety head on, we will have control over our fear, which will free us to look at possibilities and to find options leading to an optimal outcome.

Here are the steps:

- Recognize and acknowledge the new reality as soon as possible
- Describe it fully
- Identify all the fear and emotions that surface
- Reframe this reality from multiple perspectives
- Review the options and possibilities
- Select an optimal response – not reaction!
- Realign your attitude

To counteract the instinctive desire to keep our egos safe from the truth, we need to remember that we create the world we live in. Our world, our well-being is determined by our choices, by the way we interpret the events that happen to us, and the people we give our power to. That is the truth we must accept and live with courage.

## Self-Efficacy

Albert Bandura, who we met in the previous chapter, is known for his concept of self-efficacy. Self-efficacy refers to the confidence people have in their own capacity to confront the challenges they face. It is an affirmation of one's autonomy as an agent in life. A belief in oneself and one's agency that "I can do this" makes a difference when the time comes for courageous action, insists Bandura (2016).

The significance of self-efficacy lies in the individual's belief and confidence that his or her actions make a difference. People reflect on and measure whether they achieve the goals they set out to achieve, whether they can influence outcomes and whether their agency has potency. When people believe in their causative capabilities and that they are contributors to the conditions that affect them, he claims, this advances their development and their adaptive capacities.

By contrast, Bandura explains how when people experience that their ideas, their voice and their suggestions are not heard and do not make a difference, they become disengaged, subdued and even depressed. They take a minimal interest in outcomes and morally disengage. They override their inner self-sanctioning mechanisms by claiming that they have become victims and are forced to disconnect.

The deadening world of bureaucracy dehumanizes people in that they become cogs in a machine serving the whims of those in power. They lose interest in outcomes, minimally performing their tasks and deliberately repressing, denying or rationalizing any wrongdoing, thereby shutting down or shutting out any personal moral responsibility or call for courage.

There are steps we can and must take to ensure that we avoid or extricate ourselves from situations where we do not or cannot experience self-efficacy. Any experience of not being able to make a difference robs us of our self-esteem, our self-confidence and the vitality we need to develop and grow. Comfortable as it may seem, it is a bad place to be in! Change the job, change the relationship, change the group and find your freedom to be your agent of your life. Cultivating your courage depends on it. So does your life!

## Practicing Willpower

What about our willpower? Italian psychiatrist Roberto Assagioli tackles this question in his book *The Act of Will* 2010. He begins by commenting on humans' lack of knowledge and control of their inner being. He claims that the growing gap between our external powers and internal powers is one of the most profound causes of the continuing evil that afflicts our civilization. He argues that only the development of man's inner powers can offset the dangers of the external forces that threaten the survival of humanity. He claims that one aspect that demands priority is recognition of the potency of a person's own will. The will is not only central to a person's personality and connection to his core self, but it is the will that decides what is to be done.

The will gives us the power to say yes or no. We experience our will during an inner struggle when something inside us urges us to take a specific course of action. This is when we experience "willing." This willing may include insisting we take no action, that we deliberately shut down or shut out that which we do not want to face. That is still an action of the will – an action we might call "weak-willed."

It is the will that gives us the power to choose, hence our referring to whether we have willpower or not. Assagioli points out that we are aware that we have a will, and this self-awareness indicates the connection between our will and the core of who we are. He claims that we must train our will to engage us in constructive and life-giving rather than evil actions. The will needs to be disciplined and trained in perseverance, tenacity and patience. The will also needs training in being courageous. It needs to be repeatedly directed to access our capacity for courage, and in doing so helps us to cultivate the courageousness that is part of our existence.

In *The Willpower Instinct* (2013), Kelly McGonigal, a psychologist at Stanford University, discusses our struggles with temptation, addiction, distraction and procrastination. She hosts classes that provide strategies for self-control and the delaying of immediate gratification in favor of wiser choices.

McGonigal emphasizes that stress is the enemy of willpower. Stress makes us feel tired or pressured. To utilize our willpower, we need to slow down, pay attention, pause and plan. When we rush to get something done and over with, we usually take the easy way out. Stress adds to tiredness where we are too tired to resist temptation. Our self-control muscle does not kick in. When we feel bad about ourselves, she says, this leads to us giving in. The brain looks for relief and a promise of reward even when it means succumbing to temptation or unethical pursuits.

Self-control is energy expensive, she writes, so it is easier to ignore it. She emphasizes the need to pay attention and not to run on autopilot.

Developing our willpower to pay attention, to be present and mindful, helps us to cultivate our courage. Once again, here is a recommendation to take up a mindfulness practice – see page 138.

## Claiming Our Personal Authority

In the previous chapter, we discussed the intimidating power of authority and how it often inhibits our courage. We also questioned whether at times we submit to authority or cede our own authority to others to avoid having to make a difficult decision or circumvent taking personal accountability for handling challenging situations.

Taking up our own personal authority is a sign of maturity. As Jungian psychologist James Hollis writes in his book *Finding Meaning in the Second Half of Life: How to Finally, Really Grow Up*, 2006, many of us choose not to grow up in certain aspects of our lives. Taking up our personal authority, he writes, is a significant one that many of us shirk. We shirk it, because it is the ultimate one. Once we claim our own personal authority, we agree to be accountable for every choice and every aspect of our lives.

Hollis defines personal authority as "finding what is true for oneself and living it in the world" (Hollis 2006, 39). Once we take up our personal authority, meaning we recognize our own agency in our life, and we stand behind that fully, Hollis claims, we will finally have grown up. Alas, too few people are prepared to grow up, and to be willing to be self-authorizing. They are always looking somewhere for permission or approval. They are not prepared to take responsibility for their own destiny. They lack the courage to be their own person. That is where many of us are stuck.

To follow Hollis's lead, we can ask ourselves in which parts of life have we not grown up. Where in life are we stuck? In what parts of life do we choose to cede our sense of self, our principles and our power? How and in what way does that suit us? What do we fear? What are we trying to avoid?

Once again, know thyself is the key to courage and freedom. Can we take the time to reflect on and nonjudgmentally to ask ourselves what purposes not growing up serve and what things would be like if we behaved differently? Can we begin now, with the first step being more attentive to our personal authority and how we use it, and how we don't? Once again, step by step, let us grow up and live into our authority. Then there will no longer be anyone to blame for anything – not the environment, not the government, not society, our jobs, our friends, our partners or our family. Our motto will be "I am in charge of my life. I take responsibility for every choice I make, physically, emotionally, psychologically and spiritually. The Buck stops here, right here with me."

Hannah Arendt, who we met in Chapter 3 where we discussed "terribly normal people" and the "banality of evil," discusses courage in another thought-provoking book, *The Human Condition*. She affirms that it is courage, as articulated by the Greeks, that makes freedom possible. The Greeks, she claimed, understood that the difference between a free man and a slave was courage. Unless we live a courageous life, we are in fact slaves.

Courage, she writes, is the willingness to act and to insert oneself into the world and begin a story of one's own. It is about leaving one's private hiding place and showing who one is by being prepared to both disclose and expose oneself. Courage is our authority to be who one is and to act as one is (Arendt 1970).

There is no better way to cultivate courage than to begin to live out of our personal authority.

## Courage and Mindfulness

What is mindfulness? Simply put, mindfulness is paying attention to our attention moment by moment. In each conscious (aware) moment of our lives, we are our attention. We are consciously experiencing whatever we are attending to, namely thoughts, emotions, feelings and sensations. Our attention is our experience.

By paying attention to our attention, we are experiencing our experience. Our attention could be absorbed with happy or sad thoughts. It could be thoughts of regret, guilt or envy. It could be emotions of excitement, anxiety, confusion or despair. It could be feelings of hurt, pride, fear or joy. It could be sensations of attraction, pain or irritation. Whatever we are experiencing, by being mindful, we are fully present to that experience (Beerel and Raffio 2018).

The power of mindfulness lies in its direct experience. By paying attention to our attention in the moment, as things are taking place, the true mirror of our existence is held before us. This mirror is uncompromising. We get to see our ego and its antics. We are confronted with who we really are, how we really think, what triggers us, what makes us afraid, what gives us hope and meaning, our rapid impulses and how we sell ourselves out moment by moment.

With mindfulness we observe in real time, our own betrayals, lies, greed, insecurities, perversions, deflections and the cowardice behind many of our words and actions. We notice how we miss cues, skip over details, succumb to our fears, react out of patterned behaviors and dismiss the need for reflection and deliberation.

One of the greatest benefits of mindfulness is that we get to slow down. We create space between stimulus and response, allowing us time to breathe and stall our usual rapid-fire reactions.

Mindfulness is also the mirror that reveals our shadow selves – those parts of us we tossed into the basement as not being part of the persona that we have so artfully crafted for public consumption. We also find in this basement some gifts and possibilities that we have not embraced or lived into for some reason or another.[1]

Lastly, for our brief discussion here, mindfulness is about compassion. As we observe ourselves and learn about who we truly are, we are called to be compassionate. Mindfulness is not another opportunity to beat ourselves up or to cringe at our limitations or to embrace self-loathing. On the contrary, by being compassionate, we heal the inner wounds that led to some of our insecurities and fears, and we acknowledge that we are not perfect and yet we are still okay. We are, in fact, way better than okay! We are courageous because we take the risk of choosing time and again. We make decisions and sometimes we fail and fall, but we get up, and keep trying. With mindfulness we realize we have a lot of goodness within us, and as we move closer to the source (our core selves), and find our inner freedom, we find we have an almost infinite potential for more (Beerel 2020). There is bounteous literature that confirms the benefits of a mindfulness practice and how it engages our souls, makes us far more attentive and present, and cultivates our courage.

## Choices, Courage and Ethics

Have you ever thought about how many decisions we make every day? Thousands! Life is one continuous series of decisions, and each choice shapes the narrative of our lives and defines our character.

What we define as difficult choices or decisions are those that trigger our fears. They invariably challenge our sense of freedom – either external or internal. And our desire is to always to make decisions that result in our happiness. Sometimes this seems impossible to do. These so-called difficult decisions call particularly on our ethical principles and our courage. Our ethical principles – which include advancing goodness, honesty, justice, moderation and compassion – and our courage challenge us to act on these despite our fear. A person who makes virtuous choices (remember Chapter 5 on courage), where virtuous choices are ones that have as their goal to advance goodness, well-being and flourishing, has character, an honorable character.

Being an ethical person demands courage. Ethics asks us to make wise decisions, not self-interested ones or ones motivated by our need to be liked. This requires setting aside our egos and making a choice that may leave us vulnerable. It requires us to work through the systemic barriers that serve as force fields pulling and pushing us in various directions, many of which are scary as they render us out of control. There are the pressures of organizational culture and the implicit pact of what it means to belong. There is the power of the group and the understandable fear of becoming an outsider. Bureaucracy adds to feelings of alienation and loss of autonomy. Then there is the power of authority and our own personal baggage and projections associated with authority. Added to all this is our anthropomorphizing tendencies where we distance ourselves from our own moral agency and hand it over to "the company." And then of course, there is our own self-interest, our ego that gets in the way.

Jacob Needleman, an American philosopher and religious scholar, explores our struggles to be good in his deeply inquiring text *Why Can't We Be Good?* (2008). Here he discusses our ethical responsibilities for the choices we make. Everything matters, he writes. Every step we take in life is a step toward a life of conscious moral action – or not. It is only genuinely conscious action, that is, mindful action that is moral action, he writes. Needleman claims that before we ask ourselves the question of what we ought or ought not to do, our first question has to be "who are we?" What kind of human being do we want to be? What kind of character are we developing?

Taking the ethical high road takes character and, especially, courage. It takes courage to advocate taking a path that others do not want to take. It takes courage to break with precedent. It takes courage to challenge the law and lawyers. It takes courage to set aside one's ego and be vulnerable. It takes courage to speak up, to give voice to our principles, to seek out creative solutions and to take actions that sometimes place us in positions of vulnerability. It takes courage to work at living fully out of ourselves. Being ethical and courageous goes hand in hand and together they provide the foundations of our character.

## Cultivating Our Courage

This chapter is about cultivating our courage, one step at a time. Courage, like most things, begins with the small things. People who perform big, courageous acts usually have a history of little acts that over time have developed their abilities to handle larger challenges.

Seldom do we applaud ourselves for the many small courageous acts we engage in almost daily. We have grown up, encountered life along all kinds of pathways and by this time in our lives, made many millions of decisions. Many of those decisions took courage. Many decisions did not make us popular, give us that raise or fill our parents or our partner's dreams. Yet we made those choices and lived by the consequences – for good or for ill. In retrospect, some of our choices may not have been such good ones, but at the time we did the very best we could. It is highly unlikely any of us at the time said: "I feel like making a bad decision today; one that will ruin my career, render me a coward, destroy my relationships or make me unhappy!" More likely we fretted and strained over the difficult decisions and then did the very best we could at the time. Of course there were some bad decisions, and of course there were some that were influenced by our weak wills rather than our higher selves. At the time, doubtless we gathered whatever courage we could muster and made, what we considered, the best decision. So, we are the unsung heroes of our lives. We need to celebrate this part of us and to remember that courage requires cultivation through practice, practice, practice.

Let us remind ourselves of the Courage Framework from Chapter 5.

## A Courage Framework

- Courage is a moral virtue and as such is an end in itself. It is not done for the sake of anything else other than to advance goodness, flourishing and well-being. It is a selfless act.
- Courage lies in its wisdom, not its bravado. It is a choice resulting from a discernment guided by wisdom and prudence.
- Courage is not fickle and impetuous – it is the act of a person with a courageous character.
- Courage is the willingness and a commitment to act in the face of extreme danger.
- It is the mean between cowardice and over-confidence.
- Courage is not fearlessness, bravado or daring.
- Courage is always mediated by reason.
- Courage exhibits fortitude and endurance and often patience.
- There is a nobility and beauty about courage in that it is about facing the truth of a situation.
- Courage means confronting a challenge or conflict that is nonlife-giving and seeking to give it life.
- There is a self-transcendence in courage where one is called to act from one's highest self. It is a call from the soul.

If we take the steps laid out in this chapter, we can consciously and intentionally cultivate our courage by:

- Accepting what cannot be changed with serenity
- Through self-awareness, paying attention to our ego and its defensiveness and challenging it head on when it is not serving us well

- Facing our vulnerabilities and sense of inadequacy and recognizing that we can constructively compensate for them
- Acknowledging new realities and unpalatable truths, reframing what they mean to us and looking constructively at our options
- Developing our self-efficacy so that we have the confidence that we can and do make a difference
- Strengthening our willpower largely through a mindfulness practice
- Claiming our personal authority by living our story, our way, and being prepared to face the consequences even when they are dire
- Mindfully paying attention to our choices and striving to make decisions that advance goodness, well-being and flourishing.

If we take these steps, one moment, one step and one decision at a time they will become habitual acts that will shape and strengthen our character. As a result, we will find the happiness we long for by being the very best self we can be.

At the heart of it all is the need to take ownership, accountability and control over who we are. We can never control others, but we can control ourselves by how we respond to what is happening around us. If we can cease to abdicate our self-control by looking to others to make us happy, to provide a smooth and convenient path to our goals, and to give us the life we think we deserve, by being courageous and living a life of character we will be a gift to ourselves and a great gift to our very broken world.

## Your Turn

- What is the one thing that you cannot control, that challenges you the most?
- Have you ever found yourself or someone you work with in a situation where the ego is inhibiting your or their ability to make ethical or courageous choices?
- Do you find yourself overcompensating at times? Are you able to question the vulnerabilities you are trying to cover up?
- How good are you at facing unpalatable realities? Are there any that are confronting you now?
- Do you have a sense of self-efficacy in your life? What about at work?
- Are you able to claim your personal authority and to be accountable for every aspect of your life?
- Have you recently made any choices that called on your courage?
- Do you have a mindfulness practice?
- Has this chapter inspired you to intentionally cultivate your courage?
- What small step could you take today that would strengthen your courage practice?

## Note

1 For a detailed explanation of the shadow and how it affects our lives, see Annabel Beerel, *Rethinking Leadership: A Critique of Contemporary Theories* (Abingdon, Oxon: Routledge, 2021), 303–18.

## References

Arendt, Hannah. 1970. *The Human Condition*. Chicago, IL: University of Chicago Press.

Assagioli, Roberto. 2010. *The Act of Will*. Amherst, MA: Synthesis Center Press.

Bandura, Albert. 2016. *Moral Disengagement: How People Do Harm and Live with Themselves*. New York: Worth Publishers.

Beerel, Annabel. 2020. *Ethical Leadership and Global Capitalism: A Guide to Good Practice*. Abingdon, Oxon: Routledge.

Beerel, Annabel, and Tom Raffio. 2018. *Mindfulness: A Better Me; Better You: Better World*. New Hampshire: Self-published.

Freud, Sigmund. 1990. *The Ego and the Id*. New York: W.W. Norton & Co.

Hollis, James. 2006. *Finding Meaning in the Second Half of Life: How to Finally, Really Grow Up*. New York: Avery.

Kahneman, Daniel. 2013. *Thinking Fast and Slow*. New York: Farrar, Straus and Giroux.

McGonigal, Kelly. 2013. *The Willpower Instinct*. New York: Penguin Group.

Needleman, Jacob. 2008. *Why Can't We Be Good?* New York: Penguin.

# Chapter 9

# Courage for the Leadership Team

## The Slippery Slope

It was back in 1985. I had just emerged from business school proudly waving my MBA certificate that classified me as "one of those business type smart ones." That was in the old days, now I think one can buy those certificates online. After graduating, within no time I landed a job in the City of London in corporate finance.

My first assignment was to create a business plan for a medium-sized manufacturing company that was looking at its growth options. I loved preparing business plans, something in which I had developed some expertise when I worked for a large conglomerate in South Africa. Delighted to show off my skills, I plunged into the company's documents with great enthusiasm. After three long, intense days of evaluating the company's prospects from every angle, plus having several back-and-forth discussions with the client, by the end of the week I had a draft plan of which I was proud. I contacted my boss and the following Monday we met to discuss the project.

"You mean you have a draft already?" he asked in disbelief.

"Yes, I think you will find it quite robust," I said boastfully as I waved a file full of spreadsheets and text in front of him.

"You were not supposed to finish the project in under three weeks. That is what we quoted them. Three weeks work. Why did you finish it so quickly?" he asked, clearly annoyed.

My boss, Robin, who was also a senior partner in the firm which no one was allowed to forget, was a short, middle-aged man with a rapidly receding hairline and greying temples. He had the habit of jerking his head and biting his lip. Smiles were

DOI: 10.4324/9781003459644-10

rare and usually only when he had made an ironic comment – he reveled in irony – which was usually followed by a smirk and jerks of self-appreciation.

Robin wore the same dark blue suit every day along with a white shirt and a navy tie. He rarely took off his jacket, and most certainly never in a meeting. As we were meeting, he was tightly clad in his navy outfit despite the stifling summer heat.

"Oh, I had no idea I had to take three weeks," I countered. "And, anyway, isn't it great that we can tell them that we have something to discuss as they are clearly anxious to get going and that we have come in under budget?"

"That is not great at all," Robin growled. "How do you think we earn money around here? We try to come in on budget or a slight overrun if that is justified. But to come in at half the price would be ridiculous, ludicrous beyond belief," he all but snarled.

Robin then donned his dark-rimmed glasses and reviewed what I had done. I waited patiently. After what seemed an eternity, reluctantly he agreed that I had done a thorough job. With a sigh, he said: "Okay. Leave this with me. I am sure there are some hours I need to put in to bring it up to par. I will handle this with the client and let you know how we get on." With that I was dismissed.

I returned to my cubicle more than annoyed. I had expected to be praised for my hard work, for beating the deadline and coming under budget. I had imagined it would be wonderful to complete something ahead of schedule and to give the client a break on the price. Wasn't that the way to build good client relations? To build trust? To show that one was looking out for the client's best interests? Isn't this how one gets more work? Clearly this surly fellow called Robin did not think so. All he saw was the need for more projects in the pipeline which equated to having to do more work and incur added marketing effort and cost. Why not just come in on budget and the client would be none the wiser and one's reputation would be upheld?

Now, Robin was probably going to fiddle around with what I had done to justify the hours that went into the quoted budget. What a waste of time!

I learned later that we invoiced the client a few hundred pounds over budget to account for the partner's higher hourly rate.

What would I do if it were my company, I wondered? Would I have the courage to give the client the break and to trust I would make up the money elsewhere? Or would I also try to sneak in a few pounds or dollars here and there to boost my profits? What would I do?

That's what it is all about, the courage to be true, I thought. This must be how the slippery slope begins.

## Why People Cheat, Steal and Commit Fraud

Stories abound of the millions of Americans mired in low-paying jobs, struggling to make ends meet while watching the fruits of their labor get funneled to wealthy CEOs and investors. A new report by the Institute for Policy Studies (IPS) titled

Executive Excess 2023 analyzes 100 large public corporations with the lowest wages in 2022. The report found that at these corporations, a group that includes many of the nation's largest employers, "CEO pay averaged $15.3 million and median worker pay averaged $31,672." That's a ratio of 603 to 1.

One egregious example is Dollar Tree, a company that employs nearly 200,000 people, where the median wage is just $14,702, but its CEO, Michael Witynski, received $13.98 million in total compensation in 2022, a ratio of 951 to 1.

As rents escalate and living costs increase weekly, the average family can barely live on $31,672, let alone $14,702. Does this excuse them for taking any opportunity, even if it is illegal or corrupt, to help make ends meet?

Adding to the plight of lower-level workers is the enormous price gouging in the food industry. Undoubtedly, food companies face legitimate increased costs and unique shortages due to supply chain blues, but these aren't eating into their profits as expected. In fact, many of the largest publicly traded companies have never had higher profit margins. Such record earnings suggest that food companies have sufficient market power to pass all their higher costs, and then some, onto consumers. One would imagine that in these circumstances competitors would offer lower prices – except there are no competitors! As with several other industries, the few large food companies have excessive monopoly power enabling them verily to dictate prices without challenge.

**Who Is Responsible for Sky-High Inflation?**

Worried about sky-high airfares and lousy service? That's largely because airlines have merged from 12 carriers in 1980 to only four today.

Concerned about drug prices? Between 1995 and 2015, 60 leading pharmaceutical companies merged to only 10.

Upset about food costs? Four large companies now control 85 percent of beef processing, 70 percent of the pork market, and 54 percent of poultry.

Worried about grocery prices? Just three giants – Albertsons, Kroger, and Walmart – control 70 percent of the grocery sales in 167 cities.

Robert Reich (former US Secretary of Labor) Blog, Friday July 26, 2024, *Debunking the Myth About Inflation.*

Taking a different perspective, everyone knows that insider trading of stocks is illegal; however, members of Congress, who have oversight and often control legislation that can have significant effects on an industry, consider themselves immune from this rule. The *New York Times* (September 2022) reported that 97 members of Congress from both sides of the aisle have traded in companies in which they have influence.

While Congress passed the STOCK Act in 2012 as an attempt to combat congressional insider trading, the STOCK Act is widely regarded as a "failed solution" that is in desperate need of an overhaul. Nevertheless, despite renewed calls for reform, Congress has resisted imposing restrictions on itself. This resistance to congressional insider trading laws is likely to persist in the future, regardless of which party is in control. This leaves open the question of whether meaningful reform will eventually be passed, or whether Congress will refuse to put forth self-regulating legislation that serves to their personal detriment.

Then there is the growing exposure of the blatant conflicts of interest that taint the impartiality of the US Supreme Court justices. Despite ample evidence of gifts, preferential treatment, exotic travel and substantial interest free loans that are forgiven, nothing of substance has yet been done, so conflicts of interest persist.[1]

How does the average citizen respond when either he or she is struggling for economic survival and/or he or she witnesses that those in power only serve their own interests? (Remember Lisa Newton and *Permission to Steal* in Chapter 3). Does this behavior excuse people for saying "Everyone is cheating therefore it is okay if I do it too"?

No – we are not excused. The unfortunate facts may provide an explanation why having the courage to resist temptation is so challenging, but we are not excused. An explanation is never an excuse. As my father always used to say, "Two wrongs do not make a right."

Being courageous is by no means easy – in fact it is most often damn difficult. However, courage lies at the root of who we are when we self-affirm the best of our humanity. Sinking to the lowest ethical denominator does us even greater personal harm than it does to our failing society.

## An Epidemic of Greed

In the Introduction, we discussed how "Greed Rules" that everything is up for sale and our systems are now designed to promote avarice. What has led us to become so greedy? What forces or circumstances result in human greed? Psychologists tell us that greed usually arises from early traumas such as parental absence, inconsistency or neglect. Low self-esteem coupled with feelings of anxiety and vulnerability leads people to seek a substitute or some compensation for the love and security they lack. In essence, greed is an effort to fill an emptiness inside. Does that mean we are a society consumed by our emptiness?

The well-known psychologist Rollo May (1909–1994) thought so. In his book *Man's Search for Himself*, 2009 (first published in 1953), May writes of American's feelings of emptiness which comes from a sense of inner vacuousness that arises from a conviction that the individual cannot direct his own life. He is now subjected to the powers of public opinion where he must fit in, and his life is one of daily stagnation – getting up to the alarm, going to work, coming home, eating, sleeping and doing the same again, day after day.

People, wrote May, no longer know what they want or what they feel. They are totally outer directed and dependent upon what others expect of them. The only thing they know how to do is to amass material wealth as that too helps them to both fit in and be a "somebody," they do not know how else to be. Inner direction has been all but lost. Other social critics claim that the increase in greed is because our modern society has become so materialistic. Because we have lost a sense of who we are and because we are so distant from ourselves, we desperately seek reassurance elsewhere. The emptiness inside has become a nationwide problem wherein self-worth is measured by material accumulation rather than by character.

Often greed and narcissism go hand in hand. Greedy people are highly self-centered and are experts at manipulating people and circumstances. Greedy people see the world as a zero-sum game where the winner takes all, and they are determined to be the winners. The justification for their behavior is legion and serves to suppress the inner sanctions of self-condemnation – remember Chapter 3 and our discussion of power, greed and corruption.

Hoping for a shift in this mentality, Collier and Kay penned their book *Greed Is Dead* (2021), during the onslaught of COVID-19. In their text, they assert that while the 2020s might represent "Peak Greed," the pressure of the COVID-19 pandemic is likely to return people from extreme individualism back to a sense of community (Collier and Kay 2021). They acknowledge that the combination of individual selfishness and over-confident top-down management has badly damaged societies, but they insist, the future can be different.

This was in 2021. As we look at the societal terrain in both the US and the UK, Peak Greed has far from taken a turn for the better. If anything, the COVID funds so generously doled out by governments plus the fear of uncertainty heightened by the pandemic has generated even greater corruption and greater greed.

Colliers and Kay's book was written to inspire a process of positive change and to provide ideas of how we, individuals, can participate in this change. Alas, the book focuses mostly on what they saw as impediments to a healthy society, many of which have not changed or, if anything, have worsened – CEO pay and bribery of the highest order being two prime examples.

## The Challenge of Leading

As a reminder, the main thesis of this book is that the prime leadership skill that is required, and required urgently, is courage. Courage to face reality and courage to deal with people's opposition and resistance to adaptation and transformation.

Throughout these pages, I have placed many corporations and industries under the magnifying glass only to reveal rampant corruption, dishonest and greedy leadership and cowardly complicit employees. As we reflect on the many stories, what is evident is that corporate leadership is in desperate need of both character and courage. CEOs and their leadership teams have a huge influence on the culture and the quality of employee behavior in their organizations – recall our discussions on authority in Chapter 8 – a responsibility they dare not ignore or forget.

As spelled out in several chapters, the role of organizational leadership is daunting as the challenges are immense and continue to escalate. Intense global competition and the speed of technological innovation and its impact create unique challenges that need to be navigated in and across increasingly complex and far-flung systems. Change is occurring so rapidly now that everything is in a continuous state of flux, impermanency and uncertainty. This change, as we have investigated from many angles, generates fear. Once there is fear our courage is challenged. Leaders' ability to manage their own anxiety in times of uncertainty and change has a significant impact on the organizational system – see the discussion on page 152, Self-Differentiation.

In the previous chapter, I set out several steps for cultivating or enhancing our capacity for courage. Those steps apply to us all including, and perhaps especially to, CEOs and their leadership teams. Further, I propose that leadership team discussions and meetings should always include the following questions:

- What change signals or new realities can we identify right now and how should we respond? Which ones can potentially impact the health of the organization? If the answer is unknown, appoint several people to investigate. Do not let these signals, no matter how subtle, drift away into oblivion.
- Is there any troubling or bad news that we fear or know of that should be shared and discussed?
- Are we sharing the right information with our employees at the right time? Do they feel a sense of personal agency associated with their jobs?
- Have we violated any ethical principle that we know of in the past week? Are any ethical challenges in front of us right now?
- How many of us feel stressed and how might we help one another to reduce this stress?
- What major decisions are we facing right now and are we choosing to act courageously?
- Are we cultivating character among our employees? Are we hiring based on character as much as on achievement and potential? What evidence do we have of this?

If one regularly added these critical discussions to the usual feedback on numbers, people and projects, what a difference that would make!

## Character – A Reminder

The Greek philosophers challenged us as to the kind of life we should choose to lead and were unequivocal in claiming that what makes us admirable human beings is the quality of our character. It is who we are, not what we have or what we have achieved, that matters. This quality, they said, is evident in the extent to which we practice the moral virtues (excellences) of prudence, courage, justice and temperance (moderation). The more we practice these virtues, the more ingrained they become, and over time, they shape and define us.

A person of character is someone who strives to make good choices, where "good," according to their definition, means choices that seek to advance well-being, flourishing and harmony. These kinds of choices are not easy ones as there is usually no one simple choice or decision that satisfies every situation and every stakeholder interest. Good choices require some combination of wisdom, discernment, prudence (practical reasoning), courage and justice. Good choices take effort, and as we know, when we are tired, stressed or afraid we don't want anything that requires effort. Part of character is persistence and fortitude, so it behooves us – personally and as leaders – to make the effort. It is also why we have leadership teams to support one another in making good choices during challenging times.

Becoming a good decision-maker requires consultation with others, reflection and self-awareness of our personal limitations as discussed in the previous three chapters. Our limitations include our fears and vulnerabilities, the need to be liked, our capacity to face the truth and our ability to claim our personal authority.

We also noted that a person who has a well-formed character is someone who acts as an autonomous agent. This means they are not only self-aware, but self-determining, and self-reflective. They are desirous of authoring their own lives by living from a place of inner freedom.

David Brooks, in his book titled *The Road to Character* (2015), refers to two opposing sides of our nature which he refers to as Adam I and Adam II. Adam I is the career-oriented, ambitious side and Adam II is the internal side focused on moral qualities and the building of character.

Brooks's book excoriates the traits associated with Adam I and exalts the tendencies of Adam II. He claims that we all need to focus on the Adam II side of our natures otherwise we will slide into self-satisfied moral mediocrity. He discusses our desire to have people think well of us and claims that character is developed once we engage in the moral struggle with ourselves. He proposes that we ask what life wants to express through us and stresses the importance of developing our inner selves along with a robust attitude to life.

Character, according to Brooks, results from our own inner confrontation wherein we struggle with our weaknesses. It comes from self-conquest and develops due to self-control, self-mastery and self-examination along with the important element of humility.

So, nothing new here, just a reworking of the ideas of the early Greeks, including the very masculine bias with a twenty-first century twist. Brooks does not go deeply into how challenging it is to be a person of character and to be self-defining in a world that is so polarized and so intent on judging and negating people who do not conform with their own ideas or opinions.

## Self-Differentiation

In Chapter 1, we discussed Edwin Friedman and how he critiqued American leaders as showing a general failure of nerve to be self-differentiating and self-determining.

Self-differentiation is about being rooted in oneself rather than being fixated and dependent upon one's followers. Leaders, Friedman claimed, must rise above the fear of standing alone. They must recognize that saboteurs – those terrified of change – are always lurking. They must be their own well-differentiated selves who can admit mistakes without cowering to a storm of protest. They need to be able to hold their own ground and not lose their identity to the mob. They also need courage to have difficult conversations around ethical and moral matters and to hold steady in the face of resistance and even personal attack.

### *The Differentiated Self*

A big question is how one develops this differentiated self. For guidance we turn to Dr. Murray Bowen's Family Systems Theory as explained by Roberta Gilbert, MD, in her book, *Extraordinary Leadership: Thinking Systems, Making a Difference* 2009.

According to Family Systems Theory, it is within the family system that we learn and develop our anxiety management strategies. Many adults still use these strategies developed in childhood often without being aware of how conditioned and reactive their responses are.

Gilbert describes the differences in people's anxiety management strategies and their impact on effective leadership. As we know, our strategies include fight, flight, freeze, over-or-under compensation or the strategy of triangulation which means roping in some outsider or third party for assistance or relief.

For many adults in the West, institutions, organizations and corporations of all sizes have come to replace the family system as the primary relational context. Think of how many people say how much they appreciate and want a family culture at work. Of course, many organizations, especially bureaucracies, do not meet people's relational needs but that does not take away their desire nor stop them from acting out at work as if they were partaking in a family drama.

Gilbert refers to fusion as the level of interdependency and reactivity of family members to one another (Gilbert 2009, 7). The greater the fusion within the system, the greater the emotional charge among its members and the greater their reactivity. Groups use fusions to eliminate anxiety, but the intensity and expectations stimulated by fusion often create added anxiety of its own.

According to Family Systems Theory, the quality of people's relationships and the difference in people's ability to adapt in life are dependent on their emotional maturity as measured by their ability to self-differentiate. Self-differentiation is measured by the individual's ability to contain his or her emotions, and not to succumb to old family-learned patterns and to get dragged into the emotional reactivity of others. A self-differentiated individual can stand apart from the group and yet still be part of it. The self-differentiated individual can stand alone. For the leader, self-differentiation means being able to retain one's executive functioning without succumbing to the expectations and emotional needs, and sometimes the attempted emotional blackmailing, by the group.

## Scale of Differentiation

The scale of self-differentiation maps the extent to which a person's emotions and intellect are fused. On the scale, the levels of functioning are like the rungs of a ladder that go between two columns of emotion and intellect from a hypothetical zero to 100. At the bottom of the ladder emotions and intellect are fused; that is, all intellectual functioning is driven by emotions. In the middle this is less so, and at higher levels emotions and the intellect are more separate.

What must be made clear is that emotions are not bad. They are important, are needed and must be heeded. Where they take over one's ability to make thoughtful decisions, or where they overwhelm one's ability to think clearly and rationally, they do not serve us well. Leaders who are emotionally driven or easily emotionally swayed are unlikely to be good decision-makers or good at handling uncertainty or leading change.

At lower levels of the scale, all behavior and all thinking are emotionally driven; people are undifferentiated and in effect have never left home. Here emotions are so strong that independent thinking is not possible. Decision-making is impaired, behavior is impulsive and relationship difficulties are rife. Leaders who fall into this category avoid conflict, want to be loved by others, have poor boundaries and become defensive when challenged (Anderson and Hamman 2024).

As one moves up the ladder there is less ambient anxiety, relationships work better and people are freer to be their individual selves.

The higher up the ladder, the more people are self-differentiated and as such more secure. They act according to their principles rather than their or anyone else's emotions. The more self-differentiated one is, the more one can regulate one's anxiety and the more personal authority one claims.

According to Bowen, based on his research and experience, the majority of people are below 40 on the scale. He claimed that if one ever met someone at 50, one was lucky, and someone at 75 on the scale would only come along once in every few hundred years (Gilbert 2009, 72). Bowen's findings support Friedman's critique that very few leaders are self-differentiating and self-determining.

## Self-Differentiation and Effective Leadership

Gilbert, like Friedman, claims that containing one's anxiety is a critical element of effective leadership. Leaders who are emotionally driven and cannot manage their own anxiety and, worse still, are unaware of the strategies they adopt, will default to old patterns of reactivity which has a negative impact on their ability to lead the group or organization.

Effective, high functioning leaders rank higher on the scale. They lead by well-thought-through principles. They are not easily swayed by others, and they are not dependent on the approval of others.

Self-differentiation enables the leader to hold boundaries, not be overwhelmed by emotional processes, not be dependent on the approval of others, and not to adopt authoritarian means especially in challenging times as a means of squelching conflict.

For leaders to be able to lead effectively, especially during times of change where there is heightened anxiety, they need to stand emotionally apart from the system while remaining in relationship with it. They must avoid getting caught up in the anxiety management strategies of the group and they must have outgrown some of the emotional reactions learned from their own family system and that are created by the organization.

Leaders must be their own well-differentiated selves admitting mistakes without cowering to a storm of protest. They need to have the courage to challenge a group and break the pact of collusion, and create new precedents, new norms and new conventions. They also need to accept that sabotage comes with the territory and that they need to be able to withstand its divisiveness and its intensity.

If leaders cannot be self-differentiating and self-determining they will be unable to raise the organizational system to a higher level of functioning and it will simply lurch from one state of reactivity and resistance to change to the next. High resistance to change will remain an impediment to healthy growth. Effective leaders are able to transform their systems through continuous adaptation.

To become a self-differentiating leader requires self-examination, self-mastery and courage!

## Climate and Culture

The CEO is responsible for establishing the climate of the organization. This means he or she sets the tone, the spirit, values, attitudes and style of communication. For example, if the CEO parks his yellow, convertible Ferrari in a specially designated lot in front of the head office building, this communicates oceans to employees as well as customers, and suppliers. The climate is obvious!

The climate is the critical backdrop to the organization's culture. The organization's culture is the embodied values, principles and practices underlying the social fabric of an organization. It refers to the behaviors that flow from the established climate. A company's culture unites people around shared assumptions, beliefs and practices. Reward systems, such as stock options, and both implicit and explicit rules relating to behavior have a huge impact on the organizational culture.

The leadership team typically takes their cues from the CEO. If the CEO is a numbers person, everything will be about the numbers. If the CEO is brash, endorses risk-taking and panders to the stock analysts and stockholders or those who have money, the leadership team will be pressed to do the same.

**Rite Aid's Demise**

Based on multiple reports in the media, it seems that Martin Grass, CEO of Rite Aid, lived a life of flagrant luxury that included, among other things, daily commutes via private helicopter to the company's Camp Hill, Pennsylvania headquarters. In 1998, Grass and his executive team engaged in a massive fraud which involved creating a complex web of fictitious financial statements which resulted in artificially inflating Rite Aid's net earnings to the tune of $1.6 billion.

Both Grass and the executives who participated in the fraud were given prison sentences.

In March 2023, the U.S. Justice Department, based on whistleblower information, found that for a period of at least five years Rite Aid had filled "hundreds of thousands" of illegal prescriptions for drugs including opioids. In October 2023, Rite Aid filed for bankruptcy.

If the CEO lacks candor, shies away from difficult conversations and is economical with the truth, members of the leadership team are likely to follow suit. If, by contrast, the CEO is self-determining, courageous, faces unpalatable truths, is open and is prepared to be vulnerable and transparent, members of the leadership team will emulate this behavior. Alas, as we know, there will always be an outlier or two.

The crucial question for every CEO and his or her leadership team member is do they have character – good, old fashioned character ala the Greeks as we have discussed? Are they honorable and courageous and do they endeavor to use the organization to advance goodness and to make the world a better place for well-being and flourishing? Or is it all about the bottom line, about how much money they have, their gargantuan salary packages, their retirement accounts and the multiple things they can afford?

I concur with many other critics that the invention of stock options must be one of the most ethically damaging inventions ever concocted. It has a huge impact on the organization's culture and unfortunately fosters the "numbers are all that matter" attitude.

In my leadership consulting and coaching experience, I continue to be astounded by the fixation people have on the share price once they hold company stock. I have noticed how they now only care about revenue and profits, rather than quality and service. Sell to anyone, anyhow is the slogan right down the line. Some of them have the stock ticker price window open all day and they check the price as often as they do Instagram or Facebook. With this mindset why would they challenge the CEO and the leadership team if they were fiddling the books? In fact, why not help by fiddling the books themselves?

Individualism and materialism have undoubtedly fostered a culture of greed. Everyone wants more, more money, more things, more convenience and more attention. And everyone seems to fear that they won't have enough. Few people seem to escape this dynamic.

## A Culture of Fear

As we review the demands of leadership, the need for self-differentiation and the many barriers to courageous behavior, we must consider the nature of organizational fear. A review of the corporate scandals provides ample evidence of the organizational (group) cultural pressure to conform and to be silent. Outspokenness is not welcomed. As Marianne Jennings mentions in her book referenced earlier, *The Seven Signs of Ethical Collapse*, a culture of fear prevails in way too many organizations. And where a culture of fear exists, courage is stifled.

All organizations are containers of fear. This is a natural phenomenon and not specific to any one type of organization although some organizations, due to their culture and internal dynamics, experience a greater intensity of fear than others. Here are some components of the fear element ever present in organizational life:

- People are inherently anxious creatures, and they bring with them their existential fear about living and dying.
- They fear being overwhelmed by the group and losing their voice or independence.
- They fear whether they will meet organizational goals and performance standards.
- They fear whether other people in the organization will like them even when they insist, they do not care.
- They fear whether the job they have is really going to take them where they want to be, even when they are unsure where that is.
- They fear the power of their superiors who can radically influence their future. (We discussed the fear of authority in Chapter 3.)
- They fear being laid off when it does not suit them.
- They fear being their full selves at work lest this challenges cultural norms.

It must be noted that members of the leadership team are not immune to some of these fears. In fact, due to their position and visibility, their fears around meeting competence and performance expectations are likely to be higher than most employees. This is understandable. Once again, self-awareness and the courage to own one's fears are paramount. Failure to do so will affect the team members' abilities to self-differentiate.

So, what is the lesson for us here? Organizational life raises the *ante* when it comes to fear. It is hard to be courageous or ethical when one is experiencing fear, and even more so when one is in denial that one is in fear. Fear prompts the survival instinct which is about self-preservation at all costs. From a leadership perspective, a major challenge is how to create a climate and culture that reduces levels of fear in the system and how to re-channel the energy of fear into creativity. One major influencing factor is the extent to which leaders regulate their own anxiety as discussed under self-differentiation above.

## Fear and Power – The Deadly Mix

Leadership is a process of influence. Leaders use a variety of tactics to exercise that influence. The desired outcome is buy-in and commitment. This is not always readily attained no matter how well meaning and how open and power-sharing the leader is inclined to be.

What is of relevance for our discussions is how the leader holds his or her power and how he or she uses it. If a leader identifies with his or her power, if it is a defining source of self-esteem, it is likely to be abused. If a leader is inclined to use "power over" others, he or she is likely to be authoritarian and controlling. If a leader uses power manipulatively and fosters a highly political work environment, this reflects the leader's emotional insecurity and immaturity, poor ego strength and limited psychological capacity.

By contrast, if a leader encourages others to participate in the power they have, it is highly probable that they will achieve more and that work will be more effective all round. Empowering workers to assume more responsibility invariably results in a more harmonious and effective work environment. Encouraging others to feel they can succeed, thus enhancing their sense of self-efficacy, helps them to grow and to develop and evolve more complex psychological structures.

Leaders who understand the dynamics of authority will be sensitive to the way they use their power and the strategies of influence they deploy. This requires psychological strength and courage, especially in the face of resistance, in whatever form that might take.

Fear is at the base of all that is destructive and unethical. Fear leads to greedy, corrupt, abusive, deceitful, intemperate, callous and inconsistent actions. Fear is the root cause of many irrational, hasty, thoughtless and unkind behaviors. Fear-based actions and behaviors are always power-seeking. Power-seeking behavior stems from a desperate desire for control. People imagine that when they have control, they can manage or get rid of their fear and all the things that make them fearful. This is of course an illusion.

The source of hubris is fear, not confidence. Bullies are deeply fearful. Domineering, arrogant, strident, rigid and evil people are fearful. Narcissists fear how empty they feel inside. Fearful people in positions of power are dangerous because they use their power dangerously. During times of radical uncertainty and change they become even more dangerous as they feel less in control and even more exposed for not knowing all the answers (Beerel 2009).

Leaders often set themselves up to be perfect, indestructible and self-sufficient. Once they attain power, many enjoy its benefits and invariably, through lack of character, a low sense of self-worth and poor self-discipline, they want more, and more. Power is the ultimate aphrodisiac. It can be as addictive and as deadly as fentanyl. Our media is filled with stories of power addicts. We just have other names for them. Sadly, many of them are CEOs.

Once a leader who has the power to influence others is hooked, the consequences are usually dire. Their personal image management takes a great deal of energy and invites fear as to whether it is sustainable or not. They question whether they will be found out to be less perfect, brave, or smart than they have everyone believe.

The fear-power dynamic makes everyone a victim. Those in power are victims to the power plays required to hold on to their power. Those not in power, but anxious to participate in the power hierarchy, are victim to the power plays required to get power. Those without power or not aspiring to have power become a victim to those who have or aspire to have power.

A culture of fear where power dynamics reign supreme destroys all ethical sensitivity and moral courage. Fear dulls sensitivity. Fear discourages imaginative thinking, limits the capacity to observe and learn, and depresses the human spirit. A culture of fear does not promote creativity or adaptation. A culture of fear supports resistance to change. Leaders who promote a culture of fear destroy the healthy spirit of the organization and resort to power for abusive purposes (Beerel 2009).

The leader and his or her leadership team need to be highly sensitive to the issue of power, how they hold it and how it is interpreted by others. They must have the courage to operate from their personal power rather than their positional power and above all they must have the courage to work with their own fears and to be compassionate with the fears of others. They should also understand that real power is found in inner freedom, and that takes courage!

## The System – Bad Barrels Create Bad Apples

In Philip Zimbardo's chilling book *The Lucifer Effect: How Good People Turn Evil*, 2007, he spells out the details of the Stanford Prison Experiment (SPE), discussed in Chapter 7, and highlights the power of the System. It is the System, he insists, that creates the Situation in which the individual finds him or herself. Social psychology research agrees in that it shows that situational power triumphs over individual power almost every time. Simply put, bad systems create bad situations which create bad people with bad behaviors. Bad systems corrupt even good people.

Bad barrels create bad apples. We talk about bad apples, seek them out and then prosecute them which serves to deflect from the fact that they are the product of bad systems. Look at how often individuals are singled out as being the problem, and are then punished, while the System creators look on with deceitful self-satisfaction.

**Definition of Evil**

> Evil consists in intentionally behaving in ways that harm, abuse, demean, dehumanize, or destroy innocent others – or using one's authority and systemic power to encourage or permit others to do so on your behalf.
>
> (Zimbardo 2008, 5)

What if we were to put the System on trial? Who are the barrel makers? They are the power elite. They are the people at the head of the hierarchy, the senior members of government, the politicians and the CEO and his or her leadership team. The power elite are those who in one way or another create the conditions of life for their constituents. They are the group that readily focus on the "who" question, who should be blamed, who should take the fall or who was the bad apple while they smugly exonerate themselves from all culpability. How many organizations are not guilty of this dynamic? Recall Boeing in Chapter 4 and how they blamed two employees for deceiving the FAA about the 737 MAX flight control system. And how many CEOs and leadership teams don't encourage fierce competition, arrogance and aggressiveness? I could surely name a few.

We need to change the question, says Zimbardo, from "who was the perpetrator?" to "what were the conditions that contributed to certain behaviors or reactions?" We need to review the combined complicity of those in charge of creating a dysfunctional system that creates the circumstances where people lose their sense of self. Where the System owns them, and they become dead to themselves. Remember *1984*!

Zimbardo explains how the System creates rules and roles. And that in a system the rules readily take on a life of their own. He also mentions how quickly people step into their assigned roles and how many are unable to shake off those roles even when the role expectations include unethical conformance, corruption and/or evil. Put someone in a uniform and in no time their roles suppress their individuality. Think of the Nazi guards, Stalin's henchmen, and closer to home, think of the brutality of some members of the police force. Once the students assigned as guards in the SPE donned their uniforms, things changed drastically.

Zimbardo, who investigated the torture and prison abuse at Abu Ghraib,[2] draws frightening parallels between the guard-prisoner dynamic there and that of the SPE.

If one reads the details of the SPE described in Zimbardo's book, we see how those subjected to the power elites in the experiment (fellow students) either had mental breakdowns or became mindlessly obedient, enduring horrific intimidation and torture with minimal rebellion.

Zimbardo states that because the System has an enormous part to play in affecting people's behavior this does NOT excuse or condone their actions. It merely provides a deeper understanding of how the line between good and evil is crossed.

Zimbardo ends his book with advice on how not to lose oneself to the power of the System. Four things stand out: remaining continuously mindful, practicing self-awareness, exercising critical thinking and holding onto one's personal authority. All themes we have discussed throughout the chapters of this book.

The reflection for the leadership team here is obvious: what type of system are you creating? Are domination, political maneuvering and fear part of the culture, or is your system one that promotes freedom, growth, creativity and courage?

## Inspiring People to Speak Up

In 2006, Mary Gentile, PhD, a former professor at Darden University, launched an innovative business leadership program titled "Giving Voice to Values" (GVV). Gentile responded to the spate of corporate misdemeanors between the 1990s and early 2000s by taking a different approach to that of typical business ethics classes. Gentile's main premise is that most people want to speak up when they encounter unethical behaviors at work but refrain from doing so as they believe they cannot make a difference – recall the self-efficacy issue we discussed in Chapter 7.

In the GVV program, business students are taught how to develop scripts and implementation plans for giving voice to their values when they experience a values conflict. The idea is to build students' confidence and to develop their skills of speaking up. The program places great emphasis on taking positive action by communicating through constructive engagement and persuasion.

In her program, Gentile eschews using ethical principles as guidelines or moral rules. She emphasizes the importance of how the person feels about business behaviors, and provided there is some ethical issue at stake – helping students define what is ethical she does not clearly explain – they are encouraged to voice their concerns.

While I applaud Gentile for coming up with a program that is aimed at advancing people's courage – she does not use this term! – I have some reservations about the program. These include her lack of any discussion of making this GVV part of a person's character. Speaking up – when appropriate – should become part of who one is and not something one does when it suits one. She also does not discuss the issue of courage which is clearly what this program is about.

My bigger concern is that the emphasis on personal values can make the conversation a highly relativistic one. Voicing my values becomes an issue about me and what I value rather than the ethical principles that are being violated. A conversation focused on values is likely to arouse people's defenses as there is now a contest between "your values and mine." By contrast, a conversation that explores the ethical principles at stake not only is more open and less adversarial, but enables both parties to learn something from the discussion.[3]

I wholly support Gentile's intention which is to raise cultural awareness when there is discordance or when people want to discuss goodness and rightness at work. As I mentioned in Chapter 4, instead of having whistleblower hotlines and ethics seminars, organizational leaders should foster a culture of open communication where people can dialogue freely around ethical principles and behaviors in the workplace. They should encourage people to challenge decisions or question actions that appear any way unethical.

## Your Turn

### *Courage Reflection for the Leadership Team*

Here is a list of questions that a leader and his or her team may wish to pose to themselves – individually in private reflection, together as a group, or both:

- How important is your being a leader with authority to your sense of self-esteem?
- Do you reflect on how you use your power?
- Are you someone who has a demonstrable character and who role-models courage? What is the evidence?
- How well do you deal with uncertainty and change?
- Even though you have opportunities in your position, are you able to resist temptation?
- Do you mostly make good choices where good means advancing well-being and flourishing of those you impact?
- Would you describe yourself as a self-differentiating leader?
- Are you able to look at and even discuss your fears as a leader?
- Do you promote justice at work? Can you provide evidence of this?
- Are you able to practice moderation when it comes to pay or money matters?
- Are you transparent about any conflicts of interest?
- Are you someone who relies mostly on your personal authority and not on your formal authority or the authority of others?
- Do you avoid difficult conversations? Can you be candid?
- Do you encourage openness and candor at work?
- Does your leadership team regularly discuss its fears?
- Does the leadership team regularly discuss both personal and organizational challenges around uncertainty and change?
- How would you describe your System?

If your leadership team could carry out this reflection regularly everyone will gain – you, your family, your organization and our society. Is that not worth it?

## Notes

1. US Senator Bob Menendez was found guilty of bribery by accepting gold bars, a Mercedes car and hundreds of thousands of dollars cash to act on behalf of business associates and foreign governments. Menendez is the former chair of the Senate foreign relations committee. *Financial Times*, July 20–21, 2024.
2. The George W. Bush administration said that the abuses at Abu Ghraib were isolated incidents and not indicative of US policy. This was disputed by humanitarian organizations including the Red Cross, Amnesty International and Human Rights Watch; these organizations stated that the abuses at Abu Ghraib were part of a wider pattern of torture and brutal treatment at American overseas detention centers, including those in Iraq, in Afghanistan and at Guantanamo Bay. Documents popularly known as the Torture Memos came to light a few years later. These documents, prepared in the months leading up to the 2003 invasion of Iraq by the United States Department of Justice, authorized certain "enhanced interrogation techniques" (generally held to involve torture) of foreign detainees. The memoranda also argued that international humanitarian laws, such as the Geneva Conventions, did not apply to American interrogators overseas. Several subsequent US Supreme Court decisions, including *Hamdan v. Rumsfeld* (2006), have overturned Bush administration policy, ruling that the Geneva Conventions do apply. https://en.wikipedia.org/wiki/Abu_Ghraib_torture_and_prisoner_abuse.
3. I discuss how to have difficult conversations about ethical issues in my book *Ethical Leadership and Global Capitalism: A Guide to Good Practice* (Abingdon, Oxon: Routledge, 2020), 299–302.

## References

Anderson, Derek W., and Jaco J. Hamman. 2024. *The Essence of Leadership: Maintaining Emotional Independence in Situations Requiring Change*. New York: Routledge.

Beerel, Annabel. 2009. *Leadership and Change Management*. London, UK: Sage Publications.

Brooks, David. 2015. *The Road to Character*. New York: Ransom House.

Collier, Paul, and John Kay. 2021. *Greed Is Dead: Politics After Individualism*. New York: Penguin Books.

Gilbert, Roberta M. 2009. *Extraordinary Leadership*. Falls Church, VA: Leading Systems Press.

Jennings, Marianne M. 2006. *The Seven Signs of Ethical Collapse*. New York: St. Martin's Press.

Newton, Lisa H. 2006. *Permission to Steal*. Malden, MA: Blackwell Publishing.

Zimbardo, Philip. 2008. *The Lucifer Effect*. New York: Random House Trade Paperbacks.

## Recommended Reading

Beerel, Annabel. 2020. *Ethical Leadership and Global Capitalism: A Guide to Good Practice*. Abingdon, Oxon: Routledge.
Beerel, Annabel. 2021. *Rethinking Leadership: A Critique of Contemporary Theories*. Abingdon, Oxon: Routledge.
Miller, Christian B. 2018. *The Character Gap*. Oxford, UK: The Oxford University Press.
Ryan, Kathleen D., and Daniel K. Oestreich. 1998. *Driving Fear Out of the Workplace*. San Francisco, CA: Jossey-Bass.

# Chapter 10

# Primary Research Results

**Part A Review of Student and Adult Courage Questionnaires with a View to Their Relationship to Courage**

## Objectives of Survey Review

The objective of this chapter is to elicit what the responses to the Courage surveys reveal regarding their understanding and appreciation of the concept and practice of courage. I also attempt to glean whether courage is a factor that plays a significant or at least some intentional role in survey participants' lives.

## Courage Framework Reminder from Chapter 5

- Courage is a moral virtue and as such is an end in itself. It is not done for the sake of anything else other than to advance goodness, flourishing and well-being. It is a selfless act.
- Courage lies in its wisdom, not its bravado. It is a choice resulting from a discernment guided by wisdom and prudence.
- Courage is not fickle and impetuous – it is the act of a person with a courageous character.
- Courage is the willingness and a commitment to act in the face of extreme danger.
- It is the mean between cowardice and over-confidence.
- Courage is not fearlessness, bravado or daring.
- Courage is always mediated by reason.
- Courage exhibits fortitude and endurance and often patience.

DOI: 10.4324/9781003459644-11

- There is a nobility and beauty about courage in that it is about facing the truth of a situation.
- Courage means confronting a challenge or conflict that is non-lifegiving and seeking to give it life.
- There is a self-transcendence in courage where one is called to act from one's highest self. It is a call from the soul.

## Definition of Courage

Courage is a trait of character that motivates and guides a willingness to rationally, selflessly and actively confront danger, adversity, severe hardship or radical uncertainty despite great personal risk in the service of advancing goodness and well-being.

## Conclusions Drawn from Survey findings

Below are the overall conclusions drawn regarding students and adult responses to the surveys.

Sample size – 45 students and 45 adults
Gender: male 25% female 75%
Age groups of adults, students (all undergraduates) unknown:

| <30 | 0 |
|---|---|
| 31–40 | 5% |
| 41–50 | 35% |
| 51–60 | 40% |
| >60 | 20% |

The adult questionnaire differed slightly to that of the students in that they were asked four questions not posed to the students, hence the slight difference in the numbering.

### *Overall Conclusions*

- Courage as a concept is poorly understood. It is not something that people readily see in themselves or in others.
- Respondents do not uphold courage as a desirable personal trait or as an important aspect of daily living. It is not in their daily consciousness, nor is it part of their regular dialogue or reflection.
- The sample groups failed to identify any general role models or any role models in business that stood out for their courageous character.

- In answering the surveys, respondents contradicted themselves multiple times. For example, they claimed (68%) that they refrained from speaking the truth so as not to hurt others, yet they gave themselves much higher scores when it came to challenging authority and holding difficult conversations, which are all about challenging people about the truth.
- The importance of being liked by others was scored highly, which confirms the Stage 3 Thinking we discussed in Chapter 7. The need to be liked is a great inhibitor to being self-determining and courageous, yet many respondents claimed to have been whistleblowers.
- Respondents' dislike of uncertainty confirms why people cede their authority to others and why few people are truly courageous.
- A further contradiction noted is that 50% responded that they "only sometimes" could go against what other people were prompting them to do even if they disagreed with it, yet 100% of respondents answered that they were accountable people.

These are some of the broad conclusions drawn from the responses. What is quite clear is that courage is not a well-known concept to the respondents, and in many cases is poorly comprehended and minimally practiced.

## Detailed Analysis of Responses Based on the Courage Framework

1. **Who stands out as a person of courage? (Q. 1 students, Q. 3 adults)**

   **Purpose of question:**
   To inquire who people see as role models and to infer what qualities they admire. Could courage be one of them?

   **Comments:**
   One would hope that in a culture such as the US that promotes (or talks about) liberalism, justice and democratic values there would be many positive public figure role models. Not so. Most (61%) of student respondents chose family members, especially parents, as being those who role-model courage and 25% of adult respondents chose likewise.

   One might harbor some hope from these results that, in the case of the students, parents are helping the young develop their character where they are in some way virtuous and especially courageous. Responses to the rest of the questions do not support this hope or inference.

   In the case of the adult questionnaire, besides parents, a wide variety of names were offered where no one person stood out. What one might infer is that respondents selected someone who inspired them or of whom they had heard positive stories or comments which prompted them to choose these names. Examples included Melinda Gates, Mahatma Gandhi, Martin Luther King, my youngest child, Michelle Obama.

**Conclusion:**
No strong public role models stand out and evidence of courageous role models is lacking.

2. **What do you think is the key characteristic of a courageous person? (Q.2 students, Q. 4 adults)**

| Students | Adults |
|---|---|
| Selflessness | kindness and patience |
| Kindness | integrity |
| Strength | perseverance |

Kindness was the most popular response among both adults and students.

One adult responded: "Conviction in what is just and a willingness to act on that conviction in the service of something greater than themselves."

This respondent clearly has a good grasp of courage.

**Purpose of question:**
To inquire as to how people understand the concept of courage and its elements.

**Comments:**
While selflessness, patience and perseverance are needed to be courageous, they fall short of the defining criteria of courage.

Note:
Integrity is a popular word that people use as a synonym for just about anything – honesty, being moral, being reliable, being fair.

What integrity means is being whole, being an integrated person, being fully who you are. While courage includes some of this to be sure, its emphasis lies in our living out of our higher selves. It is a transcendent value.

Courageous people do not just have strength of character – so did Napoleon and Hitler – they have strength of character in the service of goodness and in order to take on what is non-lifegiving regardless of the personal cost tempered by wisdom and prudence.

**Conclusion:**
There is some understanding of the make-up of courage but key elements, such as virtuous intention and motivation, are missing.

3. **Can you name any business leaders who role-model courage? (Q. 3 students, Q.5 adults)**

No one – students 50% and adults 20%

Steve Jobs and Elon Musk received a few votes by both students and adults (5,3) and then there was a wide range of names including Ellen DeGeneres, Warren Buffet, Michelle Obama and Hillary Clinton.

**Purpose of question:**
To inquire whether courage is a feature of business leaders.

**Comment and Conclusion:**
Clearly no business leaders stand out as courageous role models. Steve Jobs was a remarkable visionary entrepreneur who certainly took some risks and radically impacted the technology industry. He had both foresight and charisma. According to many articles about him, he was a nightmare to work with – ego-centered, selfish and tyrannical. He was also very lucky in that his timing was right.

Elon Musk's colors are becoming all too obvious with his latest stance on antisemitism. It would be hard to call him courageous. He has indeed broken some new ground with his ideas, many of which have been funded by the taxpayer.

4. **Do you find it difficult to live with uncertainty? (Q. 4 students, Q.6 adults)**
Responses: students yes 75%, adults yes 42%, and 23% sort-of = 75%

**Purpose of question:**
To inquire whether respondents are intolerant or avoid uncertainty as being able to deal with uncertainty is an important element of courage.

**Comments:**
Based on the study of groups (psychologist Wilfred Bion), studies of leadership (many) and studies of moral disengagement (Albert Bandura), a high percentage of people have great anxiety during times of uncertainty. These psychologists point out how fearful people become and how hastily they replace uncertainty with something that provides certainty no matter how ill-conceived, facile or fallacious it might be. Alternatively, they demand that certainty be provided by an authority figure. This of course frequently results in unethical behavior by either the person or the authority figure.

Being able to act effectively during times of high uncertainty is one of the hallmarks of courage. If things are certain and future outcomes are clear, courage is not usually needed but rather an effective strategy.

**Conclusion:**
The dislike of uncertainty is not surprising. Uncertainty brings up anxiety and most people are not good at handling anxiety. As a result, we find a "fear project" – something or someone to blame or scapegoat – that we can fight, disparage, disregard or destroy (Paul Tillich, *The Courage to Be* (1952) – discussed in Chapter 6.

5. **Do you often refrain from speaking the truth for fear of angering or upsetting others? (Q.5 students, Q.7 adults)**
Responses: students yes 68%, adults 68%

**Purpose of question:**
To inquire into respondents' courage to be authentic and to speak the truth.

**Comments:**
The link between this question and courage is clear. Of course, how one speaks the truth (style and manner) and when (timing) without sounding self-righteous are important.

Courage is not inconsistent. It always shines its light on the truth. So being courageous includes being able to speak the truth consistently.

**Conclusion:**
We see here that a high percentage of people refrain from being authentic and true. It is surprising that both the students and the adults reflect the same level of hesitancy. And then maybe it is not surprising as we recall our discussion on Stage 3 Thinking.

6. **Have you ever confronted someone with more power than you on what you believed was an ethical issue? (Q. 6 students, Q. 8 adults)**
Responses: students yes 75%, adults yes 78%

**Purpose of question:**
This is similar to the previous question except here we inquire into whether respondents have the courage to speak truth to power.

**Comments:**
As commented earlier, the answers here contradict the previous question. In that case only 68% would speak the truth and yet here >=75% of respondents are willing to speak truth to power.

**Conclusion:**
It appears that neither the students nor the adults reflect on the circumstances and the extent to which they are able to courageously tell the truth.

7. **Have you ever been a whistleblower, or have you openly supported whistleblowers? (Q. 7 students, Q.10 adults)**
Responses: students yes – 21%, adults yes – 70%

**Purpose of question:**
To inquire as to whether respondents have courage regarding whistleblowing.

**Comments:**
Whistleblower research reports that less than 15% of people have the courage to be whistleblowers and less than 20% support them. Refer several texts on whistleblowing – Tom Mueller, C. Fred Alford and others.

This means that 21% for whistleblowing – or 1 in 5 – seems high and 70% seems astronomical! It would be interesting to know what the adults defined as whistleblowing, the details of the misdemeanors and in what context they blew the whistle.

For adults, the results also contradict the response to Question 4 regarding speaking the truth where 68% said they refrained from doing so as not to hurt others, yet here they state being prepared to be whistleblowers or to support them!?

**Conclusion:**
A contradiction?

8. **Have you found yourself in an unhealthy, toxic, or abusive situation because you need the work or a job? (Q. 8 students, Q.11 adults)**
Responses: students yes – 32%, adults 70%

**Purpose of question:**
To inquire the extent to which people might be morally compromised at work.

**Comments:**
Under social agentic theory, psychologist Albert Bandura (refer Chapter 7) explains how people who are disaffected feel less like moral agents and more readily engage in moral disengagement.

Social agentic theory describes an individual's ability to feel they have control over their lives, and that when they do something, they can influence the outcome. In cases where people do not experience this self-efficacy, they become disengaged and disinterested. They defer to others, especially those in authority, and they perform like robots – they just get the job done.

Bandura describes how many organizations, especially large bureaucracies, create these conditions where people feel powerless, and so their sense of any moral agency or accountability becomes totally disengaged.

Adult responses are higher than students as clearly, they have worked longer. One wonders whether their claim to have challenged those in power and to support whistleblowers really holds true if they had to stay in their toxic jobs.

**Conclusion:**
Stuck in a toxic workplace discourages courageous action of every kind and makes it very difficult for people to stand up or to stand out. It is certainly not an easy platform for whistleblowing.

9. **How much do you care whether other people admire you? (Q.9 students, Q. 12 adults)**
Responses: students >76% want to be admired, adults >65%

**Purpose of question:**
To gage the extent to which people are influenced by the need to be liked.

**Comments:**
Refer to Stage 3 Thinking – Chapter 7.

According to psychologist Robert Kegan, individuals in Stage 3 cannot reflect on emotions, feelings and situations. Everything experienced is part of a reality which is embedded in their relationship with others (Kegan 1982).

People in Stage 3 are unable to express anger as that might risk interpersonal relations and it would amount to a declaration that the person is a self apart from the relationship. Here the person is always attentive to the external world, where there is no possibility of reflection on personal obligation, satisfactions or purposes in life. Individual choice or moral conscience or obligation are totally repressed or denied in the service of the collective. Stage 3 people have no moral values apart from those of the group. Conforming, belonging and affiliation with the group are the only reality. All cognitive or emotional conflict is totally intolerable. Fear of loss of belonging is the main motivator or drive. Moral courage is not possible at this stage.

Lawrence Kohlberg's stages of moral development outline 6 stages that define increasing levels of maturity and complexity in moral reasoning.

His Stage 3 thinking is where the individual is preoccupied with being loyal to the group, conforming to their norms, and being accepted by others. At this point the person has a limited appreciation of situations as viewed by others and assumes that everyone has a similar outlook. Approval by the group is essential regardless of the consequences. The individual readily subordinates his or her own needs to the group (discussed in Chapter 7).

**Conclusion:**
There is very little possibility of being courageous with a Stage 3 mindset.

10. **Do you love the work you do? (Q. 10 students, Q. 15 adults)**
    Reponses: students yes 71%, adults 68%

    **Purpose of question:**
    To inquire into the potential moral engagement at work.

    **Conclusion:**
    Not much new one can conclude here.

11. **Are you able to initiate and follow through on difficult conversations? (Q. 11 students, Q. 13 adults)**
    Responses: students yes 71%, adults yes – 93%

    **Purpose of question:**
    To inquire whether respondents can be self-determining and engage in disagreement with others.

    **Comments:**
    This question was posed to tease out any contradiction with the question of being able to speak the truth (Q. 4) even if it might hurt others.

    The responses were: both students and adults at 68% refrain from speaking the truth, yet here they claim to be able to have difficult conversations.

    **Conclusion:**
    We note again the lack of reflectiveness of respondents, especially the adults.

12. **Do you have any defining principles that guide your choices by which you live, or does it depend on the situation? (Q. 12 students, Q. 16 adults)**
Responses: students yes 46%, adults yes 72%

**Purpose of question:**
To inquire whether any moral principle or moral virtues guide people's choices in life.

**Comments:**
Based on the several contradictions identified so far one might question whether those who say they live by certain principles do so consistently. One of the hallmarks of a courageous person is their consistency. They live for and by the truth and are always prepared to make sacrifices to see it manifest.

**Conclusion:**
Kohlberg's research and that done by others indicate that few people live consistently according to principles and certainly not young adults.

13. **If you become aware of someone doing something unethical, even if you are not directly involved, do you challenge them? (Q.13 students, Q. 17 adults)**
Reponses: students yes 61%, adults yes 60%

**Purpose of question:**
To inquire whether respondents have the courage to challenge others.

**Comments:**
This question is like the one where respondents were asked whether they would challenge someone in power who had done something unethical.

Those responses were: Students yes 75%, adults yes 78%.

Here we see again a glaring inconsistency: Respondents claim that they find it easier to challenge those in power than others.

**Conclusion:**
One might again conclude that respondents are neither clear nor consciously aware of how they make choices and whether they engage in courageous or honest interactions.

14. **Can you say "no" when you need to despite being prompted by others that you should say "yes?" (Q. 14 students, Q. 18 adults).**
Responses: students yes 50%, adults yes 45%

**Purpose of question:**
To inquire whether respondents have the courage to be their own persons.

**Comments:**
These responses are alarming, but they also confirm the discussions on Stage 3 and the responses on wanting to be liked and admired. It also begs the question that if one cannot say "no" can one really speak truth to power or challenge those who are doing something unethical?

To be courageous one must be self-defining and self-determining, where one can claim one's own authority. According to psychology texts and discussions on authority and obedience, most people need to work on being more self-determining. It is not possible to be a courageous person if one is not self-determining, to be able to stand apart, and to stand for principles aimed at advancing goodness.

It is also notable that adults are less able to say "no" than students.

**Conclusion:**
It takes courage to withstand the pressure from others, and clearly that is something radically wanting in our society.

15. **Do you think you should always unquestioningly follow the law? (Q. 15 students, Q. 20 adults)**
Responses: students yes – 18%, adults yes 42%

**Purpose of question:**
To inquire into the extent to which people adhere to authority.

**Comments:**
This question was intended to investigate whether people felt free to challenge the law. It might have been better worded as challenging the law for principled reasons versus challenging the law because one does not like or agree with it are two different things.

A follow-up question would be on what grounds should or could the law be challenged. As it stands, we can only infer that some people do not follow the law blindly.

**Conclusion:**
Courage sometimes requires challenging the law as in the suffrage movement. Challenging the law for good purposes needs to be well grounded and researched. Challenging the law because it does not suit you is a far cry from being courageous.

16. **What do you think is the most important characteristic of an effective leader? (Q. 16 students, Q.21 adults)**
Responses: students – courage cited twice, adults – honesty, integrity and courage cited multiple times. Other terms used were passion, vision, empathy and listening skills.

**Purpose of question:**
To inquire into what respondents see as important leadership traits and whether courage is one of them.

**Comments:**
Respondents – both students and adults – selected appealing attributes that could apply to any "nice" person. I infer that they thought of their parents

when they selected these characteristics. What is missing is the key ability to act in the face of uncertainty and danger with the motive or intention to advance goodness.

It is also interesting that the attribute of 'character" does not feature at all in any responses. Character is clearly something that is not in people's mindsets. To have a character means having some positive traits, usually good or virtuous ones.

**Conclusion:**
The idea of developing one's character and living according to some virtues or principles in a consistent manner does not appear to be in the respondents' consciousness. It is not reflected in our society and alas, students do not seem to be absorbing it as a takeaway from their studies.

17. **When did you last engage in an act of courage? (Q. 17 students, Q.22 adults)**
Responses: students – today and this week 61%
adults – today and this week 32%

**Purpose of question:**
To inquire whether courage is part of people's consciousness and intentional living.

**Comment:**
One wonders what respondents define as courage and what acts they deem courageous acts. Clearly, they feel that they are courageously engaged even though they appear to be unsure of what being courageous means.

**Conclusion:**
It would seem students believe they are quite courageous despite the many contradictions in their responses. It would be interesting to explore the circumstances they face that provide reasons for courageous acts.

18. **Are you an accountable person? (Q. 18 students, Q. 23 adults)**
Responses: students yes – 82%, adults yes – 100%

**Purpose of question:**
To inquire whether respondents feel accountable for the choices and the decisions of their lives. To probe as to whether they stand by their actions and that they have made every endeavor to be as principled and courageous as possible. To personally own that they have made their lives to be whatever they might be.

**Comment and conclusion:**
I wonder whether people understand the true meaning of accountable. Based on the responses, the high level of self-deception is astonishing. The literature is full of research – psychological and moral – that points out how few people

have the "nerve" to really live a principled, accountable life. Clearly unaware of their contradictions (e.g., the inability to say "no" under pressure (Q.14)), respondents would appear to see themselves with rosy filled moral glasses.

19. **What is the one thing you value most in yourself and in others? (Q. 19 students, Q. 24 adults).**
    Reponses: students – loyalty and respect, adults – honesty.

    **Purpose of question:**
    To inquire whether any of the components of courage or courage itself is something that people admire in themselves.

    **Comments and conclusion:**
    Loyalty and respect ties in with Stage 3 thinking. Adults who focus on honesty also by and large are challenged to speak the truth so as not to hurt others – see Q.4.

    What is ignored by respondents is that one cannot be a truly honest person without being courageous. Honesty – true honesty – means aligning with the truth which most often is risky and needs courage. It means telling the truth even if it is uncomfortable for others and it means saying "no" when you are asked to do something you do not want to do or does not fit in with your principles.

20. **Do you think that if your boss or someone in authority told you to do something, even if you were uncomfortable with it, you would do it? (Q. 20 students, Q. 25 adults)**
    Responses: both adult and students – no 86%

    **Purpose of question:**
    To inquire whether any of the components of courage or courage itself is something that people admire in themselves.

    **Comments:**
    Once again, we see the contradiction where previously respondents were asked whether they could say "no" to something they disagreed with. In that question 50% of both students and adults said they could not say "no," yet here 86% believe they could stand up to their boss.

    **Conclusion:**
    This question reveals further contradictions and lack of reflection by respondents.

## Questions posed only to Adults

**Survey question 9: Since conflicts of interest occur throughout life due to having multiple roles, how do you handle them?**

Responses:

Be transparent and deal with them 70%

Only bring significant ones to light 27%
Avoid 3%

**Purpose of question:**
To inquire whether adults have the courage to be honest and transparent about potentially competing interests.

**Comments:**
These results contradict all research and texts on leadership, teams, culture and having difficult conversations. The general statistic is that well over 80% of people avoid dealing with uncomfortable issues and having difficult conversations. Most people are highly conflict-averse.

Further these responses contradict other responses on avoiding being truthful or challenging people engaging in unethical behavior.

**Conclusion:**
Once again people deceive themselves with regard to their true courage and honesty.

**Survey question 14: Which is more important to you, honesty or loyalty?**
Responses:
Honesty 87%
Loyalty 23%

**Purpose of question:**
To inquire where adults' preferences lie – truth or bonding.

**Comments and Conclusion:**
See my discussion of Stage 3 in Chapter 7.

**Survey question 19: Has anyone tried to persuade you to do something dishonest where the dishonest action would be beneficial to you?**
Responses:
Yes 46%
No 54%

**Purpose of question:**
To inquire into the level of temptations adults are presented with at work.

**Comment and Conclusion:**
The "yes" percentage seems low given the high amount of deceit and corruption in most organizations. Could this be a matter of willful blindness?

### Part B Summary of CEO and Senior Executive Interviews

**Sample details:**

| | |
|---|---|
| Total | 18 |
| CEOs | 10 |
| For-profit quoted companies represented | 4 |
| For-profit private companies represented | 6 |
| Nonprofit companies represented | 8 |

Geography: 2 NYC, 1 Virginia, 1 California, 1 PA, 12 NH, 1 Ireland.

## Interview Guiding Questions

1. **How would you describe courage? How would you define a courageous act? What are its critical elements?**
   Respondents' descriptions included grace under pressure; a lack of ethics; the ability to make a decision regardless of whether the outcome impacts me, or those I love negatively; and a courageous act entails living to a standard, regardless of the outcome.
   Others added that courage is the ability to speak up, to ensure social justice, to be consistent, to have hard conversations, to deal with the unknown, to tell the truth and to face fear of adversity or loss.
   One person said you know courage when you see it, while another said it is to take a stand no matter the cost, and to be fearless.
   A female CEO said courage means having character and the ability to overcome obstacles.
2. **Do you think that in general our macro environment is one that reflects a time of courageous insight and action? Are you seeing evidence of courage in any sector – political, economic, environmental, technological or social?**
   One CEO responded with "in my entire professional/adult life, I've never seen less courage. The total absence of courage may very well be at the root of what's broken in both government and capitalism today."
   Without exception, all interviewees agreed that evidence of courage is missing and that corruption is on the rise.
   Some mentioned growing corruption in the health care sector, overbilling and false claims. Others discussed lack of social justice, that people are highly reactive and that they are less responsive. Several mentioned discrimination and one person spoke about the breakdown in society due to their being less religious, less family ties and less purpose of why we live. She claimed that "we have lost our way."

3. **What experiences have you had where you had to exhibit courage? Could you perhaps describe the most challenging of these experiences explaining what factors made them complex and personally challenging?**
   Only a small percentage of interviewees could provide specific examples. A recurring theme was sexual harassment among employees, board members and even clients abusing sales staff.
   Some people mentioned that they had been asked to do things not expected, that people did not speak up or stand up at meetings but just went with the majority, and one person mentioned the difficulty in creating a "courage culture."
4. **As a CEO, do you find that there are certain circumstances that generate ethical tensions that invariably call on your capacity for courage and fortitude?**
   I managed to extract the following from the various narratives.
   - How to deal with competing interests
   - How to take the high road – which was not defined
   - The importance of having a human approach to leadership
   - The need for discernment and collaboration
   - Being prepared to take risks
   - How not to make everything a business problem as opposed to an ethical one
   - How to handle board members that are looking for inappropriate benefits
   - How to support those people who do speak up

   Corruption in the United States is apparently at its worst in almost a decade, according to a new global report released by Transparency International. Advocates attribute the drop to declining trust in democratic institutions and poor oversight of pandemic-related financial aid (Transparency International 2021).
5. **Why do you think that corruption has escalated? Have you seen evidence of more corruption in your industry?**
   This is what I was able to extract from the discussions:
   - People are looking for comfort
   - Double standards exist everywhere so people abuse the system
   - People want the easy way out
   - Power reigns without compassion
   - The US is losing the "we" spirit

The reader will no doubt draw some of their own conclusions from the feedback I have provided.

I would simply add that I think organizations, their leadership and management teams and all employees would benefit from sessions on the topic of courage and character.

## Reference

Transparency International. 2021. https://foreignpolicy.com/2021/01/28/report-transparency-international-corruption-worst-decade-united-states/.

# Chapter 11

# A Return to Courage and Character

## Trousered Apes and Urban Blockheads

Several years ago, I agreed to teach a class on leadership to students completing their final year in Business Studies at a highly respected Catholic college. A week prior to the beginning of the semester, I joined 30 other professors and instructors in a seminar on student support services and classroom protocol. For three hours we listened to the drone of the Dean of Students as she flashed her way through mind deadening PowerPoints. There were student grinds, student counselors for those experiencing stress, and evening workout sessions for students to complete their assignments. There were sick bays where students could drop in if they needed some quiet or help with a migraine. If they fell behind in their work, they could appeal to a student counselor to help them to catch up. The same applied if they were getting bad grades, they could request help from a free campus tutor and the professor was duty-bound to reevaluate and regrade their next attempts. Plural!

As I listened to the categorization of student help, my anxiety escalated. What had I got myself into? Would these students be open to learning anything or would they just find someone to get them through the tough spots so that they could pass. With all this support what incentive was there for them to stretch, to try, to take risks, to learn about failure, to be open and curious and not just to muddle through?

My first class was the usual attempt to stir up enthusiasm for the course while also pointing out the need for student commitment and self-discipline. This did not go down well. Many of the students persisted in texting and sneaking peaks at their computers. I predicted this was going to be a challenging semester. It was.

DOI: 10.4324/9781003459644-12

In 1943, C.S. Lewis (1898–1963) penned a book titled *The Abolition of Man*. His focus was on the then English school system and how it no longer inculcated character and moral values in its students. The approach of some teachers, he lamented, is turning students into "trousered apes and urban blockheads" (Lewis 2010, 12). Current education, wrote Lewis, is developing "men without chests and then expecting of them virtue and enterprise" (2010, 19). It is enabling young people to develop without any sense of value or sensibility or awakening them from their "slumber of cold vulgarity." It is turning everything into materialism and rationalism.

Students, Lewis argued, need to be guided on how to wrestle with their emotions and to apply critical thinking to their choices. They need to learn how to make judgments and to question what makes things good or bad; otherwise they will fall sway to the propagandists and demagogues. (Note this was Lewis lamenting 80 years ago!)

What Lewis described is what I found myself wrestling with in that leadership class – many trousered apes and urban blockheads who had already spent three years of comatose attendance in classes and were hoping to cruise through the final round. Thankfully, after several weeks, I awoke a few. I lost a few too, particularly those on sports scholarships but with those who remained we ended up having a fiery class which they came to enjoy. Some of them may even have learned something.

William Deresiewicz, former professor at Yale (until 2008), provides a scathing critique of the education at elite colleges in his book *Excellent Sheep* (2014). Students, he writes, are talented and driven but are mostly anxious, timid and lost with little intellectual curiosity and a stunted sense of purpose. Since we live in such a meritocracy – see Sandel in the following section – everything is about grades and resume building. Character building does not exist. The colleges treat the students as customers and not as students where the students are pandered to rather than challenged. Education has become a shopping mall where everyone is looking for the best deal.

Students are pressured to be achievers and not taught to use their minds. There is no cultivation of curiosity, or critical thinking. They are not taught to have moral imagination, to appreciate choices and their consequences, and the tussle between cowardice and courage. Their beliefs and self-image need to be challenged and not self-indulged, he writes.

Instead, their big goals are to be successful, which means becoming head of a law firm, or a CEO, or winning an impressive title. They are not developed as leaders of the future who aspire to leave the world a better place. And even if they are not leaders, Deresiewicz asks, what about becoming educated citizens who understand and aspire to promote justice and virtue rather than materialistic values?

I can only echo Lewis and Deresiewicz's disappointment and frustration. Alas, it is not just students that lack moral imagination and critical thinking, it is a large majority of adults (the students' parents) including, in my experience, many high-level executives who earn outrageous salaries and have minimal if any real leadership skills and the best attributes that come with that.

Surely part of education is shaping the person's character, guiding them in discernment and deliberation and getting young people to understand the notion of virtue, how it leads to freedom and their being all that they desire to be. Students need to learn about ethical reflection and moral courage. They must be exposed to diverse perspectives and taught how to tolerate complexity and uncertainty.

It is when people are young that their characters begin to mold. It is then that they can learn that their role in life is something larger than themselves and their personal success. If we do not educate the young people in the virtues, character and courage, what kind of leaders will they be?

## Loss of Virtue and Loss of Courage

### *From Virtue to Materialism*

There are many theories explaining our loss of virtue and character. Some critics claim we have lost connection with our higher spiritual selves and therefore we have no interest in self-awareness, self-mastery or self-discipline. Virtuous behavior, as I have belabored, now lies in being successful or being seen as someone who has made it.

Here are a few theories that explain this shift.

## The Protestant Ethic and the Spirit of Capitalism

Max Weber's *Protestant Ethic and the Spirit of Capitalism* (1996) posits that it was the combination of the Reformation and Enlightenment movements that gave rise to the capitalist spirit.

Weber explains how the Reformation movement ignited by Augustinian priest Martin Luther (1483–1546) challenged the ubiquitous hold of the Catholic Church over every aspect of people's lives. This movement, he claimed, shifted the focus of ethics and morality from one communicated and meditated by the Church and its priestly agents, to one where the individual must deal directly with God and develop his or her own ethical conscience. Luther insisted that salvation could no longer be acquired through good works, obsequious attention to dogma or regular confession. People had to form a direct relationship with God, and via his or her own conscience resolve the existential angst around salvation alone. No priestly intermediary could advocate on one's behalf or assure one of one's heavenly reward.

The Protestant approach, adopted by both John Calvin (1509–1564) and the Pietists, placed religion squarely in the personal domain. Ethics, stripped of abstract and universal principles, became a highly personal struggle in deciding what was good and right. Contrary to the Catholic Church, Luther exalted work by claiming it a "calling" from God.

Calvin argued that only a life of good works could provide the conviction of a person's own salvation. There was no guarantee as one's fate was predestined. The very best one could do was to bring all actions, including economic ones, under relentless control and scrutiny as reflections on one's personal conduct. Economic motives were no longer considered alien to the life of the spirit. The capitalist was no longer distrusted as one who had grown rich from the misfortunes of his neighbor. Now it was not the accumulation of riches but rather their misuse for the purposes of self-indulgence that became the enemy of the God-oriented life. With self-discipline and sober behavior, money-making could be carried out for the greater glory of God. In the Calvinist schema, economic life became endowed with a new sanctification.

Another Protestant movement, Methodism, under its leader John Wesley (1703–1791) exhorted its followers to gain all they could, save all they could and do works of mercy. Strict self-control and diligence in work provided self-assurance of a heavenly afterlife.

By the mid-eighteenth century, religious fervor was no longer directed at the Church and its demands but was now injected into economic life. This too was shaped by the rapidly advancing Industrial Revolution which ushered in a new class of capitalists. This emerging class, inspired by the Protestant ethic of ascetic and thrifty behavior, began to accumulate vast amounts of capital. This intense worldly activity counteracted the feelings of religious anxiety previously ameliorated by the Church and the sacraments.

Weber concluded his seminal work on a dismal note, however. He anticipated that the pursuit of wealth, stripped of the religious and ethical meaning that Protestantism tried to give it, would result in a pre-occupation with external goods (materialism). The pursuit of wealth, he believed, would no longer lie on the "saint's shoulders like a light cloak, freely thrown aside at any moment" but would become an "iron cage" (Weber 1996).

Luther's hope that the world would become a monastery backfired in that the monastery has now become the world. The life of inner worldly asceticism has become one where the spirit of moderation has been abandoned in favor of unlimited accumulation of material goods as assurance of one's salvation.

## *My Property Equals My Moral Worth*

John Locke (1632–1704), an English Enlightenment philosopher, insisted that all humans have the right to life, liberty and property. He challenged the feudal system claiming that when a person worked on a property he was entitled to ownership. It is "proper to me."

Locke's influence resulted in property becoming an extension of the individual. It works like this: the more time and work invested in a property, the more it says something about the owner. The more property one has, the more conscientious one must be and certainly the happier one must be. (Remember the new Protestant spirit!)

We can see how this led to an expression of personal moral worth. Owning property has become a way of sustaining ourselves, expressing our freedom and, through free exchange, experiencing our happiness. If we combine this new understanding with the emerging idea of free markets and the free exchange of property, we can see how this creates happiness for everyone. Wealth equates to happiness which is morally praiseworthy.

## The Dark Side of Meritocracy

Renowned Harvard professor of philosophy Michael J. Sandel (who we met in the Introduction), in *The Tyranny of Merit*, 2020, critiques American's meritocratic society which he claims can be traced back to the creation of the Protestant Ethics discussed earlier.

In a society driven by merit, the conviction lies in that those who land on the top believe they deserve their success, while those left behind deserve their fate. In this world, the winners – those who have power and wealth – kid themselves that they were self-made, that it is through their talents and their hard work that they have come by their achievements. They have no humility. They have no grasp that either they had opportunities that others didn't, for example, being able to attend an Ivy League college, or that they have talents that the market currently rewards. They have a smug conviction that their fate reflects their merit. They are one of the chosen – the elect!

Worldly success, à la the Protestant Ethic, is a sign of salvation. And, as Sandel points out, American society is built around this belief. Wealth is morally praiseworthy, and poverty is a sign of indolence. One example is the healthcare system, where the rich people, because they can afford better healthcare, deserve to live longer. At colleges, the rich or the offspring of rich alumni, are more readily admitted. Sandel claims that the system is rigged to perpetuate the privileged, and the American education system serves as the premier sorting machine for promoting that privilege.

The alleged American dream is that it is the land of ultimate upward mobility. Sandel points out that this is a fallacy and that many countries such as Canada, France and Denmark make it easier to rise from poverty and provide greater equal opportunity across the board.

A system of meritocracy and the ethic of utilitarianism go hand in hand, as we shall see.

## The Rise of Utilitarianism

Contrary to the virtue ethics approach that focuses on the character of a person, and the rule-based approach that focuses on the intention behind a person's actions, consequentialist ethical theories focus on consequences. Moral worth is determined solely by the outcome or the results of one's actions.

The most widely known and applied consequentialist theory is referred to as utilitarianism. The utilitarian approach to morality views an action or practice morally praiseworthy if it leads to the greatest possible balance of good consequences, or to the least possible balance of bad consequences. Good and bad are relativistic concepts not based on any universal principles. Goodness is now based on a utilitarian equation and is no longer focused on advancing goodness, well-being and flourishing. We love saying "This is for the greater good." But what does good mean and how is it measured? Who decides?

Utilitarianism, like virtue ethics, considers the pursuit of happiness as the ultimate goal of all our actions. An important matter to bear in mind is the changed understanding of "happiness" (see the following section). Happiness has evolved from something attained by living virtuously to a more subjective measure of satisfying an individual's personal feelings of well-being, for example, being wealthy, being popular or being successful.

Business ethics relies largely on utilitarian principles and this more relativistic understanding of happiness. The "bottom line," that is, the amount of money we have made, is the ultimate goal, and the greatest utility is a "good" bottom line supposedly providing us with ultimate happiness!

## *Twenty-First-Century Happiness*

According to our Greek heritage, there is an important connection between four concepts, namely, happiness, the soul, virtuous choices and a good life. Nowadays we just seek happiness.

One thing that stands out in our twenty-first century world is how many people are searching for happiness. Speakers, artists, writers and TV hosts provide all kinds of advice on how to quell our fears, find our true selves and realize happiness. Self-help books that provide the "Ten Steps to Happiness" adorn many bookshelves. There are now even Happiness Institutes! By contrast, the Greeks kept it simple. They said the answer to happiness lies in living a life of self-examination, moderation, taking care of our souls and acting virtuously. Flourishing and well-being will follow. Happiness is a consequence, not a planned result or a possession.

But how do we experience happiness today in a culture addicted to conspicuous consumption where more wealth supposedly leads to more happiness which makes us morally praiseworthy? Instead, what we are seeing is many people drowning in debt, unhealthy, depressed, anxious regarding their future, feeling alienated at work, stressed by their family commitments, and worrying about retirement.

A high percentage of young people are scared, lost and feel hopeless. Suicide statistics worldwide are the highest ever and rising. Despair is everywhere. So, where is this happiness?

A key insight here, raised by both Plato and Aristotle, and reiterated by others, is that happiness itself cannot be pursued. If anything, its pursuit leads to a greater sense of frustration, failure and unhappiness. It is by being in a certain way, such as living a virtuous life, helping others and especially nurturing our souls, that happiness results (Beerel, *Ethical Leadership: A Guide to Good Practice* 2020). It is also by living a virtuous and courageous life that citizens create a vibrant society, are able to support and withstand the challenges of being a democracy.

## How Democracies Die

In the Introduction, we discussed Sir John Glubb's analysis of the Stage of Decadence which always heralds the collapse of a society. I challenged us to consider whether the US is in that stage. Is our democracy moving from decadence to dissolution?

In *How Democracies Die*, Steven Livitsky and Daniel Ziblatt draw on decades of research and a wide range of historical and global examples over the past almost 100 years to extract the key factors that foreshadow the collapse of democracies. Their findings include overall economic decline, loss of productivity, extreme inequality, corruption and greed, general moral decadence, and a growingly powerful oligarchy. A major contributing factor to society's collapse is the lethargy and disenchantment of citizens who demonstrate growing ignorance about what is really going on and are readily swayed by demagogues. They are uneducated and not bothered by their lack of awareness. They readily adopt a mass mob mentality and are always looking for someone to blame. They have no real vision of the future and exhibit no personal accountability.

In *The Crisis of Democratic Capitalism*, 2023, Martin Wolf, CBE, chief economics commentator at the *Financial Times*, does not mince his words regarding the predatory nature of capitalism as currently practiced. Besides denouncing the massive incomes that motivate executives with short tenures armed only with their self-interest, he writes about how many of them have power with no accountability to anyone and how corporations have huge political influence which they use purely to serve their own agendas. He also writes about the incompetence of many citizens and how they have no idea of how to engage in the public sphere. Understanding the nature of good citizenship is something of which they have no notion and sadly no interest.

In John F. Kennedy's Pulitzer Prize–winning book *Profiles of Courage*, 1961, Kennedy wrote that a true democracy puts faith in its people elect, people who are expected to exercise conscientious judgment, to do what they must despite personal circumstances and despite obstacles and dangers. To be courageous, Kennedy wrote, does not require exceptional qualifications, or a magic formula. It is an opportunity that sooner or later is presented to everyone, and the only place that a person can turn to for courage is his or her own soul (Kennedy 1964, 225). Do we have the courage to turn to our souls?

We do not need books, speeches or the media to confirm what we experience every day. Our society no longer honors or cultivates character, courage or a commitment to self-mastery or personal excellence.

## A Return to Virtue, Courage and Character

Despite my criticism of current society and of many corporate leaders, the more time I spend with my clients and my friends having real conversations, the clearer it is to me as to how people long to be more in touch with their inner selves and to live more truthfully, openly and courageously. Many despise the moral identity and ethical behaviors of the groups to which they belong, and they hunger for opportunities to live a noble existence. They realize too that when they lose their souls, for whatever reason, their capacity for courage is diminished.

So, how might we bring virtue and courage back into our lives – both personally and in the public sphere? How might we take our roles as educated, engaged citizens more seriously?

What is the most effective way to ignite our moral imagination, and to make us desire living a life of excellence, a life of courage? A life where we understand that by advancing goodness, we will achieve the happiness we long for, and the real "invisible hand" will work its magic, and everyone will benefit.

How might we nourish the emptiness inside that leads to both loneliness and greed? And how can we inspire young people so that they retain their child-like curiosity, their willingness to take risks, and their hunger to learn for the sake of learning and not just to get some certificate that assures them of a job? How might we teach the art of living well and the idea that character is our most important possession?

Massimo Pigliucci's book *How to be Good: What Socrates Can Teach Us about the Art of Living Well*, 2023, begins with the question as to whether virtue can be taught. He explains that virtue and courage are teachable concepts à la Socrates/Plato mostly through role-modeling by leaders. Since it is a well-known fact that we are strongly inclined to model our behaviors on people we admire, where can we find admirable leaders who we can emulate?

Pigliucci adds that critical reflection and focusing on developing our ethical sensitivity also support character development and the cultivation of courage. Critical reflection lies in us challenging our assumptions and questioning with an open mind and heart as to whether they are appropriate and accurate and reflect wisdom.

Hannah Arendt claimed that thoughtlessness is a large contributor to lack of courage, and as we have discussed, some of that thoughtlessness is our defense from facing what we don't want to face. There is also our habitual distractedness that takes us from living mindfully. This distractedness and sometimes outright denial of new realities or new truths create that willful blindness that invariably costs us dearly. This distractedness also robs us of our moral imagination and our empathy – important ingredients of a courageous life.

Most importantly how might we grow up? How might we cease from being so dependent on what others think, being liked, finding our self-worth outside ourselves and instead claim our personal authority? Can we cease betraying ourselves, being subservient to those in charge or aligning ourselves with the group in efforts to fit in and belong, and turn to belonging to ourselves?

What will it take for us to find the courage to be self-determining and self-differentiating? Can we integrate the *Serenity Prayer* into our daily lives where we accept what we cannot control but have the courage to change the things that we can?

Can we begin by knowing that existentially courage is part of who we are? Can we commit to a mindful life where we live with both attention and intention and where we practice courage in the small things, day by day or even moment by moment? Can we cease finding external enemies to fight and tackle our inner ones first and by so doing cultivate our courage, thereby gaining our inner freedom, the true path to happiness?

We know that it is much easier to be courageous together than alone, so can we support one another in our courageous efforts to advance truth and goodness? We do not need to intentionally place ourselves in challenging situations; there are plenty of them if one is truly paying attention.

This book began with my hunt for courage. And the journey through these chapters took us through some dark places. However, I hope my ideas and reflections have brought some light to that journey, that what I have shared with you will inspire you to live your life even more courageously and from an ever-greater place of inner freedom, and that you will become the happiness you long for.

T.S. Eliot reflected in his poem "Little Gidding" (1942) that the end of our exploring will bring us back to the place where we started, which we will then know for the first time.

We started with Paul Tillich's assertion that courage is part of who we are. Courage is our ability to affirm ourselves despite fate and fear and the reality of death, and it is this self-affirmation that makes love of others possible. It is courage, that act of the heart, that gives us the ability to love. And being able to love makes us deeply happy.

What greater incentive do we need than that?

## Your Turn

- How would you describe your character?
- Do you support or encourage other people to exhibit moderation?
- Are you able to say "no?"
- What does happiness look like to you? When do you experience deep inner happiness?
- Has this book inspired you to reflect on your courage?
- Can you think of ways in which you can bring more courage to your personal and professional life?

## References

Beerel, Annabel. 2020. *Ethical Leadership and Global Capitalism: A Guide to Good Practice.* Abingdon, Oxon: Routledge.

Deresiewicz, William. 2014. *Excellent Sheep*. New York: Free Press.

Kennedy, John F. 1964. *Profiles of Courage*. New York: HarperPerrenial.

Lewis, C.S. 2010. *The Abolition of Man*. Las Vegas, NV: Lits.

Pigliucci, Masimo. 2023. *How to Be Good*. London, UK: Basic Books.

Sandel, Michael J. 2020. *The Tyranny of Merit: Can We Find the Common Good?* New York: Picador.

Weber, Max. 1996. *The Protestant Ethic & the Spirit of Capitalism*. Los Angeles, CA: Roxbury Publishing Company.

# Index

Printed in the United States
by Baker & Taylor Publisher Services